Muḥammad
The Unknown Man

Atabek Shukurov

Shukurov Publishing

Muḥammad:

The Unknown Man

ISBN 978-1-64606-443-4

Phone; +44-7792468389 +44-161 4781005

Email; @
shukurov.publishing@gmail.com,info@shukurovpublishing.co.uk,
info@shukurovpublishing.com

https://www.shukurovpublishing.co.uk

Written and translated by Otabek Shukurov. Editing and Calligraphy by Rasheed Gillespie. Graphic designing by Rula Shukurova.

Contents

Introduction 1
Chapter 1 3
...as a Son 3
Chapter 2 28
...as a Grandson 28
Chapter 3 34
...as a Father 34
Chapter 4 46
...as a Grandfather 46
Chapter 5 55
...as a Step-father 55
Chapter 6 57
...as a Brother 57
Chapter 7 60
...as a Relative 60
Chapter 8 65
...as a Neighbour 65
Chapter 9 68
...as a Husband 68
...as a Master 75
Chapter 11 90
...as a Friend 90
Chapter 12 102
...as a Guest 102
Chapter 13 114

...as a Host 114
Chapter 14 120
...as a Teacher 120
Chapter 15 131
...as a Leader 131
Chapter 16 142
...as a Prophet 142
Part II 155
Introduction 155
Chapter 17 157
...Oppressed 157
Chapter 18 168
...Victorious 168
Chapter 19 180
...Supportive 180
Chapter 20 185
...Loving 185
Chapter 21 189
...Loved 189
Chapter 22 204
...Smiling 204
Chapter 23 208
...Laughing 208
...Angry 217
Chapter 25 221
...Sadness 221

Chapter 27 223
...Crying 223
Chapter 27 233
...Facing his Mortality 233
Chapter 29 243
Death of the Prophet Muḥammad µ 243
Index 247
Personalities 247
Places 255
Bibliography 258
References 269

Part I

Introduction

Were I or any of us living today to commit our biographies to paper, there would doubtlessly be reems and sheaves of pages we would prefer burned to ash, never to be seen by mortal eyes. This truth is undeniable, and the only difference between any of us is the exact number of those regrettable pages – whether they would fill volumes or mere chapters. As for the well-known noble and righteous characters of history, such pages would number few indeed. But as for the Prophets π, whose station exceeds all of the aforementioned, the books of their lives contain not a single leaf in need of abrogation – or so Muslims believe. And the best of them, namely Muḥammad b. ʿAbdullāhμ, left neither jot nor tittle of which any of his nation could feel ashamed.

On the topic of character, a well-known and authenticated reminder transmitted to us from the Prophet μ goes along the lines that, "the best from among you is the one who is best to his family."[1] Hiding one's true face (to whatever extent) for the sake of social acceptability or interpersonal palatability is an activity, we feel safe in assuming, undertaken by most people much of the time. But doing so expends mental and emotional energy, the stores of which are pointedly finite, and one simply cannot carry on indefinitely; the mask must fall away eventually. There are also, quite naturally, individuals and groups from which a man feels no need to conceal his true self; sometimes the mask need not be donned at all. And so, it stands to reason, the surest way of ascertaining a man's true character is to consider his public conduct and how he acts around friends and acquaintances alongside scrutiny of how he performs in more private and intimate settings, such as in his roles of father, son, or spouse.

Because the objective of this work is to highlight, using authentic sources, the manifold aspects (too-seldom mentioned in Muslim circles, and scarcely if at all brought to the attention of a wider non-Muslim audience) of the Prophet's µ life that were common to the roles filled by the typical man – and how he fiylled those roles in the shiningly exemplary way referenced in the Qur'ān – rather than present the more familiar, chronologically-ordered biography or examination of how he operated in the capacity of Prophet and fulfilled his duties as Messenger, I have chosen the title *Muḥammad: The Unknown Man.*

Now let us avail ourselves of this God-given Paragon of Excellence µ and get to know him…

Chapter 1

...as a Son

While a plethora of information will be available about a given famous historical personality regarding the period during which they actually achieved their fame, what can be known about the time leading up to then – such as their childhood and formative years – tends to be, by comparison, next to nothing. Perhaps surprisingly, because the corpus of *ḥadīth* literature's sheer amount and detail of information about his life after the age of forty (when he was sent forth on the mission of divine messengership), the biography of the Prophet Muḥammadµ is no exception to this tendency.

Despite the foregoing, the aforementioned scarcity of information is only relative; enough has reached us to form a detailed-enough sketch of the Prophet's µ earliest years via deduction from how he behaved with his "parents" later in life.

In the city of Makkah, at the age of eighteen, Āminah bt. Wahb ι married a young (twenty-one at the time) noble of the Quraysh clan named ʿAbdullāh b. ʿAbd al-Muṭṭalibκ. Not long after their union, the young husband set off on a caravan journey to the region then known as al-Shām (comprising modern-day Syria, Lebanon, Jordan, and Palestine), as he often did in his occupation as a trader. However, ʿAbdullāh became severely ill on his way home. When the caravan made its stop at

Yathrib (decades later to be renamed Madīnah al-Nabī, or City of the Prophet) on the route back to Makkah, he passed away.

Now, we know that, as accords God's wisdom, Muḥammadμ was orphaned at a very young age; as we now know, his father ʿAbdullāhη died three months before his birth. His mother Āminahι also died when he was just six. The time during which he could have been properly called "son" was tragically short, yet he demonstrated the nobility of his character not only with the various surrogates with whom he was blessed, but also his own biological mother decades later – as will be demonstrated.

Typically, human nature dictates that a person will tend to distance themselves as much as is practical from those of a lower social or economic status. Slaves, usually occupying the lowest rung on the social ladder we exhaust ourselves trying to climb, thus would have found themselves the most ostracized; freed-slaves tended not to fare much better. But such a one, as a matter of fact, was the Prophet's μ first non-parental caregiver – an Abyssinian lady by the name of Thuwaybah. She had been a slave of one of Muḥammad's μ uncles, a man who went by the moniker of Abū Lahab, but she was freed as an expression of his joy when she brought him the news of the birth of the nephew for whom he would ironically end up with nothing but animosity. For several days thereafter, she nursed the new-born Muḥammadμ from herself, becoming his first milk-mother.

Notwithstanding the short duration of her wet nursing duties and her low social standing, Muḥammadμ established and adhered to a tradition of sending her gifts, such as clothing items and other necessities, until she passed away (historians disagree over whether this was as a Muslim or not). Even thereafter, the tradition was not abandoned; he μ would inquire after her living relatives, sending them provisions and gifts. This continued until such time as he asked if she had some relations yet alive and the reply finally came back in the negative.[2] The Prophet's μ level of gratitude and depth of sincerity can be well-appreciated simply by his treatment of the freed-slave who wet nursed him for just a few days.

Arabian society, being largely rooted in desert life, was centred around hospitality and generosity, but it was also highly patriarchal, so individual virtues like physical strength, mental endurance, and martial skill were prized above most others. At that time in history, being quick-witted and eloquent were also sought-after qualities as poetry was not only the great Arabian pastime, but a major source of cultural pride as well. To that end, urbanized Arabs had long since instituted the tradition of sending their offspring, at an early-enough age that language was yet being acquired, out to the desert with a Bedouin family (or one from one of the more isolated villages) to be reared (including wet nursing) as their own for two years. In exchange for perfecting the language and inner qualities of the city-dwellers' children, the foster family would receive usually-handsome payment and a certain level of prestige for themselves – depending on whose child they had the honour of hosting.

Becoming a full-fledged orphan at the age of six was as much of a tragic anomaly for a seventh-century Arab as it would be for anyone today. But an aspect of the Prophet's μ childhood we have ample information about is one that he had quite in common with the children of any well-enough-to-do family of settled Arabs – as the Quraysh of Ḥijāz were – at the time.

When the proper time came to do so, ʿAbd al-Muṭṭalibη took his grandson to the part of town where prospective foster parents would select, or be selected by, city-dwelling families. One after another approached ʿAbd al-Muṭṭalibη to ask whether the young Muḥammadμ was his son; upon finding out the true nature of their relation – and the boy's status as an orphan – each would invariably move on to another family. This continued for the entire day until every foster family had a city-dweller's child placed in their care and departed. But ʿAbd al-Muṭṭalibη still held out hope and remained in the area, on the lookout for latecomers. And, due to the hunger-induced sluggishness of their riding animal, there did come one couple late indeed.

Under a now-low-hanging sun, exhausted from their protracted expedition, Ḥalīmah bt. Abī Dhu'ayb al-Saʿdiyyah ι and her husband al-Ḥārith b. ʿAbd al-ʿUzzah η happened upon a grandfather shouting, in desperation at the prospect of his beloved grandson missing his opportunity to benefit from a taste of desert life, "who will take my son?"[3]

We have on record this Ḥalīmah's ι entire recounting of the tale, as follows: "I set off to Makkah with some of the other women of Saʿd b. Banī Bakr in the hopes of getting for myself a milk-son. I was riding my elderly grey mule. We had with us an old sheep for milking, but it was no good but for a few drops at a time. My own new-born baby was with me at the time, and he kept us from sleeping at night for his constant crying from hunger; I had no milk in my own breast to feed him, and what little milk we got from that old sheep even we grown folk hoped to have for ourselves!

"Now, when we finally arrived at Makkah, each of my travelling companions who had reached ahead of me were offered Muḥammad. But they refused to take him. We usually hoped to receive a good payment from the fathers, you see, but he was an orphan. 'What could his widowed mother have given us?' they would have said. So it happened that all the women took a child but me by the time we started back home, but I refused to leave empty-handed! So I said to my husband, 'I'll have to go and take that orphan.' So when I came back, child in hand, my husband asked if it was him. 'Well, he was the only one left I could find,' I replied.

"But my husband encouraged me saying, 'you did the right thing. Perhaps God will grant us some reward through him.' And that He did. I remember it still, that no sooner than I placed him on my lap to suckle, my breasts were filled with milk, so much so that he and his milk-brother both drank their fill! Not only that, but when my husband went to milk our old sheep that evening, *its* udder was full as well. We got such milk from it as we never had before, and all of us on the journey went to sleep with full bellies that night. At all of this my husband remarked, 'it seems you've picked a blessed soul indeed!'

"On the trip home, rather than lagging behind on a starving mount as we had on the way to Makkah, we paced well ahead of the rest of the caravan. Our travelling companions, in their good nature, tried to convince us to slow down a bit; they couldn't believe we were even riding the same mule.

"When we finally got back to our village, I swear to God the surrounding land was barren. People would send their animals out to feed, and our shepherd would take ours out at the same time. By the end of the day, their sheep would come back still hungry and thirsty, with barely any milk. But my sheep would always return satiated and quenched, and we would drink our fill from them. So the other villagers would tell their shepherds to graze their sheep where we took ours; but theirs still came back hungry, and ours full!"[4]

After two years of wondrous bounty – for Muḥammadµ and his milk-family alike, as he was said to be extremely eloquent despite not being a trained poet, and his time in the desert no doubt played a large part in that – Ḥalīmahı returned her now two-year-old charge to his own mother, as custom dictated, in Makkah. But she convinced Āminahı to send him back with them for another four years;[5] were he anything but an exemplary son, this would not have been so even despite the benefits his Presence μ brought. The second time they made their way back to Makkah to return a six-year-old Muḥammadμ, there seems to have been some sort of plague epidemic. Fearing for the boy they had both grown to love, Ḥārithη this time convinced Āminahιto send him with them yet again. They kept him for another two years without even collecting a fee[6].

As accorded Arabian custom, one's milk-mother was kept in nearly the same standing and esteem as one's biological mother, and historical compilations are replete with episodes of just how strongly the Prophet μ adhered to this custom, highlighting the filial piety and compassion with which he dealt with Ḥalīmahι later in life.

Now, it is exceedingly common that a person will betray their own relatives without a second thought if it means some personal gain or avoiding even the most minor embarrassment; how much more easily would this be done to some poor nobody from nowhere? This sad fact of humanity brings to mind a story told me by one of my own teachers about a destitute man from one of the "backward" (as some people see them) Asian countries. He sent his son to England to study at a university, and he worked day and night to pay his son's tuition. After graduation, the son took a flight home and his father was at the airport when he arrived to pick him up. Since most of his wage went towards his son's education abroad, the father was still quite poor and hadn't the means to appear otherwise, so his clothes were old and tattered. When the son's friends – all being from wealthy families – who had travelled with him saw the man waiting, they asked who he was. Embarrassed, the son replied to their queries in English, "he is our driver!" Despite not being fluent in English, the father understood the son's simple answer; he was heartbroken.

Contrast the above with the following. Once, Ḥalīmahı came to the Prophet µ – after his marriage to Khadījahı, so he was around twenty-five years old – complaining about the particularly hard times upon which her village had fallen. The land had become especially barren and their livestock were dying off at an alarming rate. Upon hearing this distressing news, Muḥammadµ promptly spoke with his wife – who was actually quite a wealthy, prestigious woman – and she gifted Ḥalīmah ı with forty sheep and camels.[7]

Another example of the Prophet's µ refusal to forsake his milk-mother despite the differences in their respective socioeconomic stations occurred when he was around sixty years old, when he went to Makkah for either an *ʿumrah* (minor pilgrimage) or his *Ḥijjah al-Widāʿ* (the Valedictory Pilgrimage). He µ was in Jiʿrānah– a place about fifteen miles from Makkah – distributing meat to the people gathered there when suddenly came a lady into their midst. When he caught sight of her, the Prophet µ immediately stopped what he was doing and removed his outercoat, spreading it on the ground so she could sit comfortably. A young boy (at the time) called Abū Ṭufaylη watched these events as they unfolded, holding his piece of camel meat in silent amazement. When he was finally able, he asked someone who that woman was for whom the Prophet µ had shown such reverence. They replied knowingly, "she's his milk-mother."[8]

Yet another similar event was witnessed and entered the historical record, in which Ḥalīmah'sι husband came to sit with the Prophet µ, so he removed his coat and placed it on the ground to make a seat for his milk-father and himself. When Ḥalīmahι herself arrived on the scene, the Prophet µ quickly opened the coat from the other side, spreading out a seat for her as well. Some moments later, his milk-brother joined the group, so the Prophet µ stood up, offering his own seat, and he sat back down in front of them in the dust.[9] Even after being raised to the pinnacle of human potential in being bestowed with prophethood, our Beloved µ persisted in deferring, with utmost sincerity, to his milk-family for the duration of his life. This was from the signs of deep gratitude which characterized the sonship of Muḥammadµ.

The third of our Mentor's µ milk-mothers was yet another Abyssinian slave woman, this one belonging to the Prophet's µ mother Āminahι. Her name was "Umm Ayman" Barakah bt. Thaʿlabah ι, and the Prophet µ inherited her from his mother when she passed away, freeing her upon his marriage to Khadījahι. During ʿAbd al-Muṭṭalib's η guardianship over the young Muḥammad µ, she would look after him when the need arose, acting as a sort of babysitter.

In his relationship with Umm Aymanι, Muḥammadµ found yet another opportunity to demonstrate his utter disregard for those artificial class distinctions whereby some justify their demeaning and mistreatment of others, for even though he was a high-born son of the Banū Hāshim family of the venerable Quraysh clan, he would say astonishing things about this particular freed-slave, such as, "she is my own mother after my mother,"[10] and "she is the only one of my relatives yet living."[11] He µ even sought to have her married to a worthy, righteous man by broadcasting that, "whosoever wants to marry a woman set to enter Paradise, then let him marry Umm Ayman." Zayd b. Ḥārithah η, the adopted son of the Prophet µ, responded to this advertisement and married her as soon as he was able.[12]

We also have on the authority of one Anas b. Mālikη, who was a household servant of the Prophet µ, that the latter used to frequent Umm Ayman's ι home, wherein she would offer him food and milk – of which he would partake unless fasting – and they would sit together joking and laughing.[13] Because this was a constant habit of the Prophet µ, and his closest Companions tended toward a keenness for emulating even the most mundane of prophetic customs, Abū Bakrη and ʿUmarη on one occasion suggested to one another a visit to Umm Ayman's ι house sometime after the Prophet's µ passing;

perhaps they hoped to provide her with some laughter as their Master µ had in days past. But when they arrived, Umm Aymanι began crying. Mistaking the impetus for her tears being grief over the Prophet's µ death, the two sought to console her, gently chiding her, "why are you crying? Don't you know that what God has prepared for the Prophet is better than what we have her?"

Her reply, "rather I am crying because the revelation has stopped," demonstrated that her connection to her milk-son was not only maternal but consisted also of the deepest conviction of the genuinely faithful. At this realization, the *Shaykhayn* (an abbreviated way of referring to both Abū Barkη and ʿUmarη at once) joined her tears with their own.[14]

That what any of us would view as just another freed-slave and babysitter was honoured with the Prophet's µ consistent attention and a title more tremendous than any official bestowal (i.e. "my mother after my mother") forces one to consider the sonship of Muḥammad as befitting of one word if no other: genuine.

The final one of the Prophet's µ mother-figures we shall mention, until we finally discuss his biological mother, was a truly angelic personality by the name of Fāṭimah bt. Asadι. She was the wife of Abū Ṭālibη, the uncle of Muḥammad µ who adopted him after the demise of ʿAbd al-Muṭṭalibη.

It seems that the Prophet's µ character never tended toward pursuit of satisfaction or engaging in selfish competition; even as a young boy he demonstrated an extraordinary degree of forbearance. So whenever food was served at a family repast, and the rest of the children rushed forward to secure their own shares, Muḥammadµ would often not get to start eating until the others had finished – sometimes he may not have even been left with quite enough to satisfy his hunger.[15] Now, Abū Ṭālibη already had several children, but this never prevented him and Fāṭimahι from treating Muḥammadµ as yet another one of their very own. Thus, when he noticed, to his chagrin, these goings on, he requested that his wife set an ample portion aside for Muḥammadµ and offer it to him before the others so he could enjoy himself with the rest of them. She did so happily, and Muḥammadµ never failed once in expressing his deep gratitude for their various gestures of consideration; indeed, he treated them as if they were his natural parents.

The Prophet's µ sincere love and genuine appreciation for his foster-mother was such that, when his own first (and most beloved) daughter ο was born, he thought it only appropriate to honour her with the name Fāṭimah. And when the time came for the multitude of righteous and noble suitors to come seeking her hand in marriage, he refused them all in favour of the son of that same beloved foster-mother, ʿAlīν.

In our estimation, the truest gauges of the Prophet's μ exemplary sonship to Fāṭimah bt. Asad ι happen to be quite well-attested, as they actually occurred after the advent of his prophethood. We can rest assured that the Prophet μ saw and treated his foster-mother as his very own by the powerfully illustrative episode of her death and burial; in fact, three of the Prophet's μ closest companions – his household servant Anas η and his two cousins ʿAlīν and ʿAbd Allāh b. al-ʿAbbās κ – all had unique and intimate vantage points on the following events.

When came Fāṭimah's ι time to finally pass on from the life of this world, the Prophet μ was heard whispering, "O my mother, may God shower you with His mercy! You were my mother after my mother, you kept yourself hungry that I be fed, you would rather your garments were old to buy mine new. You passed yourself over for every goodness in my favour, and you never did it but for the sake of God and the life hereafter!" One can scarcely imagine any of this being uttered with dry eyes; he μ continued, "O God, O Who Gives and Takes Life, O Infinite and Undying, forgive my mother Fāṭimah, daughter of Asad; allow her every excuse, and widen the place of her body's final resting! This I ask You through Your Prophet (i.e. himself μ) and all previous Prophets, O Most Merciful and Compassionate!"[16]

Thereafter, during the preparations of the body for interment, the Prophet μ offered one of his own garments to be used as a *kafan*, or burial shroud.[17] And when he, naturally, led her *janāzah* – funeral prayer – he performed seventy *takbīrs* (i.e. pronouncements of the Arabic formulaic declaration "*Allāhu akbar*," or "God is Most Great"). Once the prayer was over and Fāṭimah's ι body was placed in the bottom of the grave, the Prophet μ made his way down into it as well and set about pointing towards the corners and sides of the shaft; it seemed as if every time he did this, the bottom became wider and straighter in the place toward which he indicated.

These finishing touches now complete, the Prophet μ did something next that astonished those of his Companions present – something which he neither did before nor since.

Pause here to contemplate a moment; could you, dear reader, really envisage climbing down in a grave and lying next to its occupant – a corpse?

Because this is precisely what the Prophet μ did at that moment. So many times a little boy needs the comfort of his mother's lap, or to lie next to her during a cold or frightening night, and this Fāṭimahι was the one next to whom the young Muḥammadμ had lain so often. And this he did one final time, despite his advanced years and long since having severed ties of dependence – and now as Prophet of God and Master of a Nation, no less. He lay there for a time, crying and whispering prayers.

When the Prophet μ finally clambered back to the surface, his eyes were still full of the tears that had left glistening trails streaked through the dust on his face. To commence the process of filling in the grave, he took a handful of earth and cast it in – a final farewell.

Shortly thereafter, and probably at the gathering that forms after a burial, ʿUmar b. al-Khaṭṭābη, who never passed up an opportunity to seek the Prophet's µ purpose in whatever he did, caught up with him and posed his question by announcing, "O Prophet, I saw you doing something for that Lady that you've never done for anyone else…"

Graciously as always, the Prophet µ explained, "O ʿUmar, that Lady was as much my mother as the woman who gave birth to me. Whenever AbūṬālib hosted guests and would call us all in to eat, that Lady would always save a portion just for me. After Abū Ṭālib, she gave me the best treatment in this world. So yes, I put my own garment on her in hopes that she could be clothed in the clothing of Paradise, and I lay down in her grave to ease its tightness and loneliness.

"I tell you truly: Gabriel has informed me from my Lord that she is one of those set to enter Paradise. He also told me that God has ordered seventy thousand angels to hold their own funeral prayer over her."[18]

Contrast the above with the state of affairs in our day. Children tend to completely forget, much less praise and show gratitude for, the generosity and kindness of their parents. To quite the contrary, the caring that goes above and beyond what a non-parent could fathom is somehow transformed into cause for blame for hardship and one's own failures. Although the

Prophet's µ biography reads like a laundry list of tragedy after setback after calamity, for the woman who raised him longest he had nothing but good to say. He climbed into her grave to keep her company one last time and recounted even the smallest of her kindnesses and considerations to his close friends. It is hoped that by this, a small glimpse of Muḥammad's µ magnanimity can be caught.

Despite being enfolded in love while yet in his grandfather's care, in the home of his daughter's namesake the Prophet µ had a complete family; let us now shift the focus from the mother of that noble household to its father, Muḥammad's µ full uncle Abū Ṭālibη. Mirroring the behaviour of his own father toward the young Muḥammadµ, Abū Ṭālibη too developed the habit of being able to sleep only in the company of his nephew µ, and he too took him wherever he went as far as was practicable. He also found his family in the curious position that, if they all ate together with Muḥammadµ, they would all feel satiated with whatever they consumed; but without him they would feel hungry even after devouring plenty. This led Abū Ṭālibη to institute a peculiar house rule: "let no one touch the food until my son comes!"[19] So, not only was the Prophet µ made every meal's esteemed dignitary, he was also called *son* with pride by a man who already had sons aplenty. "Indeed you are a blessed one!"[20] Abū Ṭālib η would often gush, probably unprovoked as loving parents often do to their young children.

Abū Ṭālibη was unabashed in his fawning over his young nephew, and one eyewitness account of such an occasion has reached us, wherein it is narrated that "once, I came to Makkah during a time of great dearth and drought. The heads of Makkah's tribes had come together to deliberate on a solution. Some of them suggested offering a sacrifice to Lāt and ʿUzzah (two deities in the pre-Islāmic Arabian pantheon). Others suggested a worship ritual dedicated to Manāt (another important idol).

"But one of them rebuked the others, saying 'O people, what are you doing? Where else do you think you'll find your solution but with some of the descendants of Ibrāhīm and Ismāʿīl you have in your midst?'

"To which they replied, 'do you mean Abū Ṭālib?'

"'Who else?' went the emphatic response. So, off they all went to the aforementioned man's house as I followed closely behind. Upon arrival, they knocked on his front door, and out stepped a terribly handsome man.

"The impromptu delegation of supplicants addressed him, saying 'O Abā Ṭālib, you have seen that there is drought in the valley, and that famine has stricken its citizens! So come out and perform the *istisqāʾ* (a special, formulaic prayer for rain) for us!' At that, Abū Ṭālibη disappeared into his house, reappearing a few moments later with a young boy whose face shone as brightly as the Sun bursting through a canopy of dark clouds. A few of his other children were around him, no doubt curious as to the cause of the commotion outside their home. Abū Ṭālib proceeded to pick up the radiant boy of his into his arms and carry him to the Kaʿbah with all of us in tow. He hoisted the boy up and held his back against one of the Kaʿbah's walls. He began whispering his prayer for rain while gesturing with his finger toward the young man thus held aloft.

"I should add that before he started all this, there wasn't a cloud in the sky, not as far as the eye could see. But as soon as he started his recitation? Clouds formed and drew in above us from all directions, and they opened upon the valley a downpour that practically filled it!"

Later in his life, Abū Ṭālibη referenced this event in a verse of poetry he composed in honour of his cherished nephew μ:

The radiant one by whom rain is called, a guardian of orphans and refuge for widows;

The new-born moon takes its light from the face of this man of the line of Hāshim – he is the one who bestows and grants to them.[21]

This episode from the Prophet's μ life is a demonstration of his abiding righteousness, known to those closest to him even at a young age. A matter had literally come down to life and death, as drought and famine for Arabians – most of whom already lived well below what we might consider the poverty line today – spelled destruction if prolonged. The people most drastically affected took as their final recourse the wisdom of Abū Ṭālibη, and as we saw, his solution involved a ritual that requires intermediation ("*tawassul*" in Arabic) of one possessed of peerless piety and wholesomeness.

Today, Muslims might use in this capacity the names of people whose righteousness is not known by first-hand experience and long-term, intimate relation, but by word of mouth (and believed by benefit of the doubt). And indeed, the closer we are with acquaintances, friends, and family, the clearer their flaws and foibles become; respect naturally diminishes thusly. It may even unfortunately transpire that familiarity breeds contempt. But Abū Ṭālibη, who knew Muḥammadμ as a father knows his own son, hung the weight of desperate lives on the righteousness he nevertheless knew was manifested in his nephew μ (despite having numerous other sons to choose from, mind).

Because Abū Ṭālibη was a trader, and he kept to his own father's tradition of hardly going anywhere without Muḥammadμ by his side, it so happened that once, the two were with a caravan in the Levant when it had stopped to water and rest the animals. A Christian priest met them there and proclaimed, "you have amongst you one of the righteous."

One of the Arabs responded, saying "as a matter of fact, we do have with us one who shows great hospitality towards guests, pays the ransoms for hostages, and does good to all people."

At this, the priest reiterated emphatically, "indeed you have amongst you one of the righteous!" He gestured towards the young Muḥammad µ and asked, "who is the father of this child?"

The group of Makkans motioned toward Abū Ṭālibη, prompting him to speak up. "I am his father."

At this the priest must have furrowed his brow in consternation, saying half to himself, "but he should not have a father."

Abū Ṭālibη, perhaps not fully understanding the priest's confusion, nevertheless clarified, "well, no. But he's my brother's son, you see." At that, satisfaction began to show on the priest's face, though concern tinged the tone of his inquiry as to what had befallen the boy's father. "He died while his wife was yet pregnant," Abū Ṭālib responded.

"Ah, now you have revealed the truth of the matter," the priest solemnly pronounced. "You must take your nephew back to your own city, for there is a group in this area of those who will recognize him as I have. And they will know, as I know, that he will become a great person in the future; they are an envious lot and will endeavour to bring harm to him."

"What you have said is a warning from God!" Abū Ṭālibη exclaimed as he hastened to prepare himself and his young charge µ for their express journey home.

"O God, I beg that you preserve Muḥammad!" the priest intoned as the two set off in accordance with his advice. He died soon after.[22]

The above episode is a further demonstration of the robustness of Abū Ṭālib's η bond with his nephew. Some random, unfamiliar priest's advice could have easily been ignored, or dismissed with a promise to take extra care in that foreign land. For the two to embark on their own back to Makkah at that juncture meant nothing but added hardship, cost, and personal risk. But such was Abū Ṭālib's η concern for the Prophet μ that he gladly, even hastily, incurred the aforementioned.

And such was the adolescent Muḥammad's μ dedication and gratitude to his beloved uncle that he, soon as he was able, took a job shepherding to supplement Abū Ṭālib's η income which, while ample, was often quickly exhausted by the sheer amount of his dependents. So a pre-teenaged Muḥammadμ would take charge of various Makkan families' flocks and lead them away from the city to graze; what little money he received in return for this great responsibility and difficult task,[23] he spent on his cousins and foster-parents. And when he was finally old enough, around eighteen years of age, Muḥammadμ took on the even-greater responsibility of leading Abū Ṭālib's η trade caravans to al-Shām (in the summer) and Yemen (in the winter).

Even after he married and finally left Abū Ṭālib's η house, taking on the added responsibilities of husband and head of his own household, Muḥammadμ never abandoned his duty to the uncle and aunt who had raised him as their own son. In a great show of not only concern, but taking initiative as well, he went to one of his other uncles, ʿAbbāsη (who was himself another wealthy merchant), and said, "O uncle, you can see that your brother Abū Ṭālib has a large family, too large to provide for on his own. I think you and I are in a position to help him. What do you say?" ʿAbbās agreed, of course, and asked what the Prophet μ had in mind. "Let us each take one of his sons, so it will be easier for him to look after the rest of his children. I will take ʿAlī, and you could take Jaʿfar," he explained. ʿAbbās agreed, and they did so. The two sons of Abū Ṭālibη were around five and fifteen years old at the time, respectively[24].

Increasingly in modern times, we find that children have become over-dependent on their parents, even well into their thirties (I know some personally). Despite the pleading of their parents, who work day and night to maintain the household, they themselves neither work nor study, seldom even lifting a finger in the execution of daily chores. In some cases, these same leech-like offspring go so far as to openly disrespect their parents with insults and shouted ingratitude. This is all in stark contrast to the Prophet μ, whose perfect example of sonship was such that he did everything he possibly could, as soon as he possibly could, to relieve the burdens of whom he regarded as his equal to his parents.

We saw earlier in this chapter the severity with which the death of Fāṭimah bt. Asadι had stricken the Prophet μ. This same year, none other than her husband and the Prophet's μ beloved uncle and foster-father Abū Ṭālibη passed away, as well as his wife Khadījahо. The extremity of his love and gratitude for the aforementioned was matched only by the extremity of grief by which the Prophet's μ heart was wracked at their deaths; thus that entire year rightfully earned the title "Year of Sorrow."

We have on record in the Islāmic tradition many well-authenticated sayings of the Prophet χ extolling the virtues of motherhood, and the paramount importance placed on honouring that position. One such goes that, "Paradise lies at the feet of your mothers."[25] Mothers specifically even get a special mention from God Himself in the Holy Qur'ān which can be rendered into English as, "thus have We enjoined upon humankind the best possible conduct with their parents; in hardship did their mothers bear them, and painfully were they born…"[26] to the end of the verse. And so, in acknowledgement of this Qur'ānic precept, and in keeping with the Western tradition of "saving the best for last," we move finally in this chapter to the Prophet's μ own mother, Āminah bt. Wahbι.

We know that the Prophet μ spent scarcely any of his childhood with his mother before her death in his sixth year of life, so one might feel safe in assuming that we have no way of knowing how he behaved with her. But even so, we yet have accounts of his relationship with her well after her passing, even after his being called to divine messengership. And in these accounts, we can see – perhaps unsurprisingly – the Prophet's μ application of the Qur'ānic prescription of "the best possible conduct" (or "*iḥsān*" in Arabic) with one's parents.

Were we to reflect on our own mental and emotional states, most of us might countenance having strong enough feelings of pain and loss to weep only on the days of death and burial of our parents – even after being blessed with decades to spend with them. And on the rare occasions we might find ourselves visiting them in their graves, many wouldn't even be able to muster tears then, even after a few years.

Now, there is no reason to assume the Prophet μ visited his mother's grave any less, but what we actually have on record is that he visited her when he was on his way to al-Ḥudaybiyyah, after the Liberation of Makkah, during *ʿumrah* (a lesser pilgrimage to the Kaʿbah outside of the Ḥajj season), and during his *Ḥijjah al-Widāʿ*. The first of these recorded visits took place when the Prophet μ was fifty-six years old.

It was on one of these occasions that the Prophet μ approached a grave and sat next to it, so those accompanying him – around a thousand people – sat around him, keen as his companions always were to observe his behaviour in every situation. He began moving his head in the way a person does when engaged in conversation, and after a short while he began crying as no one had ever seen him cry before. Finally, ʿUmar b. al-Khaṭṭābη approached the Prophet μ and asked why he was weeping so. "This," the Prophet μ responded sorrowfully, "is the grave of Āminah, daughter of Wahb!"[27]

On another occasion, it was another of the Prophet's μ star pupils – a companion by the name of ʿAbdullāh b.

Mas῾ūdη – who witnessed a similar scene. This time, as the Prophet µ made his way to the graveyard in Makkah, he asked those accompanying him to wait for him before proceeding to a particular grave. There he sat, there he conversed, and there he wept. He wept so forcefully and for so long that it gave his companions a fright such that they too began to weep uncontrollably. On his way back, the Prophet µ was asked, "why were you sobbing so, O Messenger of God?"

"Did it scare you?" the Prophet µ asked comfortingly. The gathered companions answered in the affirmative, some still wiping tears away. "Well," continued the Prophet µ, "that grave you saw me speaking and crying at was that of none other than Āminah, daughter of Wahb – my mother!"[28]

These are only the few occasions that have been narrated through the ages to reach us today, and we can see the deep sadness that gripped the Prophet µ every time he visited his mother's final resting place.[29] This was a woman with whom he spent almost no time, but who nevertheless bore him with hardship, and with pain gave birth to him. And so he honoured her with his sincere heartache and tears at every opportunity.[30]

Chapter 2

...as a Grandson

There is an understandable, if unfortunate, dearth of information on the Prophet's µ grandparents, and even less on his relationship with them. But what little that has reached us in this regard paints a picture of the same warmth and affection most of us today experience with our own grandparents.

For three of his grandparents, we have only names. His maternal grandmother was Barrah bt. ʿAbd al-ʿUzzah[31], and his maternal grandfather was Wahb b. ʿAbd Manāf[32]. His paternal grandmother was Fāṭimah bt. ʿAmr,[33] who was also the mother of the Prophet's µ uncle Abū Ṭālibη.

However, the grandparent about whom we have the most information – particularly about their interactions with the Prophet µ – is his paternal grandfather, a man named Shaybah b. Hāshimη[34]. As an interesting aside, his own personal name means "hoary-headed" as he was indeed born with some white hairs on his head. He was born in Yathrib, and his father passed away in Gaza. He and his uncle, a man named al-Muṭṭalib, relocated to Makkah at some point and upon entering the town, people began to mistake him for al-Muṭṭalib's slave, thus earning him the nickname by which he is better known even until today – ʿAbd al-Muṭṭalib. He would quickly correct them, saying "he is not my slave, rather he is my brother Hāshim's son," but the appellation stuck.[35]

When the Prophet μ was six years old, his mother Āminahı passed away, whereupon he was taken in by this grandfather of his; this is perhaps what allowed so much of what follows to be preserved.[36]

Once, when the Prophet μ was still quite young, ʿAbd al-Muṭṭalibη sent him off on his own to retrieve a fugitive camel. His task took so much longer than his grandfather expected that by the time the Prophet μ returned, ʿAbd al-Muṭṭalibη had spent the better part of the day sick with worry, blaming himself for whatever misfortune he feared must have befallen his beloved grandson. When the young Prophet μ did finally accomplish his mission and return safe and sound, his grandfather wasted no time in solemnly swearing never again to let him out of his sight, much less send him solo after lost livestock.[37] And as far as we know, he kept this oath, going so far as to sleep exclusively next to his dear lad Muḥammadμ despite being the head of the Quraysh clan, thus enjoying such sacrosanct privacy that none else dared disturb his slumber or even enter his quarters.[38]

Daylight hours were no different, as he would make the Prophet μ his escort on any and every sortie from their home.[39] And as he was the head of the Quraysh, he also had reserved for himself a seat next to the Kaʿbah which none else had the honour of occupying but Muḥammadμ. And when they would sit together, in that seat or others, ʿAbd al-Muṭṭalibη could be heard proclaiming, with the same sort of delighted pride with which any grandparent today would be familiar that "this is my son, and he will soon establish his kingdom!"[40]

Because the environs of the Kaʿbah were so public and heavily-trafficked, much of the tender interaction between ʿAbd al-Muṭṭalibη and his favoured grandson μ was on display, thus the couple following episodes we have on record also took place under the shade of the Kaʿbah itself.

As mentioned previously, ʿAbd al-Muṭṭalib's η spot on his couch near the Kaʿbah was inviolable. Often, when he occupied it, his own sons would sit around him, forming a sort of entourage. So, when a young Muḥammadμ would break that sacred circle to sit with his beloved grandfather, his uncles would rush to remove him – no doubt with the good intention of saving their father from the disturbance of which young boys are so often the cause. But ʿAbd al-Muṭṭalibη would quickly refrain them saying, "leave my son alone! I swear to God he's got a bright future ahead of him!" He would thereafter gather Muḥammadμ up and set him down right next to him, often stroking his back idly. Or he would simply sit, watching in delighted amusement whatever the young boy did.[41]

As he was head of the Quraysh, delegations from various Arab tribes would come to ʿAbd al-Muṭṭalibη, if for nothing more than the honour of meeting with him. And so it was that once, a group of men from the Banū Mudlij came to greet him under the Kaʿbah's shade. A peculiar thing for which this tribe was well-known was producing men with the ability to ascertain an individual's lineage, age, and other various details via an examination of their feet; it must have been shortly after they offered their salutations to ʿAbd al-Muṭṭalibη that little Muḥammadµ – as he was surely by now freely allowed to do – came to sit with his grandfather. When he straightened his legs, revealing the soles of his feet, the Banū Mudlij men caught sight of them. One of them must not have been able to contain himself and remarked, "how amazing! I've not seen a footprint bearing more resemblance to that marking the Maqām Ibrāhīm than that of this boy!" Composing himself, he turned to ʿAbd al-Muṭṭalibη and sincerely advised him to "take good care of him, because he should grow into a great man."

Pleased with this prediction from what he must have considered an authoritative source, ʿAbd al-Muṭṭalibη turned to his son Abū Ṭālibη and counselled him saying, "keep this in mind!"[42]

Another harbinger of young Muḥammad's µ eventual rise to paramountcy – specifically prophethood in this case – came from some young scholars of *Ahl al-Kitāb* (probably Jews given their strong presence in the Ḥijāz at that time in history, but maybe Christians) with whom he had spent some time playing. There must have been something about the youngster that compelled them to inform ʿAbd al-Muṭṭalibη of their observations; he passed them along to his slave Umm Ayman, who was at that time acting in the capacity as a sort of step-mother to Muḥammadµ, addressing her thusly: "O Barakah, keep an eye on my son! I was told by some scholars of People of Scripture that he shall be the prophet of this nation."[43]

Finally, when ʿAbd al-Muṭṭtalib's η passing became imminent, he summoned his sons to dictate to each of them his final will and testament. When came Abū Ṭālib's η turn for instruction, his father addressed him concerning Muḥammadμ saying, "O Abā Ṭālib, take care of this lone child who was deprived both of his father's love, and more than but a few years with his mother. Treat him as your own flesh and blood! I have chosen you especially for this task; you've been the closest to him from the rest of his uncles, and you are from the same mother as his father. O Abā Ṭālib, if you live to see him grow to participate in the world of men, then ensure you support and follow his every endeavour, because I'm convinced that he'll attain such a position of esteem that no other descendant of our forefathers could. O Abā Ṭālib, I'm not aware of any of our ancestors who lost both father and mother as he did, so take care to keep him from feeling loneliness!"[44]

Not long after, ʿAbd al-Muṭṭalibη passed away; Muḥammadμ was only eight years old. Umm Ayman later recounted that she saw him μ behind ʿAbd al-Muṭṭalib's η bed, crying at his passing.[45] Muḥammadμ as a loving grandson kept the day of loosing his beloved grandfather in his memory for the rest of his life, and he has acknowledged it after becoming a prophet when was asked "do you remember the death of ʿAbd al-Muṭṭalib " by saying "yes!, I was eight then."[46]

Thus ended the chapter of our Beloved's µ life as a grandson – a chapter filled, as we can see, with the tenderness and love known to anyone who was ever privileged enough to be singled out for showering with a grandparent's adoration.

Chapter 3

...as a Father

Historians disagree on exactly how many children the Prophet Muḥammadμ had, but there is agreement on four daughters and three sons.

Zaynabι was the first of the Prophet's μ daughters – popularly the first-born of all his children – born when he was thirty years old, which would have been five years after marrying Khadījaho. She supported her father μ in his divine mission and migrated to Madīnah. She passed away in the year 8AH/629CE.[47]

Qāsimη was the first of the Prophet's μ sons born, according to most, when the Prophet μ was thirty-one years old, with some historians taking the position that he was actually first-born rather than Zaynabo. But he was the very first of the Prophet's μ children to pass away. It is commonly accepted that he died before Muḥammadμ was even called to prophethood, with some historians holding that he passed away while yet a breastfeeding baby.[48]

The third child of God's Messenger μ was a daughter, who was known by the *kunyah* (the Arabian equivalent of a nickname) of Umm Kulthūmι. Some say her name was Āminah, but the most widely-held view is that her given name cannot now be known. Before Muḥammad's μ first receipt of divine revelation, Umm Kulthūm had been betrothed to one ʿUtaybah b. Abī Lahab. But as soon as the Prophet µ came out in opposition to the paganism and oppression of his fellow Quraysh, ʿUtaybah broke off the engagement so he could openly criticize and impede the Prophet µ.[49] But later on, three years after the migration to Madīnah, Umm Kulthūmı was married to ʿUthmān b. ʿAffānŋ – one of the Prophet's µ closest companions. She passed away six years later in 9AH/630CE, with the Prophet µ himself leading her *janāzah*.[50]

Muḥammad's µ fourth child was another daughter by the name of Fāṭimah al-Zahrā'o, who was named after the Prophet's µ foster-mother. Historians disagree over her date of birth; some argue that the Prophet µ was forty-one at the time, while others say thirty-five. Either way, we know that many of the Prophet's µ noble companions later sought to marry her, even two of the most well-known – the Prophet's µ two immediate political successors Abū Bakrŋ and ʿUmar b. al-Khaṭṭābŋ. But they were all politely refused in favour of the Prophet's µ much-younger cousin and adoptive son, ʿAlī b. Abī Ṭālibv – none other than the son of Fāṭimah's o namesake. According to the most prevalent opinion, she passed away six months after the Prophet µ, in 11AH/632CE.[51]

Ruqayyahı, whom a minority of historians regard as the eldest the Prophet's µ daughters, was famously beautiful and was for a time engaged to ʿUtbah b. Abī Lahab. He cancelled their engagement for the same reason his brother broke things off with Umm Kulthūmη[52], shortly after which ʿUthmān b. ʿAffānη proposed to and married her.[53] She participated in both of the Muslims' migration events – first to Abyssinia,[54] then to Madīnah – dying shortly after the latter in 2AH/624CE at the age of twenty. Her passing coincided with the Expedition of Badr, hence the Prophet μ was only present for her funeral.

ʿAbdullāhη was the youngest son from Khadījaho.[55] Unfortunately, the only things mentioned about him in the annals of history are disagreements over whether he was born before or after the bestowal of prophethood upon Muḥammadμ, and whether he was given the different names of Ṭāhir or Ṭayyib[56]. Other historians posit that Ṭāhir and Ṭayyib were two other sons born to the Prophet μ, each one the second of two sets of twins; the other alleged twins were named Muṭahhar and Muṭayyab.[57]

The last child to be born to the Prophet μ was a son by the name Ibrāhīm. His mother was Māryah the Copt ι (al-Qibṭiyyah in Arabic), an Egyptian Christian maid-servant sent to Muḥammadμ from al-Muqawqis, the administrator of Alexandria, as a gesture of goodwill after receiving a letter inviting him to Islām. Ibrāhīm was born in 8AH/629CE and died as an infant. Some reports give his age at the time of death as seventy days, others six months, and still others one year and ten months.[58]

Those who would have sought to undermine the Prophet's μ credibility as a genuine messenger of the Almighty χfalsely attributed a further two sons to him by the names of ʿAbd Manāf and ʿAbd al-ʿUzzah. We know from much more credible sources that the Prophet's μ immediate family, including he himself, never participated in the idolatry practiced by the majority of the Quraysh; they and several other well-known families followed a set of beliefs that identified them as what is referred to in Islāmic literature as *Ḥunafā'* (singular of *Ḥanīf*), or Abrahamic monotheists. Therefore, that the aforementioned two theophoric names would be chosen by Muḥammad for any of his children is an unrealistic suggestion at best (and deliberate slander at worst).

Because all of his children (and some of his grandchildren) but Fāṭimaho passed away during his lifetime[59], and her husband was also one of the Prophet's μ own household, most of his recorded interactions with his children centre around her. That the Prophet μ was as dutiful, compassionate, and loving a father as he was a son and grandson shall hereunder be illustrated in great detail.

Numerous sources inform us that it was the Prophet's μ consistent practice to pay the members of his immediate family a visit before setting off on a journey of any significant length. These sources also inform us that a part of this practice was to make the home of his daughter Fāṭimaho his last stop before leaving and his first upon return. Muḥammad had the immense love that any father would for all of his children, but Fāṭimah's o relationship with her father was a uniquely close one. This could have been attested to by anyone who observed the family together, but none other than one of the Prophet's µ dearest wives, ʿĀ'ishah bt. Abī Bakrι, narrated for posterity the following glowing report, which vividly illustrates the sincerity and love – bearing in mind that Arabian culture made a man's displays of affection for his children an oddity – with which the Prophet µ approached fatherhood.

"I have never seen anyone who more resembles the Prophet µ in character, habits, and manner than his daughter Fāṭimah. Whenever she came to visit him, he would always stand to greet her with a kiss, ushering her in to sit where he had been sitting. And whenever he went to visit her, she would do likewise"[60].

"When the Prophet became bed-ridden in his final illness – thus unable to greet her accordingly – she leaned over to kiss him after sitting next to him. He must have said something to her in those few seconds, because when she sat back up, she was crying. A few moments later she leaned over again, only to sit back up laughing. Now, I used to hold her in such high regard, and view her with such awe, that I was a bit taken aback to see her displaying such emotionality. So, some time after the Prophet had passed away, I could no longer resist and finally asked her about that incident. She told me that when she had started crying, it was because the Prophet had told her that he had deduced that he wasn't much longer for this world; and when she laughed afterwards, it was because the Prophet had told her that she would be one of his first relatives to join him."[61]

What a father our Prophet μ must have been, that not only did his daughter cry upon receiving news of his imminent death, but she was overjoyed only moments later at the prospect of soon re-joining him in the life hereafter – nevermind the implication such news brought of her own impending demise!

Not only did the Prophet μ love, honour, and cherish his children, he even stepped in as something of an amateur marriage counsellor when the need arose. On one occasion, ʿAlīv expressed something in a way which Fāṭimaho found unfavourable – so much so that she vowed to go and immediately protest his conduct to none other than the Prophet μ. When she left their house, ʿAlīv covertly tailed her and concealed himself where he could overhear his wife's conversation with her father. After quietly listening while his daughter presented her complaints, the Prophet μ responded gently, "my dear daughter – listen to me, and understand. It could be that he took that harsh tone because you displeased him somehow; it often happens that the lady who does so brings about the behaviour you described."

Upon hearing this and being confronted with the realization that his behaviour was the impetus for the Prophet's μ implication that his beloved daughter was possibly a disappointing wife, ʿAlīv vowed never again to express any displeasure with Fāṭimaho.[62]

Another occasion of some marital discord between the Prophet's µ daughter and his cousin this time brought *him* to *their*home. When he arrived, they greeted him and laid out a mat upon which to rest. He reclined on it and invited the two to do the same, one on either side. Still sensing some tension between his beloveds, he took ʿAlī's hand and placed it on his belly, doing likewise with Fāṭimah's. He then proceeded to converse, advise, and joke with the couple until no tension was left, and their condition was well as ever.

Someone who had happened to see the Prophet µ approaching ʿAlī's house with signs of distress on his face but leaving in a much lighter mood couldn't help himself and inquired as to the reason. So the Prophet µ answered, "how could I not be happy after reconciling between the two most beloved people to me!"[63]

How many of us fathers would see our daughter upset with her husband and jump to support her arguments, or stoke the flames of her anger with our own, consequences be damned? Instead, the Prophet µ forewent the impulse to lash out and not only abated his daughter's anger, but proceeded in every case to bring a happy resolution to situations that – for people who were products of a temperamental culture – could easily have ended in divorce.

Our historical record is all but brimming with the love Muḥammadµ had, and expressed, for his children and grandchildren. But this love was tempered by deep wisdom and a commitment to justice and charity for those less fortunate.

And despite the austerity it entailed, he consistently prioritized success in the life hereafter over the luxuries of the world.

Now, as has been mentioned, the Prophet µ made it an imperative of his that he should visit his daughter Fāṭimaho just before setting off on any sort of expedition, after visiting his other immediate relatives; likewise he made sure to see her first upon his return. On one of these returning visits, he approached Fāṭimah's o house and, seeing an elaborate curtain hung on her door and silver necklaces hung around the necks of his grandchildren Ḥasanv and Ḥusaynv, he instead went away without entering. Making the reasonable assumption that the reason for the Prophet's µ hasty departure was displeasure with what he saw, Fāṭimaho proceeded to tear down the curtain and rip the necklaces from her children's necks.

Naturally, the two young children came shortly thereafter running to their grandfather crying, holding the pieces of their formerly-prized necklaces in their little hands. At this, the Prophet µ told his servant Thawbānη to gift the silver fragments that used to be necklaces to one of the poor families of Madīnah. "These are my relatives," explained the Prophet µ, "so I dislike that they should trade any measure of bliss in the hereafter for some fleeting extravagance in this world. Go now, Thawbān, and buy a couple of simple necklaces made of nerve fibre for my grandsons, and for Fāṭimah two bracelets of elephant bone."[64]

So, what albeit minor injustice the Prophet µ perceived in his grandchildren having silver necklaces while other children in the same city were destitute, he was obliged to rectify. But out of compassion for his grandchildren – heartbroken over the loss of their ornaments – he yet compensated their loss. It may not have been like for like, but all children that age understand is that their mother broke something they enjoyed, and their grandpa replaced it. Analysing this scenario, I can only be amazed at how deftly the Prophet µ manoeuvred through all the variables – love for his family, equity with the city's poor, raising his grandsons' spirits, and gifting his daughter – and emerged with a positive outcome for all involved.

The moments immediately preceding our own death, if it is our lot to experience them for what they are, must arguably be the most disconcerting and terrifying of any other. The Prophet µ though, as was his Way, refused to give in to selfish concerns near his own time of passing, instead focusing all his mental and emotional energy on comforting those loved ones who surrounded him. When he began to fade in and out of consciousness at one point, for example, Fāṭimaho exclaimed "woe to me, my sorrow for my father's pain!"

When he was able, the Prophet µ responded, "do not worry; from after today, there is no more pain for your father!"[65] At another point around that same time he saw her crying, so he called out to her "don't you cry, O my dear daughter! Just remind yourself, 'to God we belong, and to Him is our return!' Indeed, whoever does so will be compensated."[66]

Despite his own pain and impending mortality, his priority was the soothing of his daughter's sadness.

Even at a time when the pain of loss would overwhelm any of us who are parents – at the death of a child – the Prophet's µ main concern was soothing the anguish of others and seeing to their emotional health. When the Prophet µ returned from the Expedition of Badr only to discover that his own daughter Ruqayyah had passed away, he went to her grave and said sorrowfully, "go and join our predecessor ʿUthmān son of Maẓʿūn," as the death of that particularly close Companion η was still quite recent. A group of women nearby overheard him, could bear it no longer and began to weep. ʿUmarη, who was also present, made as if to begin beating them with a stick for what he assumed was a grave breach of protocol, but his hand was stayed by the Prophet µ who – through and despite his own grief – advised him gently, "leave them to their tears!" Turning then to the group of women, he reminded them that "it's perfectly alright to cry, but don't let yourselves start with that Satanic wailing of the idolaters! What flows from hearts and eyes is a sign of God's mercy; but what is expressed on tongues and hands is from Satan."[67] At about that time, Fāṭimaho came and sat beside her father at the grave site, and when she herself began to cry over her sister, the Prophet µ held her and wiped her tears with his sleeve.

The Prophet's µ care for others despite his own pain shone through when his daughter Zaynab died as well. At a time when most of us would be lost in sorrow, the Prophet µ personally supervised the preparation of his own daughter's body for burial. He approached the group of women carrying out the actual preparations and advised them, "wash her an odd number of times, three or five. The last time should be with camphor or a mixture containing camphor. Inform me when you've finished." When they did so, he presented them with his *izār* (a large square cloth used as a garment) for use as Zaynab's *kafan* – no doubt in hopes that something of him would remain with her.[68]

As was glimpsed above, the Prophet μ forbade his followers from the extreme mourning rituals and customs of the idol-worshiping Arabians, and some mistook this prohibition for a general moratorium on any display of sadness, no matter how unintentional or sincere.

At some point, the Prophet's μ young son Ibrāhīm had been sent to the home of a blacksmith known as Abū Sayf to be looked after and breastfed. When the Prophet μ would come to visit the infant, he would pick him up, kiss him (which, as mentioned previously, was a fairly un-Arabian thing to do), and breathe in the smell of smoke in his hair. When the Prophet μ came to see him after he had taken ill – and was in fact dying – tears began to flow from his eyes as he picked him up and whispered, "O my dear son, I am not in a position to change anything set in motion by God."

ʿAbd al-Raḥmān b. ʿAwfη, who had accompanied the Prophet μ, was shocked to see this and asked, "even you do it, O Messenger of God? Didn't you prevent us from crying?"

Through tears the Prophet µ answered, "O son of ʿAwf, I forbade from scratching and beating the face, ripping the clothing, and wailing like demons. But this is from compassion, and the one who has no compassion receives none. And if it were not true that the ones who go before and the ones who follow meet again regardless, I would feel even more sad than I do now." After being interrupted by a sob, he continued "truly, the eye is in tears and the heart is in sorrow, but we refrain the tongue from what displeases our Lord. O Ibrāhīm, we're so sad at your departure!"[69] The Prophet µ used to mention later on that, because he died while still a breast-feeding babe, Ibrāhīm would have two – probably angels – to complete his breastfeeding in Paradise.[70]

Chapter 4

...as a Grandfather

The Prophet µ had a total of eight grandchildren. From Zaynabι was born ʿAlīη who died as a child, shortly after his mother, according to the most prevalent opinion. However, historians differ greatly, with some positing that he was killed in the Battle of Yarmūk (15 AH/636 CE), which was actually seven years after his mother's passing – this would have been four years after the Prophet's µ death.[71] Zaynab's second child was a girl named Umāmahι. Such was her virtue that before her own demise, Fāṭimaho, her aunt, advised her husband ʿAlī ν to marry her; he did so, but they never had any children.[72]

Fāṭimah o had four children with ʿAlī b. AbīṬālibν, the first of whom was named Ḥasanν. He was born on the 13th or 14th of Ramaḍān, 3AH/March, 625CE and died in Madīnah in 49AH/669CE. Second was Ḥusaynν, born in 4AH/626CE and martyred in 61AH/680CE at Karbalā' (near Najaf, Iraq). Third came Muḥsinν, born while the Prophet µ was still alive; he died while still in infancy.[73]

One of the two daughters born of Fāṭimaho was Umm Kulthūm, according to some historians, also while the Prophet µ was yet living.[74] She went on to wed ʿUmar b. al-Khaṭṭābη, the second Khalīfah.[75] After his demise, she married her cousin ʿAwn b. Jaʿfar b. AbīṬālib, and after his death married his brother Muḥammad b. Jaʿfar. After that cousin's demise, she married his brother ʿAbdullāh b. Jaʿfar. She herself had only two children, both from ʿUmarη, named Zayd and Ruqayyah, both of whom died during her lifetime.[76]

Fāṭimah's o second daughter was named Zaynab, who was also said by historians to have been born before the Prophet's µ death. After the death of her sister Umm Kulthūm, she married the same ʿAbdullāh b. Jaʿfar and had two children with him –ʿAlī and Umm Kulthūm.[77]

Lastly, the Prophet's µ daughter Ruqayyah had a son named ʿAbdullāh, who died as a child.[78]

As was the case with Fāṭimah o, her sons Ḥasan and Ḥusaynθ feature most heavily – almost exclusively, in fact – in the eyewitness accounts of the Prophet's µ interactions with his grandchildren. He was even personally involved in arguably one of the most important aspects of their lives: the selection and bestowal of their names. Now, we have already touched on the emphasis Arabians placed on virtues associated with virility and bellicosity, so it is perfectly understandable that ʿAlīv would want to gift his sons with glorious and strong names. When his first son was born, he had wanted to call him Ḥarb, which means "war." When the Prophet µ came to congratulate his two beloveds on the birth of their first child, he asked excitedly after what they had decided to call him. When ʿAlī informed him that he had chosen Ḥarb as the boy's name, the Prophet µ immediately disagreed, saying "no, rather he is Ḥasan!" which instead means "beautiful" and connotes a sort of wholesome fullness.

When Ḥusaynv was born, again ʿAlī had intended to name him Ḥarb, but again the Prophet µ intervened, rushing to their home with congratulations and asking "where is he? What have you named my son?" ʿAlī's v suggestion was again rejected, with the Prophet µ opining, "no, not that! Rather he is Ḥusayn," which is the diminutive form of the word *ḥasan.* A third son saw a third name suggestion – Ḥarb again – from ʿAlīv overruled in favour of the name Muḥsin, in keeping with the motif; this was something the Prophet µ admitted to, saying proudly "I have named them following the pattern of Prophet Hārūn's sons – Shabr, Shabīr, and Mushabbir!"[79]

One of the most solemn duties to which the Prophet µ was tasked was the leadership of congregational prayers; indeed, this is an honour taken most seriously by any Muslim, even today. But even the dischargement of this duty never prevented the Prophet µ from acting in his capacity as the fun-loving grandpa.

Once, the Prophet µ left for the mosque to lead the night prayer with either Ḥasanv or Ḥusaynv in his arms. When he arrived, he took his place at the head of the ranks, put his grandson down, and commenced to leading the prayer. Somewhere around the middle of the prayer though, the Prophet µ led the congregation into what seemed like an extraordinarily long prostration, prompting the gathered worshipers to question thereafter what had happened; some of them worried for the health of their Prophet µ, while others assumed a revelation was descending upon him, making it impossible for him to get up. But the Prophet µ responded, likely the twinkle of good humour in his eye, that "no, no, none of that. It's just that my boy here was riding on top of me, and I didn't want to get up and spoil it for him!"[80]

On another occasion, the Prophet µ came out into the mosque carrying Umāmah bt. Abī al-ʿĀṣ – his granddaughter from Zaynab – when she was yet a child. He began praying a voluntary prayer, still holding her tightly, putting her down when bowing or prostrating, but picking her back up and placing her on his shoulders when standing.[81] The ritual prayer is one of the central aspects of a practicing Muslim's daily life, and it requires the utmost presence of mind and tranquillity of temperament; and while these conditions were undoubtedly fulfilled perfectly by the Prophet µ, he still allowed these moments of personal devotion and closeness to God to be opportunities for closeness with his beloved grandchildren as well.

Another great responsibility upon the shoulders of the Prophet µ was delivering public addresses and sermons. On one such occasion, the Prophet µ was atop the pulpit in the mosque delivering a speech. At some point, his grandson Ḥasanv toddled up the steps of the pulpit, prompting the Prophet µ to lean down, pick him, and hug him. Turning to the gathered audience, he prophesied that "this son of mine is a noble lord, and through his actions God shall reconcile two warring factions of my nation."[82]

On another occasion, the Prophet was again atop the pulpit giving a sermon when he spotted both Ḥasanν and Ḥusaynν stumbling along on a direct approach, so he decided to dismount the pulpit and meet them halfway, stooping down to hug them both tightly before picking them up and returning to the pulpit, grandsons in hand. He continued his address, saying "surely God has spoken the truth when He said, 'your wealth and children are not but a trial for you,'" quoting the Qur'ānic verse. "I saw these two walking, and they kept falling; I was unable to bear it, so I went to them instead." Then, looking at the two beautiful boys sitting at his feet, he said "indeed, you are a mercy from God, and you are to be glorified and loved."[83]

In fact, the Prophet μ seized any and every opportunity to show his affection for his grandchildren, even to the astonishment of many of his male Companions. One of them once, sitting in a gathering with the Prophet μ saw young Ḥasanν come and snuggle up to the Prophet μ, so the Prophet μ grabbed him, lifted up his shirt, and kissed his tummy.[84] Another time, one al-Aqrā' b. Ḥābisη noticed the Prophet μ grab Ḥasanν and kiss him; at this al-Aqrā'η blurted out, "I have ten sons, and I've never kissed a single one of them!"

Considering this a teachable moment, the Prophet μ simply responded, "the one who doesn't show compassion is not shown compassion."[85] This was an oft-quoted maxim in the prophetic Way, as we can see he also used it in reply to another of his Companions, ʿUyaynah b. Badrη, who saw the Prophet μplaying with Husainν by sticking out his tongue and wagging it around, eliciting delighted laughter from the child.

ʿUyaynahη saw this and remarked, "By God, if my son turned his face to me, I would never kiss it!" And so the Prophet μ replied with the aforementioned principle.[86]

Another time, some unknown Bedouin came to visit the Prophet μ; among the things he inquired about was whether he kissed his children (because, you see, this Bedouin *never* did so). All the Prophet μ could say, probably in exasperation, was "if God has lifted compassion from your heart, well… I can't help you!"[87] On another occasion, the Prophet μ took hold of either Ḥasan's ν or Ḥusayn's ν hands and shouted "*taraqqa ʿayn baqqah*!" which was a nonsensical rhyme meant to initiate a game which children used to play in that time. So, following the rules of the game, the child stamped his foot down on top of the Prophet's μ. But instead of continuing, the Prophet μ swooped the child up to his chest and kissed him, exclaiming, "O God, I love him, so You love him too!"[88]

The Prophet μ made this same sort of supplication in favour of his grandchildren many times, as we see in another well-attested tradition that the Prophet μ had gone to the house of Fāṭimah ο in search of Ḥasan ν. When he arrived, he called out "is thc tiny onc hcrc?" Λftcr a short whilc, nobody responded to his call, so he turned to leave when suddenly Ḥasan v burst forth and ran straight into the waiting arms of the Prophet µ. He picked him up and shouted, "O God, I love him! So You love him and those who love him!"[89]

Indeed, the Prophet µ absolutely delighted in playing with his grandchildren. Once, Abū Hurayrahη – who followed the Prophet µ closely in the last years of his life – saw the Prophet µ lying on his back holding up either Ḥasan v or Ḥusayn v, hand-to-hand and foot-to-foot, singing "lit-tle man, lit-tle man!" as he bounced him up and down.[90]

Another time, when one of the two grandsons was riding around on the Prophet's µ neck, someone approached and addressed the youngster laughingly, "what an amazing mount you've found, O boy!"

The Prophet µ, without skipping a beat called out from beneath his grandson, "and what an amazing rider he is!"[91] But it wasn't just play that the Prophet µ enjoyed with his grandchildren; he also enjoyed simply being close to them, as we can see in a report that once Anas b. Mālikη entered the Prophet's µ house and saw him lying on his stomach, with Ḥasan µ lying on the Prophet's µ back.[92]

Prophet Muḥammad µ didn't exclude his other grandchildren from the bottomless spring of tenderness that flowed for his family. On the momentous occasion of Makkah's liberation from the corrupt and idolatrous Quraysh, the

Prophet μ entered the city riding a mule, but not on his own. He had a passenger set snugly behind him – none other than ʿAlīη, his grandson from his daughter Zaynab ι.[93]

Zaynab's ι daughter Umāmahι was another whose special attention from the Prophet μ we have on record, but in a manner more appropriate for little girls than the horseplay he engaged in with his grandsons. Once, likely after the death of his daughter Zaynab ι, all of the Prophet's μ wives were gathered in the same house with Umāmahι (who would have been by this time under the Prophet's μ custody) playing in some sand in the corner, when someone came to the house to deliver to the Prophet μ a gift of a beautiful necklace with gold accents. The Prophet μ displayed the necklace to all present and asked, "well what do you think of this?" All expressed their amazement, that they had never seen better. With this point made and agreed upon, the Prophet μ continued, saying, "then I will give it to the most beloved to me from my family." Everyone assumed that he would proceed to present it to ʿĀ'ishahι, but he instead called Umāmahι over and hung it round her neck, brushing some dirt from her eye as he did so.[94] Another similar instance took place when the Negus of Abyssinia gifted the Prophet μ with several exquisite pieces of jewellery, amongst which was a golden ring he passed along to Umāmahι.[95] We can see in the aforementioned not only the Prophet's μ special care and attention for his family, but the special place he had in his heart for orphans as well.

As has been mentioned, all of the Prophet's μ children but Fāṭimah ο died during his lifetime, and several of his grandchildren.[96] On a much more sombre occasion than those above – when ʿAlīη, son of Zaynab ι was deathly ill – Zaynab ι sent a servant to fetch the Prophet μ to her house. But the Prophet μ sent him back, saying "to God belongs what he has granted, and what he takes back. Let her be patient." But when she sent for him again, he went to her. When he arrived, ʿAlīη – whose chest was trembling – was passed over to the Prophet μ, and when he saw the condition of his little grandson, he began to cry. Saʿd b. ʿUbādah η, one from the small group who had accompanied him, seems to have been under the same impression as many others who assumed that any sort of expression of grief at calamity was forbidden. But through his tears, the Prophet μ reiterated his oft-repeated principle, that "God shows compassion only to his compassionate servants."[97]

It should be clear now that, notwithstanding his position at the head of the community – the pinnacle of humanity itself, in fact – the Prophet μ never took himself so seriously as to forego enjoying every moment he possibly could with his grandchildren (in spite of what the macho cultural norms of his contemporary Arabians dictated). And despite the rigours of daily life as prophet-cum-leader, he made conscious efforts to seek out his progeny, ensuring they never felt neglected and always felt loved.

Chapter 5

...as a Step-father

Prophet Muḥammad μ had the opportunity to set an example in every role a man might fill, including one which many never get the chance to: that of step-father.

Among the earliest converts to Islām were a married couple whose names were Abū Salamah ʿAbdullāh b. ʿAbd al-Asad al-Makhzūmīη and Umm Salamah Hind bt. Suhayl al-Makhzūmiyyahκ. They were members of the group who undertook the Muslims' first emigration from Makkah to Abyssinia, continuing on to Madīnah after the Prophet μ had established himself there. Abū Salamahη fell as one of the martyrs at the Battle of Uḥud in 4AH, leaving Umm Salamah ι with two sons named Salamahη and ʿUmarη and one daughter, Zaynabι. The Prophet μ married her thereafter, adopting these three new step-children.[98]

Anas b. Mālikη reported that once, he observed the Prophet μ playing with Zaynabι, calling out and laughing "O Zuwaynib, O Zuwaynib!"[99] This is the diminutive of the name Zaynab, so he was actually affectionately calling her "dear little Zaynab," which he used to do often.

ʿUmar b. Abī Salamahφ, the step-son of the Prophet μ himself, recounted that once when he was a child under the guardianship of Muḥammad μ and they were eating together, he was picking up morsels from random places on the shared plate. So the Prophet μ advised him, "O my boy, eat only after mentioning God's name, and take from whichever part of the plate is *nearer* to you."[100]

References to his interactions with his step-children are sparse, but the two episodes above illustrate that not only was Prophet Muḥammad μ a loving step-father for them, but a caring guide and teacher as well.

Chapter 6

…as a Brother

Despite his being an only-child, the Prophet μ, as we saw previously, had many milk-mothers, and along with them had several milk-siblings.

Through Thuwaybahι, the freed-slave of Abū Lahab, the Prophet's μ milk-siblings were Ḥamzah b. ʿAbd al-Muṭṭalibη, the Prophet's μ uncle. He was wet-nursed not only by Thuwaybahι, but also by Ḥalīmah al-Saʿdiyyahι, making him something of a double-milk-brother with the Prophet μ. Abū Salamahη, mentioned in the previous chapter, was also nursed by Thuwaybahι, making him his milk-brother as well.[101] Abū Salamahη was also a cousin of the Prophet μ, as his mother Barrah bt. ʿAbd al-Muṭṭalibκ was the Prophet's μ aunt.[102]

Through Ḥalīmah al-Saʿdiyyahι and her husband, the Prophet μ was milk-related with ʿAbdullāh b. al-Ḥārithη, Unaysah bt. al-Ḥārithη, and Shaymā' bt. al-Ḥārithη (who used to sing to the young Muḥammad μ whenever she was able to hold him for a while).[103] This Shaymā'η features in one of the few recorded interactions of the Prophet μ with his milk-siblings who were not otherwise famous in Islāmic history on other merits; this episode is an example of the Prophet's μ magnanimity toward a "relation" (if it can even be called such in the modern West) so distant that he failed to even recognize her when they met for the first time since he was a child in the care of her family.

The Battle of Ḥunayn, which was an expedition undertaken against the Hawāzin tribe, its subtribe of Banū Thaqīf, and a confederation of smaller tribes including Banū Saʿd b. Bakr from the surrounding area, saw a resounding Muslim victory with many prisoners and hostages taken from their opponents. Being among them, Shaymā'ι sought an audience with her milk-brother, who happened to be the Prophet μ and general of the Muslim army on this occasion. Upon being conveyed to him, she announced herself, "O Messenger of God, I am your milk-sister!"

Not recognizing her, the Prophet μ pressed her for proof of her claim, demanding, "is there some sign by which I might know you?"

She must have smiled as she replied, "why yes! Once, I was picking you up to carry you on my hip; the sign is the mark you left when you bit me on my back!"

This seems to have sparked the memory in the Prophet's μ mind, because at that moment he removed his cloak and laid it down, inviting her "oh, have a seat, have a seat!" He proceeded to offer her a choice between two options. "Now look, you can either stay with the Muslims in Madīnah where you'll be cared for and well-respected, or I can send you back to your family in safety." She chose to go home, and the Prophet μ, true to his word as always, sent her along with gifts aplenty for her and her family.[104]

Chapter 7

...as a Relative

Preservation of the ties of kinship is one of Islām's most-emphasized obligations; the corpus of narrations from which the prophetic *Sunnah* is distilled, and indeed the Qur'ān itself, are heavy with such references.

ʿAbdullāh b. Salāmη recounts on this subject that once, before his conversion to Islām, he saw the Prophet μ after his arrival to Madīnah and just from his face, one could tell he wasn't a liar, and the first thing the soon-to-be Muslim heard the Prophet μ saying was, "O people! Spread peace amongst yourselves, feed the hungry, reinforce and reconnect the ties of kinship, keep awake at night in prayer while others sleep; this, so that you may enter paradise!"[105] Anas b. Mālikη transmitted to later generations the Prophet's μ maxim that, "anyone who wants to expand their means and lengthen their days, then let them strengthen their ties of kinship."[106] Furthermore, Abū Hurayrahη passed along to posterity that the Prophet μ said, "*raḥim* (the word for kinship) is related to al-Raḥīm(one of the names, meaning "Most Merciful," whereby Muslims call on God). God has said to these ties of kinship that, 'I will connect anyone who connects you, and cut anyone who cuts you!'"[107]

Despite the fact that one of the most heavily-emphasised measures of righteousness is the maintenance of one's ties of kinship and how well one cares for one's family, what has become globally prevalent today is disregard for one's family; even actively severing ties is commonplace.

Clearly, this virtue merits its own dedicated treatment, but as the focus of this work is the manifold roles the Prophet µ filled, the brilliant example of his role as a preserver of kinship ties and a deeply concerned and caring relative will be upheld hereunder. Previously, we have been shown the excellence with which the Prophet µ dealt with his immediate family, but the divine imperative under discussion extends even to one's distant relatives.

When someone truly loved is lost, it may sometimes be painful when others *fail* to mourn them. After the Battle of Uḥud, the Prophet µ passed by a group of ladies from the Banū ʿAbd al-Ashhal crying over the men of their tribe who had fallen as martyrs; that seems to have been the last straw, as the most difficult loss to *him* was his uncle Ḥamzahη, and the Prophet µ hadn't yet heard his name sung in sorrow by *anyone.* He would go to this group and that, asking who was among their martyrs, but nobody asked him about his uncle. He could take no more, and – stricken by grief and suffering at the loss of one of his most beloved uncles – he called out, "but who mourns Ḥamzah? I mourn him!"[108] This outpouring of emotion – that even the Prophet µ could not control – shows what a caring nephew he was.

Of one of the Prophet's µ other close uncles, ʿAbbāsη, he used to often say "he is from me and I am from him."[109] He also used to say, when referring to ʿAbbās η, that "a man's uncle is like his father."[110] Several different Companions and members of the Prophet's µ Household heard this for themselves and transmitted it to their own fellows.

This particular uncle of Muḥammad µ seems to have been especially blessed by the Prophet's µ penchant for maintaining family ties. Once, ʿAbdullāh – the Prophet's µ cousin and son of ʿAbbās κ – recounted a time when the Prophet µ invited them to his home, saying, "come with your children on Monday so that I may pray for you; God will benefit you and your children thereby!" When they arrived, the Prophet µ gifted the children with new clothes, which they excitedly donned. Then the Prophet µ supplicated for them, saying "O Lord, forgive ʿAbbās and his children from every sin – those of which they are aware, and those of which they are not. Leave not a single one out of Your forgiveness! O Lord, protect him and his children!"[111]

On another occasion, ʿAbbās η came to the Prophet µ scowling and visibly angry. "Why are you angry, uncle?" the Prophet µ asked, immediately concerned.

In an exasperated fluster, he practically shouted, "what evil have we done to our Quraysh clan, O Messenger of God? When they meet each-other, they're all smiles and pleasantries. But when they meet one of us Sons of Hāshim, it's a completely different story!"

At this – more the stress caused to uncle than anything else – the Prophet's µ face darkened, and his own brow furrowed in disgust. "By God!" he declared, "their faith shall not be perfected until and unless they love you, O ʿAbbās, for the sake of God and His Messenger!" Determined to never see his uncle in such a state again, the Prophet µ proceeded to make a public address, saying "O people! Anyone who hurts my uncle, hurts me. A person's uncle is equal to his father."[112]

Once, in a gathering with some of his Companions, the Prophet µ was approached by the great Saʿd b. Abī Waqqāṣη. Catching sight of him, the Prophet's µ eyes lit up, and he – as a show of appreciation and love – in a facetiously boastful tone called out, "here comes my maternal uncle! Let's see any of *your* maternal uncles!"[113] It certainly does the heart good to be built up in people's eyes by a family member, and Saʿd η must have felt elated to have none other than the Prophet µ himself express such pride at being his kin.

Another incident which clearly demonstrates the Prophet's µ love for his extended family, and that he sincerely missed them in their absences, was after the Muslim victory at Khaybar in 7AH/616CE when Jaʿfar b. Abī Ṭālibκ presented himself to the Prophet µ. He hugged and kissed Jaʿfar η, exclaiming, "I don't know what's made me happier, our victory today, or the arrival of Jaʿfar!"[114] This was the first time the Prophet µ had seen this beloved cousin of his since his migration to Abyssinia twelve years prior.

After the Battle of Mu'tah in 8AH/629CE, during which Ja'far b. Abī Ṭālib κ fell a martyr, Asmā' bt. 'Umaysι found herself playing hostess to the Prophet μ. She recounts that, "just before he came, I had finished tanning around forty skins, preparing a dove, and bathing my children and oiling their hair. The Prophet told me to fetch the children for him, so I did. When they came in, he hugged them tenderly and smelled their hair. But when his eyes brimmed with tears, we couldn't suppress our curiosity about his unexpected visit. So we asked, 'O Messenger, why are you crying? Have you heard anything about Ja'far and his comrades?' When he finally delivered the news that they had all just been martyred, I too began to sob."

When the women began to gather in Asmā's ι house to mourn with her, the Prophet μ headed to his own home; but on the way out he made sure to remind the arriving ladies, "do not forget to make food for the family and help out around their house; they'll be busy with what happened to their father."[115] That the Prophet μ took it upon himself to personally deliver this devastating news – and his own genuine sorrow at it – is a further demonstration not only of his humanity and humility, but that he was indeed a caring and concerned family member.

Chapter 8

...as a Neighbour

In Uzbekistan, we have a tradition: when one family proposes marriage to another family, their neighbours are practically subpoenaed to testify regarding their character. Neighbours have a surprisingly intimate relationship with each-other; even if they barely speak to one another, they are yet witness to nearly all the goings-on of a household; they see much and hear more. People we only see at work or out in public, or who we invite to our homes at pre-arranged times may typically see our best faces, but an individual's and a family's flaws are an open book for their neighbours.

Due to this unavoidable fact of life, the Prophet µ transmitted to future generations the following axiom: "the true *mu'min* (committed believer) is whoever refrains from harming people, and the true Muslim is from whose tongue and hand all have safety. By God, none shall enter Paradise whose neighbour is not safe from his evil!"[116]

God Himself has emphasized the importance of neighbourliness in the Holy Qur'ān in a verse which roughly equates in English to, "worship God without associating anything with Him, deal in the best possible way with parents, kith and kin, orphans and destitute, near and far neighbours, the companion and the wayfarer, and those over whom you are placed in charge; indeed, God loves not the conceited braggart!"[117]

A couple of episodes illustrating the Prophet's µ conduct with his neighbours show that not only did they get along with him quite well, but he was himself a concerned and helpful neighbour; and this spirit of kindness wasn't reserved for his fellow Muslims either. There was a Jewish family that lived near the Prophet µ, and the young son of that family used to come to the Prophet's µ house to do chores and run errands for him. This young boy became quite ill at one point, and it was during this time that the Prophet µ was sitting with a group of his Companions at his house. Suddenly, the Prophet µ said, "let's go and visit my Jewish neighbour." So, up they got and out they went a few houses over. When they entered the Jewish family's house, the Prophet µ asked with visible concern after the boy's condition. After being taken to the boy, the Prophet µ sat down next to his head and quietly urged him, "submit to your Lord, accept that there is no god but He and that I am His Messenger."

The boy wasn't quite sure what to do, as he was out of sorts due to his illness; he already believed in the One God, and he really had come to believe that Muḥammad µ was His prophet and messenger, but he was hesitant to say so openly in his father's presence. After the Prophet µ repeated his invitation a couple more times, the boy's father – who had been keeping otherwise silent – finally approved, saying "obey Abū Qāsim and accept it, O my dear son!"

Satisfied that these Jewish neighbours of his, of whom he had grown quite fond, were taken care of in the way which mattered most to him, the Prophet µ stood up to leave, exclaiming, "I thank God for freeing another soul from the fire!"[118]

Once, Anas b. Mālikη was witness to an event which tidily sums up what the people of a certain street thought of having Muḥammad µ as a neighbour. He and the Prophet µ were walking in Madīnah not far from the Prophet's µ home when they happened to hear a group of young girls playing a *daf* and singing the following lyrics:

> *"We are the girls of Banū Najjār; it is so lovely to have Muḥammad as a neighbour."*

Laughing, he called back to the singers who must have been unaware of just who comprised their audience, "Verily God knows I love you!"[119] Now, how many of us have neighbours who would literally sing our praises?

Chapter 9

...as a Husband

Typically, the closest person to a man after his mother is his wife. Women, being the highly intuitive, caring, and observant creatures they are, know each and every thing about their husbands. Trying to hide anything from them tends to be an exercise in futility, and they might sometimes even be aware of things regarding their husbands of which they themselves are unaware, like subconscious preferences or idiosyncrasies. It can thus be concluded that a man's wife is the best judge of his character, and for that reason the Prophet Muḥammad µ constantly stressed the paramount importance of goodness to one's wife.

The Prophet's µ own wife ʿĀ'ishahι has related that the Prophet µ never raised a hand to anyone – neither his servants, nor his wives. She was also the primary conduit through which flowed such prophetic axioms as, "the best among you is he who is best to his wife,"[120] and "verily, he has perfect security in his faith who has the best behaviour, and who treats his wife in the gentlest manner."[121]

The Prophet's µ cousin and son-in-law ʿAlīν, who was raised on an ample and steady diet of prophetic guidance and instruction, attributed the golden principle that "only the noble show respect to women, whereas only the miserable humiliate them"[122] to his sublime father-in-law µ.

God's Messenger µ even made it a point to exhort his Companions – and the rest of the Muslim community until Judgement Day – to the best treatment of one's wife in his Valedictory Sermon, saying "fear God in your treatment of women! You have taken them as a trust from Him, and you have married them by His words."[123]

The Prophet µ also is supposed to have set forth the following similitude, saying, "it is compulsory upon whomever believes in God and the Day of Judgement to refrain from harming his neighbour, and to treat women in the best way. They have been created from the rib, which is most curved at the top. If you try to straighten it, you will break it, but if you leave it as it is, it will remain bent. Therefore, treat women in the best manner!"[124] The one who passed this attribution along explained that the rib's being bent here is an allusion to nothing more than the fact that men and women are different, rather than to some deviance or maladjustment.

The Prophet µ was never one to advise his nation one thing and do another himself, rather he was commissioned by God to explain by both word and deed, to be the best *practical* example.

Because one of the most sought-after associates of the Prophet µ for instruction on his *Sunnah* after his passing was his wife ʿĀ'ishah ι, an overwhelming number of the accounts of his quality as a husband – among many other things – reach us through her testimony.

Now, it is perhaps unfortunately common – particularly among those who are assumed by outsiders to be "practicing" Muslims – that we may advertise a positive disposition while under the public eye, which all but completely evaporates no sooner than we step through the front door of our homes. We may demonstrate superhuman forbearance to strangers on the street, while subjecting our wives and children to the harshness of our true character. This tends to be the behaviour of people whose only concern is respect and reputation; but the Prophet µ, we can see, was never such a one.

When at some point someone came to ʿĀ'ishahι with a question about the Prophet's µ behaviour behind closed doors, she answered simply, "he used to be the softest man, always smiling and laughing."[125] In reply to another who asked a similar question, she recalled, "he used to serve his family while at home, only leaving to answer the call to prayer."[126] Expounding on the nature of this service for yet another questioner, she explained, "he used to mend his own clothing, repair his own shoes, milk our sheep, and do all the work around the house – just as any husband does."[127] This is in stark contrast to many husbands today who behave as despots and dictators, able but unwilling to lift their eyes much less a finger to accomplish any household duty. Now, milking the animals and stitching up torn clothing in that time were among the duties reserved from the women of a household, so ʿĀ'ishah's ι somewhat naïve assumption at the end of her response must surely have been due to the fact that she was only ever married to the Prophet µ; "doing everything around the house" has never been a typical attribute of the creature known as "husband," especially not those jobs classically recognized as "women's work."

Muḥammad µ was someone who genuinely loved spending time with his family, sparing no opportunity to find enjoyment with them even in something so simple as a footrace. ʿĀ'ishah ι also used to tell the story of how once – as a slim, younger lady – she was on a long journey with the Prophet µ and some others. At some point, the Prophet µ stopped with her, urging everyone else to go on ahead of them. When they were far enough out of sight, he turned to ʿĀ'ishah ι and said playfully, "let's race!" Ready, set, go, and they were off and sprinting until finally, the slighter and younger lady pulled ahead of the Prophet µ and won.

A few years later, though, when ʿĀ'ishah ι wasn't as petite as she had once been, she found herself on a similar journey, accepting a similar cheerful challenge from her husband. Ready, set, go, and they were off sprinting until finally the Prophet µ was victorious. Catching his breath, he laughingly chided her "tit-for-tat, O ʿĀ'ishah!"[128]

Due to the human condition itself, as well as having a marriage partner as enviable as theirs, God bless him and grant him peace, we can understand that some jealousy might have cropped up amongst the wives of the Prophet µ, but not in the way one might expect. ʿĀ'ishah ι once recounted, "I was never more jealous of anyone than Khadījah, even though she died three years before the Prophet married me. He always used to reminisce about her, saying God had ordered him to convey glad tidings of her securing a place in Paradise. He even used to sometimes slaughter a sheep and send the meat to those who had been her friends."[129] Such was his quality in being a husband, that a living wife even felt jealous of the deceased one; his persistence in being a good husband never ceased.

Once, when the Prophet μ was staying with ʿĀ'ishah ι, an old lady came to visit him. After she left, ʿĀ'ishah expressed great curiosity at the geniality and familiarity the two shared, as she couldn't recall having ever seen the old woman before. To her surprise, the Prophet μ explained, "she used to visit Khadījah and me when she was alive and maintaining a good relationship with one's acquaintances is an expression of one's faith."[130] and cordiality with the friends of a deceased spouse is all the more so. Anas b. Mālikη even observed that many times, when people would send a gift to the Prophet's μ house, he would send them away, ordering, "take this to so-and-so's house, because she used to be a good friend to Khadījah."[131]

In addition to being a playful, dutiful husband, the Prophet μ also seized any opportunity to show his wives tenderness and compassion. Now, at the time in history during which Muḥammad μ was active in his mission of social and spiritual reform, it was common for the warriors of a victorious invasion force to indiscriminately enslave their subdued foes, forcing themselves on even the elite of the womenfolk. But, in keeping with the pattern set by the Prophet's μ Way, we can see that Muḥammad µ defied this trend and set his own radiant example.

Due to the political and military drama that had played out beyond the scope of this work, the Prophet µ had led an expedition in 7AH/628CE against a confederation of Jewish tribes headquartered in Khaybar, in what is now Saudi Arabia. One of the defeated Jewish tribes was that of Banū al-Naḍīr, of whom one Ḥuyayy b. Akhṭab had been the chief (he had been killed after the so-called Battle of the Trench a year prior). He had a daughter named Ṣafiyyahι, and she was taken hostage by the victorious Muslims. During his meeting with her to discuss her situation, the Prophet µ offered her two conditions: she could either accept Islām and live as a free woman among the Muslims back at Madīnah, or she could remain a Jew and be released to what was left of her own tribe, having been decimated as they were in the battle and its aftermath. In perhaps a somewhat surprising turn of events, Ṣafiyyah ι announced that, "O Prophet, I accepted Islām even before you offered it; I knew from the start that you were a true prophet of the One God!" At that, the Prophet µ proposed to marry her himself. She accepted, and they married almost immediately.

On the journey back to Madīnah, the Prophet µ was travelling at night mounted on a camel with his new wife Ṣafiyyah bt. Ḥuyayyι sat behind him. Soothed by the cool night air and rocking gait of the camel beneath them, Ṣafiyyah ι began to doze off, nearly falling to one side. The Prophet µ quickly seized her hand, saying, "be careful, O daughter of

Ḥuyayy!" This happened several times, and it must for some reason – perhaps stirring the love and protectiveness he now felt for her – have gotten the Prophet's µ mind onto how he met this wife of his and the circumstances that brought them together. Overcome with the need to say something comforting to her, he took her hand and said, "O Ṣafiyyah… you know circumstances left me with no other choice, but I *am* sorry for what happened to your tribe."[132]

Chapter 10

...as a Master

The question of why the one sent as a "Mercy to Every Realm" µ never abolished the generally oppressive and often violent institution of slavery in one fell swoop during his own lifetime arises, understandably, in the mind of any thinking person. Although a substantial discussion on the issue of slavery in antiquity and its impact on Islām is beyond the scope of this work, it was a socioeconomic reality at the time during which the Prophet µ was active, so it needs to be at least cursorily addressed.

Now, we can see with some investigation and reflection that the Islām of Muḥammad µ actually did set its adherents on a trajectory toward abolishing the institution of slavery by both attempting to sever its supply of new slaves and establishing strong incentives for freeing those already caught in the system. But why not just free all slaves at once? Wasn't Muḥammad's µ word absolute for those who took him as their prophet and liege? It was, and historical sources attest to the depth of the Prophet's µ sincere Companions' loyalty, so why not simply speak the word, and bring the rotten edifice of slavery crashing down once and for all? Quite simply, such an immediate collapse would have caused collateral damage such that the harm would have actually outweighed the good done in the short term.

Slaves were technically dependents of their masters for food, shelter, and clothing – absolute necessities for human life. In some cases, for instance prisoners of war from foreign lands, slavery was a person's best option for protection and eventual introduction into a given society (not ideal in an absolute sense, but certainly ideal for the context). Probably thousands of homeless, jobless individuals being unleashed on the population all at once would have placed critical strain on an already fragile economy. Poverty is a major contributing factor to crime as well, and the sudden simultaneous eviction of every slave in a region would doubtlessly be impetus for unprecedented waves of theft, vandalism, and violence.

Slave-owners, who had been socialized in a world that didn't actually view slavery as a moral affront – and hence should not be retroactively blamed for engaging in it – would have also seen the forced confiscation of what they considered their property as an injustice to be actively and enthusiastically (perhaps even violently) resisted. They needed to be introduced at first to the idea of their slaves' equality with themselves (or at the very least seeing themselves as their caretakers), and then normalizing freeing them by penalizing wrongdoing with obligatory manumission, and making volitional manumission deserving of reward in the life hereafter.

Hence, we can see the immense wisdom in the slow but deliberate trajectory manifested in such Qur'ānic injunctions as the following. Manslaughter/negligent homicide carried the penalty of freeing one slave. Breaking one's oath carried the penalty of having to free a slave, or feed or clothe ten destitute persons. Humiliating one's wife necessitated freeing one slave before being able to carry on normal relations with her. Willingly freeing a slave or feeding orphans/those in need in time of famine carried the reward of safety from some measure of punishment in the life hereafter. There was a strong recommendation in place (and contract formulated) for a master to free a slave if they felt said slave could do well enough on their own.

Supplementing and demonstrating the above Qur'ānic imperatives, the Prophet's µ*Sunnah* is rife with examples. The Prophet µ was often heard sternly warning his fellows that, "it is a sin to beat or slap a slave, and this sin can only be forgiven by freeing them!"[133] In a frankly terrifying specific instance of this warning being given, one of the natives of Madīnah was once thrashing a slave of his in public, whereupon he suddenly heard a voice behind him exclaiming, "God is better able to get you than you are to get that slave of yours!"

When he turned around and saw that it was the Prophet µ who had issued these foreboding words, he cried out "O Messenger of God, he is freed immediately!"

Still seething at the conduct of his Companion, the Prophet µ severely replied, "and if he weren't, the fires of Hell would surely thrash you!"[134]

Once, someone spotted the great Companion Abū Dharr al-Ghifārīη walking along, dressed in the same clothing as the slave walking with him. He couldn't help but approach and ask why this was the case. "I once had a serious argument with him and said some regrettable things," he motioned toward the slave next to him, "and he went to complain about it to the Prophet. So the Prophet called me to him and asked why I insulted him by his mother, and told me, 'these slaves are your brothers who are just serving you for now. God put them under your care, so whoever is in charge of his brother should feed them from what he himself eats and clothe them from what he himself wears. Never order them beyond their capability unless you're willing to help them yourself!'"[135] So not only were slave-owners now expected to view their slaves as equal to themselves, they were also expected to treat them as such. This also serves peripherally as an example of the loyalty and sincerity Muḥammad's µ genuine Companions possessed.

When someone came to the Prophet µ once, seeking advice on how lenient a master should be on his slaves as far as forgiving their errors, the Prophet µ advised him, "forgive him seventy times a day!"[136] It must be understood that different languages have different conventions for how they express an arbitrarily large amount of something. In English, we use numbers like "a million" or "a ton." Arabic, however, makes use of "seven," "seventy," and "one thousand" to denote something of great or even unlimited quantity.

There is mention in the books of history that ʿAlī b. AbīṬālib ν – whose conduct and philosophy, it can be strongly argued, most perfectly reflected the Prophet's µ Way – once bought two sets of clothing; he offered one to one of his slaves, giving him the choice between the two. The slave chose the higher-quality clothing, so ʿAlīv took the lesser.

As we know well by now, Muḥammad μ was never one to give advice until and unless he could first demonstrate it himself. He had four slaves well-known to history – Zayd b. Ḥārithah, Thawbān, Salmān al-Fārisī, and Anas b. Mālikφ.

From the time of the so-called *Jāhiliyyah* – the time of savage tribal conflict, social depravity, and idolatry of the Arabs before the advent of Islām – there has been a yearly market called ʿUkāẓ after the Ḥajj season near Mount ʿArafah at which everything that can be, is bought and sold. In centuries past, this naturally included slaves. One year, a young boy of the Banū Kalb named Zaydη had been captured in a raid, entered into the system of slavery, and put up for sale in that year's ʿUkāẓ. It just so happened that, being in the market for a good young servant, Khadījah ι went, saw him, and purchased him; she later gave him as a gift to the Prophet μ after they married.[137]

Now, the raid that had resulted in Zayd's η enslavement happened while he was away from his own tribe, as he had gone with his mother to visit her own tribe to see some relatives. Therefore, news only reached Zayd's η father Ḥārithah of his wife and son's fates after some time, and he had no way of knowing what had become of them; but he never gave up hope that his son was yet alive and continued to search for him for years. And this incessant search bore fruit eventually, as he had finally tracked down Zayd's η whereabouts to Makkah, specifically the house of Muḥammad b. ʿAbdullāh μ. He asked around town about where his son's master was and was directed to the Kaʿbah. So he went with his travelling companions, who were members of his own family, and found Muḥammad μ there, as directed.

Ḥārithah approached the Prophet μ and launched into some version of the plea he had doubtlessly gone over hundreds of times in his head, saying, "O son of ʿAbd al-Muṭṭalib, you are famous as the head of the Banū Hāshim. I've heard tell of your generosity, and sincerity, that you help those who've fallen on hard times and make sure prisoners of war are well looked-after. We have come to you about my son… please, can you at least give us a discount on his price?"

"And who is your son?" the Prophet μ asked. When Ḥārithah replied that it was Zayd η, of whom the Prophet μ had grown quite fond, the Prophet μ thought for a moment and said, "would you perchance accept something else?" Ḥārithah assented, and the Prophet μ continued, saying, "I will call Zayd here, and leave the choice in his hands. If he prefers to go with you, then he is yours – free and clear. But if he chooses me… well, by God, I can't just give away someone who chooses me!"

Assuming his son would choose to go back to his family without a moment's hesitation, Ḥārithah exclaimed, "you've given me more than I could ask!"

So the Prophet µ sent for Zaydη, and asked him when he arrived, "do you know these men?"

"Yes," came Zayd's η terse reply.

"Who are they, then?" the Prophet µ probed.

"They are my father and uncle," Zayd η confirmed.

"Right, and you know who I am and how I've treated you over the years," the Prophet µ continued. "Now I'm giving you a choice… you can either go on home with them or stay with me."

Zayd's η responded to the Prophet µ immediately and frankly, "I'd never choose anyone over you; you yourself are as my own father *and* uncle!"

"What's the matter with you, Zayd?" an astonished Ḥārithah exclaimed, "you're choosing a life of slavery over your own father and uncle, your *family*?"

Zayd η calmly replied, "yes… after knowing this man, I could never choose anyone else," the firmness of finality shading the softness of his voice.

At this, the Prophet µ ushered Zayd η and his kin to the Ḥijr Ismāʿīl (the low, semi-circular wall opposite the north-west wall of the Kaʿbah) to make a public announcement. After gaining the attention of all within earshot, he called out, "O people! Know now that this Zayd is my son and heir!" Thus,

Zayd η was at once freed and adopted by the Prophet μ. His son no longer a slave, and now the heir to a Qurayshī noble, Zayd's η father left Makkah satisfied with the conclusion of his son's saga.

From that day, until the revelation of a Qur'ānic prohibition of attributing oneself to other than one's natural father, Zayd η was known as "Zayd b. Muḥammad;" after the prohibition though, he went back to being known as "Zayd b. Ḥārithah."[138]

It must be understood that, for the Arab, freedom and lineage were paramount, and the shame of having a family member in slavery was two-fold. First, it could imply some degree of impotence on their part that they were unable to resist having a member forced into slavery; second, it might also imply some miserliness on their part, that they were unwilling to pay the price of their kinsman's freedom, no matter the cost.

Arab pride was something to behold (as an extreme case in point, a bloody forty-year war known as Ḥarb al-Basūs was instigated by the killing of a single camel)[139] and freedom was something to be fiercely guarded, yet this young Arab whose own father had come for him still chose, for all he knew, to forfeit his freedom and honour just to stay with the Prophet μ. This must have been due either solely to the sheer magnitude of the Prophet μ, or Zayd η must have found the thought of returning to his own tribe too repugnant to entertain. But

Zayd's η tribe – the Quḍāʿah – was one well-known and highly-esteemed by the Arabs, famous for the poets it produced, and his own immediate family did genuinely care for him; his father went in search of him spurred on not only by dogged Arab pride, but true despair at his loss. There actually exists in the collections of Arab poetry a touching, sorrowful lament attributed to Ḥārithah, which he is supposed to have composed after initial searches for Zayd η yielded no results.

So, we can be sure that Zaydη meant what he said, and that his choice really was due to nothing more than the Prophet's μ immense personality – a personality which treated slaves better than other fathers could treat sons. A personality whose wisdom and compassion were such that after the rather generously-termed agreement between himself and Ḥārithah ended up in his own favour (after which he could have simply sent the men of Banū Kalb packing), he still found a way to greatly benefit Zayd's η former family and tribe by making that public announcement from the holiest place of the Arabs, not only assuaging Ḥārithah's shame, but heaping honours on top of it.

Furthermore, Zayd η had bestowed upon him by the Prophet μ the title of "al-Ḥibb," meaning "the beloved," which even extended to his own son Usāmah η, who was thus called "al-Ḥibb b. al-Ḥibb."[140] Who, particularly in that time and place wherein slave-owners went to the extent of keeping their slaves in their animals' stables to distance themselves from them, could countenance such closeness with their slave that they would consider them a beloved son and go out of their way to honour their former family?

Abū ʿAbdillāh Thawbān b. Bajdudη was another of the Prophet's μ slaves, albeit for a very short time. He was originally from a place called al-Sārah, between Yemen and Makkah. He was for sale in the slave markets of Madīnah after being taken hostage in a raid – similar to Zayd η – from whence Muḥammad μ bought him and subsequently freed him, allowing him to choose between staying in Madīnah as a member of his household and returning to his own family. He, too, chose to stay with the Prophet μ and developed such a fondness for him that he seldom left his side, becoming distraught were they ever forced apart.[141]

This anxiety at even the mere thought of being away from the Prophet μ for long took such a toll on Thawbānη that, at one point, he began losing unhealthy amounts of weight. The Prophet μ noticed as his complexion yellowed and his face became gaunt, eyes setting deep into their sockets, glazed over in sorrowful preoccupation. Worried for his dear freed-slave, Muḥammad μ finally inquired as to the reason for Thawbān's η deteriorating condition.

"O Prophet," Thawbān η explained wearily, "I have not taken ill, and I am not in any pain. It's just that… you see, if I don't see you for a while, I miss you terribly and I can think of nothing else until I see you again. Now, recently I got to thinking about the Day of Judgement, and that I would never see you again thereafter." Pausing to wipe the tears away that had begun to gather in the corners of his tired eyes, he continued, "and I know you'll be in Paradise, at the level of the Prophets. So even *if* I am admitted, my station will be so far below yours that I won't see you anyway; and if I don't get in at all, well there's no chance…"

But at that very moment, a fresh flood of revelation came crashing down upon the Prophet µ, the meaning of which is, "whomsoever obeyed God and His Messenger are *with* those upon whom God bestowed His favours from among the Prophets, the steadfast affirmers of truth, the martyrs, and the righteous; what excellent associates are they!"[142]

Another of the Prophet's µ household servants was an extraordinary man known to history as Salmān al-Fārisīη ("Fārisī" being the Arabic demonym for a Persian). Originally named Rozbeh and born to a Persian aristocrat named Yūdhakhshān in Iṣfahān in modern-day Iran, Salmān η was raised in a pious Zoroastrian household.[143] He was naturally inquisitive, and actively sought out the truth in religious matters whenever and however he could. He had been training for the Zoroastrian priesthood, but he came upon some Christians on one occasion, and was attracted to their rituals and the content of their preaching. He asked the men whence came their religion, and upon discovering that it was al-Shām, he set off in search of the pure message of God – as we shall see was his wont – and as soon as he was able, he escaped the home of his strict and overbearing father and anonymously joined a trade caravan whose destination coincided with his.

When he finally arrived, he detached himself from his travelling companions and began asking the common folk about who was the best person from whom to learn Christianity. The various responses all unanimously directed him toward the area's bishop, to whom Salmānη immediately betook himself, to arrange an introduction and possibly begin serving the church. However, to his chagrin, Salmān η discovered that this particular bishop was a corrupt and impious man guilty of redirecting the peoples' tithes into his own pockets. That wicked clergyman was replaced after his death, though, by one of quite the opposite temperament – a noble, God-fearing man whom Salmān η followed closely and grew to love, and from whom he learned much.

On his deathbed, this bishop called Salmān η to him and disclosed that, by his reckoning, there was none on the face of the Earth who followed the pure message of God but a particular man living in al-Mawṣil (modern-day Mosul, Iraq). So, upon the sad occasion of the bishop's passing, Salmān η departed for the company of this saint in Iraq. When this man's time was near, he referred Salmān η to yet another holy man living in Nusaybin, in modern-day Turkey. He, too, died shortly thereafter, but not before referring Salmān η to his next master, a man living in Amorium (located near modern-day Hisarköy, Turkey). Before this penultimate teacher's passing, Salmān η asked him from whom next to seek guidance.

"The time has come for the appearance of a prophet in Arabia," said the sage, enumerating the signs whereby Salmān should identify said Arabian prophet, "so go and follow him."

Thrilled at the prospect of meeting and following a true prophet of God, Salmān η sought out the next group of travellers heading for Arabia – which in this case happened to be some merchants – and arranged to pay them to take him along. But these merchants had something else in mind; they captured Salmān and sold him to someone along the way. This man sold Salmān η to his cousin, who lived in Yathrib (so this was before the Prophet's μ historical migration event).

Salmān took a circuitous and gruelling path, but through perseverance in his earnest search for guidance, he found his way to that Arabian Prophet μ when he did finally transfer his movement's base to Yathrib (thereafter Madīnah).

Longing to finally be free, if for no other reason than the ability to follow this Prophet μ, Salmān had struck an accord with his master that he would be freed if he could pay a certain amount of gold by a certain time. But the contract expired, so Salmānη remained in his bondage, kept from the fellowship he so desired. When the epic tale of this intrepid young man's journey finally reached the Prophet μ, he met with Salmān's η master, paid the requisite amount to transfer ownership to himself, and freed him forthwith.[144] From then on, the Prophet μ would say of Salmān η that, "he is a member of my family."[145]

The Prophet µ was the master of one other person (who was actually a freeman) named Anas b. Mālikη, whose family was part of the Khazraj tribe based in Madīnah. His mother was called Umm Sulaymι, and she kept close ties with the Prophet's µ family. His father, Mālik b. Naḍr, passed away before the Prophet µ and his religion's entry into Madīnah, but his mother was re-married to one Abū Ṭalḥah b. Thābitη. He was a child of about ten years when the Prophet µ finally did migrate to Madīnah, at which point he began serving in the Prophet's µ house until the Prophet's µ passing.

If the Prophet µ had he compassion and sincere nobility to treat actual slaves as his own family, then a servant in his house must have been as a son – and indeed Anas η was. When the Prophet µ migrated, had no servant to attend him, so Abū Ṭalḥah η took Anas η to the Prophet µ and presented him, saying, "my step-son is a bright lad, so why not let him serve in your house?"[146]

From then on, Anas η attended to the Prophet µ at home and on journeys. He recounted once that, "the Prophet never scolded me, not even by saying 'why did you do this' or 'why did you not do that.'"[147] In fact, Anas η used to fondly recount to anyone who asked, "for ten years I served the Prophet, and he never once blamed me for delaying or neglecting an order. If a member of his household would, though, he would rush to my aid and excuse, saying, 'leave him alone! If it's meant to happen, it will happen!'"[148]

Anasη confirmed this sterling quality of the Prophet's μ character elsewhere, relating that once when he was much younger, the Prophet μ had ordered him to go to some part of the city for something. "By God, I will not go!" the young Anas η cheekily exclaimed, but he went anyway, still wanting to obey the Prophet's μ command. But on the way, he saw a group of children his own age playing in the street, so he joined them, completely forgetting about the errand on which he had been sent. After a long while of playing, Anasη felt the palm of a large hand on his back and, turning around, saw that it belonged to none other than the Prophet μ!

Laughing at the astonished embarrassment Anas's η face betrayed, the Prophet μ jokingly asked him, "Did you go where I asked?"

"I'm going now, O Prophet!" came Anas's η shrill, red-faced reply.[149]

Many of us are quick to chastise – sometimes harshly – our own children if they make some mistake in carrying out an order, and more so if they ignore it altogether. How would we treat some servant if they did the same? Probably not with this same good-natured bemusement or a complete lack of regard for the utter failure of a servant to complete what must have been a relatively important task. But this was, after all, Muḥammad μ.

Chapter 11

...as a Friend

True friendship is a rare treasure usually obtained only by sincere persons. What most people consider friendship is merely acquaintance of varying levels of shallowness, made and kept for some social or financial benefit; such a relationship should not be assumed to be negative, though, and is only prohibited in such cases as it causes disorder or hardship for others (like the "friendship" a gang of highwaymen might have known in centuries past). Otherwise, such attempts to climb social and financial ladders by association are completely permissible.

But genuine friendship forsakes worldly benefit, is blind to wealth and poverty, ignorant of high and low society, indifferent to sickness and health, and oblivious to absence and presence. True friends are so solely for each-other's sake and remain so through times of adversity and indigence; they advise their friends in private and conceal their errors in public, guarding their honour against backbiting and slander. In most cases, we see that yesterday's friends are today's most meticulously-plotting enemies, and today's friends are nothing more than tomorrow's arch-nemeses waiting for the right reason.

The Prophet µ, however, was a *genuine* friend. There was no social, monetary, or other benefit he could garner from calling casual acquaintances "friends," as he was not only a high-born member of one of the premier tribes of one of Arabia's most prestigious clans (despite being an orphan), he was also God's Messenger on a mission being provided for accordingly from on high. Thus having Muḥammad µ as a friend meant having the truest friend a human could imagine.

Once, the famous Companion Sa'd b. Abī Waqqāṣη was beset by a serious illness in the year of the Prophet's µ Valedictory Pilgrimage; being his friend, and this illness being quite severe, the Prophet µ made sure to visit him often. On one of these visits, Sa'd η rather glumly sought the Prophet's µ advice, saying, "as you can see, I'm very ill, O Prophet, and I have no one to inherit me but my daughter. So do you think I should give two-thirds of my wealth in charity?"

"No, don't do that!" an astonished Prophet µ replied.

"Then how about half?" Sa'd η asked wearily. But after another negative reaction by the Prophet, Sa'd η suggested "alright then, a third."

"Even a third is a lot, O Sa'd," cautioned the Prophet µ. "Instead of leaving your children with just enough to keep them begging, why not leave them wealthy? You shan't maintain anyone for the sake of God except that you shall be rewarded for it – even for something so small as the morsel you place in your wife's mouth."

Sa'd η considered this for a moment before giving voice to another pressing concern – his own mortality. "O Prophet… will I remain alive after my friends?"

"Any good that you do after them will surely raise your rank," the Prophet μ replied, reassuring him that this illness, however grave, would eventually pass.[150]

In another specific incident we find that once, when one Sa'd b. 'Ubādahη was poorly, the Prophet μ came to offer him some aid, bringing dates and sesame for him and supplicating for him and the others who were present.[151]

Visiting his friends during their times of illness was a duty the Prophet μ took very seriously and was consistent in performing. Contrast that with the condition of many today, who have every means of convenient conveyance at their disposal yet still neglect visiting friends during their difficult times. Even given the modern ease with which contact should be kept, communication with people we call "friends" is still sorely lacking.

But perhaps some of us do have friends with whom we are so close that we consider them family, and we could easily imagine the grief at their passing being equal to if a sibling were to die. The Prophet μ had this in one 'Uthmān b. Maẓ'ūnη; the Prophet μ was by his side when he breathed his last, at which point the Prophet μ kissed him, eyes brimming with tears.[152] And when the time came shortly thereafter to bury his body, the Prophet μ requested that a stone be brought to mark his grave. But the person he had sent was unable to lift it, so the Prophet μ went himself, rolled up his sleeves, hoisted the stone up, and placed it at the head of ʿUthmān's η final resting place, saying solemnly, "this I have done so that I know where my brother is buried, and where to bury others of my kin."[153] Take note, *others of his kin.*

The above illustrates another truism – which is incidentally even called attention to in the Qur'ān (43:67) – that the genuine friendship shared by sincere people ends not with the worldly life, but extends even up to and beyond the Day of Judgement; and such were the Prophet's μ friendships, that he continued them even after death, visiting graves and burying family next to them to keep them company. The Prophet μ even used to visit the martyrs of Uḥud (many of whom were dear friends in life), lying beneath the soil upon which they fell in battle, at the end of each year and he would address them, saying, "peace be upon you for your perseverance! How wondrous must be your hereafter. The Prophet μ, his wife ʿĀ'ishah ι relates, used to also visit the cemetery at Baqīʿ during some of the nights he stayed in her house to pray for those friends of his buried there.[154]

And what sort of real friend sits idle while his fellows engage in hard labour or some other difficult task? Friends should want to ease each-other's burdens, and the Prophet μ with his friends was no exception. The Prophet μ was in fact witnessed, when a group of *Anṣār* and *Muhājirūn* were busy about bringing heavy stones for the construction of Madinah's first mosque, also porting masonry from point to point and motivating his crew by singing out, "O Lord, there's no good better than the good of the hereafter, so forgive these Assistants and Migrants!"[155]

Serving each-other is another characteristic of genuine friendship, and rather a rarely-found one. But when the Prophet μ was in his friends' company, he used to serve them gladly. In one episode, the great Companion ʿAbdullāh b. Masʿūdη related that once, when he was a young boy working as a shepherd, he was approached in the field by the Prophet μ and Abū Bakrη. The Prophet croaked, "boy, do you have any milk?"

"Yes, but these aren't my sheep…" young Ibn Masʿūd η replied timidly.

"Well then, do you have any sheep that haven't mated yet?" the Prophet μ asked. ʿAbdullāh η nodded and brought one of them to the Prophet μ, who proceeded to wipe his hand over the sheep's udder and commence to whispering Qur'ānic supplications; with that, milk began to gush forth. The Prophet μ quickly gathered some in a container and handed it to his good friend Abū Bakr η, urging him, "drink, drink!" After Abū Bakr downed the bowl, he passed it back to the Prophet μ who refilled it and drank himself. "Now shrink," the Prophet μ commanded the sheep's udder after the two had finished their miraculous beverage.

Understandably astonished by what he had just seen, the young Ibn Masʿūd η – who would himself come to be counted among the Prophet's μ good friends – blurted out, "teach me some of these incantations!"

The Prophet μ laughed and tousled his hair, saying, "God love you, you're certainly an inquisitive lad!"[156]

A similar incident took place during the Prophet's μ treacherous migration from Makkah to Madīnah with the exception that in addition to Abū Bakr η, there was also one ʿĀmir b. Fuhayrahη present, and the sheep belonged to one Umm Maʿbadι. In this case as well, though, he served his two friends first before quenching what must have been by that point maddening thirst.[157]

Before his migration to Madīnah and his commission to divine messengership, Muḥammad μ was, as we now know, a successful trader. As was common then as it is today, part of his mercantile success was due to having formed a partnership; in this case – as is not so common, or even advisable – his partner was also a close friend named Sā'ib b. Abī Sā'ibη. The Prophet μ often used to praise his acumen and quality as a partner, pointing out that the two never argued (which is something business partners can spend an unfortunate amount of time doing). When the Prophet μ entered Makkah upon its liberation, Sā'ib η, who had by now embraced his former partner's religion, came to visit him. The Prophet μ greeted him merrily, announcing, "welcome to my brother and partner who never argues or meddles in disturbances!"[158] As aforementioned, only publicizing the other's positive qualities is a characteristic of true friendship – and this reluctance to engage in argumentation and disorder is considered one of the highest virtues a Muslim can achieve.

Now, it should not be assumed that because a friendship is genuine, and its members sincere, that it will remain free of tension. The Prophet µ had developed a uniquely strong emotional attachment to Makkah, which was the spiritual centre of what began as the Arabs' branch of Abrahamic monotheism (notwithstanding its degeneration into full-blown idolatry), what with having been born, raised, and living there for the first fifty years of his life. When he was called to prophethood, he first reached out to his neighbours, family, and the wider community of his hometown. Despite the severity of the backlash this generated against him and his followers, he persisted in his call for ten years. He was only forced to leave when the political, financial, emotional, and physical pressure surpassed what the Prophet µ could bear; so he fled to security, and to further expand and strengthen his call, in Madīnah. In fact, as he and Abū Bakr η were leaving Makkah once and for all, the Prophet µ turned and addressed the city itself, lamenting, "O Makkah! You are so beloved to me; if your sons hadn't forced me, I would never have left you!"[159]

The natives of Madīnah, for the most part, welcomed the Prophet µ and his Makkan refugees, the so-called "*Muhājirūn*," with open arms, forging strong ties with the Makkan Muslims and pledging their moral, material, financial, political, and military support for them and their religion, gaining them the title "*Anṣār*," which means "supporters." As time went on, these relationships only grew stronger as the *Anṣār* truly fell in love with the Prophet µ and Islām to the point that they felt their community could never be complete again *without* the Prophet µ. But eight years on from settling in Madīnah, Makkah was wrested from the oppressive, iron grip of the Quraysh due to their brazen violation of an already-unfair treaty, opening it to the free spread of Islām and the potential return of the Prophet µ and his Makkah-born followers. After this endgame victory and his entry into his hometown, the Prophet µ tarried for some time there, drinking in the sights and sounds of his old familiar haunts; he needed to quench the thirst of nostalgia.

This caused his Madīnan supporters some trepidation, however, as it gave them the impression that he might opt to remain in Islām's – and his own – birthplace, never to return to them. "Now that Makkah is open to us, do you reckon the Prophet will move back here?" some of the *Anṣār* whispered nervously to each-other when, at one point during his visitations around Makkah, the Prophet µ mounted the hill of Ṣafā and performed a ritual prayer there.

"What are you saying?" the Prophet µ asked them upon finishing his prayer.

"Nothing, nothing, O Messenger!" the group sheepishly replied. But when the Prophet µ insisted, they came clean.

"May God save me from that! I live with you, and I shall die with you!"[160] the Prophet µ exclaimed, putting their fears to rest and proving that his friendship wasn't temporary or conditional on their support in claiming Makkah.

Yet another test of friendship is when two *mutual* friends have an altercation. The way a friend in the middle handles the situation is a testament to their quality *as* a friend. Such a test came upon the Prophet µ when he was sitting once with some of his Companions and suddenly Abū Bakr η rushed in upon them, anxiously grasping his lower garment, causing it to hike up to the extent that his knees were nearly showing. Observing such behaviour in the usually-mild-mannered man he'd known so well for so long, the Prophet µ muttered, "something must be bothering him."

Before the Prophet µ could ask, Abū Bakr η greeted the assembly and breathlessly addressed the Prophet µ, "Ibn al-Khaṭṭāb and I had a bit of an argument and I said something I ought not have and I apologized, but he didn't accept my apology, so I came to you!"

"May God forgive you, Abū Bakr!" the Prophet µ said thrice.

Unbeknownst to either of them, shortly after Abū Bakr's η failed attempt at reconciliation with ʿUmar η, ʿUmar η himself began to feel guilty for giving his senior – in so many regards – the cold shoulder. So he quickly betook himself to Abū Bakr's η residence to seek him out, but he was nowhere to be found. Unable to assuage his guilt, he too ran to the Prophet µ for counsel, only to find Abū Bakr η already there with a disappointed Prophet µ next to him.

"O Prophet, I was more wrong!" Abū Bakr η said quickly, feeling instantly guilty about the situation into which he had just dropped ʿUmar η.

But the attempt was to no avail. "O people! God has sent me to you, and most of you belied me except for this one. Abū Bakr bore witness to my truthfulness and supported my message with his wealth and with his self! Are you now going to offend this friend of mine?" the Prophet µ announced, indirectly addressing ʿUmar η so as not to overtly single him out for further embarrassment.[161] Everyone was familiar with Islām's short history up to that point, that Abū Bakr had been the very first person after the Prophet's µ own household (including ʿAlī b. AbīṬālib ν) to accept Islām, without question, the very moment he was presented with it. And most people would have been cognizant of the fact that it took six years for ʿUmar η to come around to the Prophet's µ call – six years of ʿUmar η doing everything he could short of getting blood on his hands to silence that call. Furthermore, Abū Bakr η was a full ten years older than ʿUmar η. The latter snubbing the former was a breach of protocol too offensive for the Prophet μ to dismiss, hence his reaction. As a true friend, he became an advocate for the one unjustly wronged while correcting the other in a socially appropriate manner, bringing an amicable close to the issue without compromising any of his principles.

A similar situation transpired during an altercation between Khālid b. al-Walīdη and ʿAbd al-Raḥmān b. ʿAwfη. "Oh, so you think you're better than me just because you started following the Prophet a few days before me, is that it?" a group of other Companions overheard Khālid η lash out accusatorily as their argument reached its boiling point. They were astonished by this, being aware of the two men's relative standing, and went immediately to the Prophet μ to seek intervention.

Now, this ʿAbd al-Raḥmānη was among the group of those who accepted the Prophet's μ call to Islām in its first month, after which he exerted himself with the rest of them in feeding the poor, protecting the weaker Muslims from their persecution – which was at that time at its peak of intensity – as well as he could, and passing the message along to others. To be a Muslim *then* meant constant sacrifice, an uphill battle with no end in sight. Conversely, it wasn't until only a year *before* the liberation of Makkah – when Muslims were no longer in such a miserable state, Islām had already begun gaining ground with surrounding tribes, and political pressure on Madīnah had begun to abate – that Khālidη came to the Prophet μ to offer him the pledge of allegiance. God Himself has revealed in the Qur'ān that which means roughly, "unequal are they among you who, from before the victory, spent and fought; their rank is greater than those who spent and fought only afterward. However, to all has God promised excellence – and He is Ever-Aware of all you do."

Thus, with all haste the Prophet μ came upon them and scolded Khālid η, saying, "leave my Companions alone! I swear by God, were one of you to donate a mountain of gold the size of Uḥud, it would still be dwarfed by what my Companions have sacrificed!"[162] In this way, the Prophet μ at once soothed ʿAbd al-Raḥmān's η hurt feelings by expressing appreciation for his extensive contributions while putting Khālid η in his place for trivializing them so insensitively. The Prophet μ was never one to miss an opportunity to show gratitude to his friends for their contributions to his God-given mission, and he publicly praised Khālid η on several other occasions for *his* as well.

Chapter 12

...as a Guest

The relationship between guest and host is like a single coin with its two sides, and investigation into a person's behaviour while a guest and their hospitality when playing host grants great insight into their character. Prophet Muḥammad µ had ample opportunity during his lifetime to fill both roles, and historical accounts of his doing so abound, so his conduct as a guest will be examined first.

Some criteria that I consider important in devising a rubric for judging the praiseworthiness of a guest include such questions as: does one accept invitations of the wealthy and poor like, or just the wealthy? Are they demanding, or are they satisfied with what the host offers? Do they act according to the occasion for their visit? And do they express gratitude to their host? We shall observe what follows through the lens of the aforementioned considerations and judge accordingly.

Once, the grandmother of Anas b. Mālikη invited him and the Prophet µ to her home for a meal. The Prophet µ gladly accepted her invitation, and after the gathering had finished eating, the Prophet µ stood and suggested, "let's all pray together." Because his host was an impoverished old woman, and the floor of her small dwelling was basically dirt, Anas η went to fetch a few of her bamboo mats which had turned black with age. He washed them, as well as he could do so quickly, and laid them down. The Prophet took his place on one of them, Anas η stood behind him forming a rank with the orphan who was also present, and Anas's η grandmother stood behind them. With everyone in their proper places, the Prophet μ commenced his prayer.[163]

Applying the rubric, we see that the Prophet μ did indeed accept the invitation of a poor person of little to no social standing to speak of whose best protection from their dirt floor was some sullied, old, uncomfortable bamboo mats, and the only other guest of honour was some anonymous orphan. Furthermore, we know from history that the sustenance of the poor in this time and place was, aside from the ubiquitous date, some bland boiled barley porridge or coarse barley bread and water. The Prophet μ would have known what kind of hospitality to expect from an indigent senior citizen, and he had several tremendously wealthy Companions – 'Uthmān b. 'Affānη, for example; and so it normally goes that an individual with rich followers and fans wouldn't be caught dead at the meagre home of some old woman whose only comfort was some raggedy bamboo mats whose better days were far behind them. Or, if they would be caught dead there, it would only be in the performance of a publicity stunt, and as soon as they had finished choking down their meal of probably stale bread and water, they would abscond at the first opportunity. One cannot countenance a pompous, insincere pretender staying not only to perform a prayer to bless the woman and her home but doing so along with some random orphan. The Prophet µ, however, was obviously not such a one.

It was a common practice, in fact, for people who invited the Prophet µ for a visit to seek blessings from him; and he always obliged by performing prayers with them in their homes. The son of ʿUmar b. al-Khaṭṭābĸ noted that on one of the occasions that he accompanied the Prophet µ on one of his invitations, the host provided them with food and afterward laid down a mat for the Prophet µ whereupon he prayed two cycles of ritual prayer (*ṣalāh*).

On another of his responses to an invitation, the Prophet µ – as was his wont – had with him several other Companions. When it came to light, on their way to the house, that one of them was in the middle of a voluntary fast for that day and thus would be abstaining from the meal their host prepared, the Prophet µ chided him, saying "your brother went to great lengths for you! Break your fast for today and make it up some other day."[164]

Arabians were, and still are, famous for their generosity and hospitality; such people greatly resent having their offerings refused (take the author's word for it; do not try this at home!), so the Prophet's µ advice to his companion was given in the spirit of being an excellent guest. Furthermore, it should be borne in mind that the Prophet's µ directive to his companion was formulated – by Arabic rhetoric standards – in the gentlest way possible by employing the plural rather than the singular imperative, which wold have served to save the recipient of his chastisement from its full linguistic intensity.

In the year 5AH/627CE, one of the most momentous battles in the early history of Islām took place, referred to as the Battle of al-Aḥzāb, or "confederates" on account of Madīnah's opposition being composed of over ten thousand warriors (thus greatly outnumbering the Muslims' three thousand) sent from various Arabian tribes to bolster the already numerically superior and better-equipped forces of the Quraysh with whom they had allied. When the Prophet μ received intelligence that this behemoth force was coming to Madīnah – which was concurrently in the middle of a severe famine – to strike at the very heart of Islām, he convened a war council with his most shrewd and martially-experienced Companions. Among them was Salmān al-Fārisīη who suggested a strategy familiar to his Persian mind, but which hadn't occurred to the others who were more accustomed to less-sophisticated tactics: that was to effectively wall off the entirety of Madīnah with a trench wide and deep enough to preclude the advance of any sufficiently large or organised mass of infantry, and of any cavalry or camelry whatsoever. This would force a disastrously one-sided pitched battle into a much more manageable siege, what with Madīnah's small population being mostly women and children. So this ingenious plan was accepted and put into effect post haste, earning this battle its other common name, the Battle of al-Khandaq, or "the trench."

It was during this time of prolonged famine piled atop feverish preparation for impending invasion that one of the residents of Madīnah, one Jābir b. ʿAbdillāhη, who spied the Prophet μ toiling away with the rest of the city in the digging of its massive trench noticed that he μ looked famished. So he set his tools down and ran to his wife, announcing to her, "I saw the Prophet, and he looks like he's starving. Do we not have anything to make him?" So she brought out their last four-kilogram bag of flour, and he slaughtered their one small sheep.

By the time he was finished with his butchery, his wife had finished grinding the barley finely enough to make into bread. As he was setting off to call the Prophet μ, his wife stopped him and said, "now don't put me to shame when you invite our Prophet and his Companions!" This was her way of warning him not to invite so many people that they wouldn't have enough to go around.

Heeding his wife's advice, Jābir η hurried to where he had seen the Prophet μ working before and approached him, whispering when he was near enough, "O Messenger of God, we have slaughtered our sheep and ground our four kilograms of barley, so come with a few of your Companions and refresh yourself."

Wiping the sweat from his brow, the Prophet μ called out – to Jābir's η horror – to all within earshot, "all you working in the trench! Jābir here has made us lunch, so let's all go and eat!" after which he turned to Jābir η and whispered, "listen. Don't cook any of your meat or bake any of your dough until I arrive."

Jābirη hurried home in a panic, and when his wife saw the multitude of exhausted men following the Prophet μ approaching their house from the trench, she turned on her husband, crying out, "what have you done? Didn't I tell you not to invite too many people? Now what are we going to do?"

"I did just what you told me to do!" Jābir η retorted. But, reforming their composure as the Prophet μ arrived and entered their humble abode, the two of them offered the unbaked dough and uncooked meat to the Prophet μ for him to bless it.

"Now, fetch the baker to ignite the oven, but don't cook anything until I tell you" the Prophet μ instructed after saying a quick prayer over the dough and meat, and placing a cover over them. He then instructed Jābir η to begin ushering people into his house, but only in small groups, and for every new group the Prophet μ placed a bit of the dough and meat in the fire and cooked them, giving them to Jābir η to distribute until the last of them had come and gone. When Jābir η would recount this episode later, he would say, "by God, there had to have been over a thousand people there that day, and each of them ate until they could eat no more! And when the last of them finally left my house, I looked and saw the dough and meat were as if they'd never had anything taken from them!"[165]

God has stated in His Qur'ān that, "certainly there has come to you a Messenger from among your selves. It torments him that you suffer; his concern is for you, and he is kind and compassionate to the believers."[166] For someone like the Prophet µ, being a guest meant guarding his host's honour when necessary. But being who and how he was, he could not stand for having his own hunger satiated while his beloved followers, who were working just as hard and facing odds just as grim, went on labouring in their hunger. So, he accepted an invitation and came as a noble guest, blessed the food as a most merciful prophet, fed the people as a most generous father, and left the food as if it were untouched for his deprived hosts as a most glorious friend.

Scarcity was a familiar feature of life for the followers of Muḥammad µ before the liberation of Makkah and the end to Qurayshī pressure it brought, so while the preceding episode was indeed miraculous, it was also surprisingly not a solitary one.

Once, Abū Ṭalḥahη (Anas's η step-father) overheard the Prophet µ in conversation with some of his other Companions; his voice must have been fainter than usual, or his tempo slower. *Something* about it told Abū Ṭalḥah's η intuition that the Prophet µ was famished, and must have been for some time. He hurried to his wife and asked, "do you have anything to eat for the Prophet?" Without a moment's hesitation, she scurried off and returned with two barley breads wrapped in her scarf. She tucked it under Anas's η shirt and sent him on his way to the Prophet µ.

When Anas η entered the mosque, he found the Prophet μ sitting, still speaking to some of his Companions. As soon as he caught sight of his faithful servant, he called out, "has Abū Ṭalḥah sent you with food?"

"Yes," Anas η replied.

"Get up and follow me, everyone!" the Prophet μ suddenly ordered the circle of Companions in which he had been sitting. Sensing that the Prophet μ intended to go to his mother's house, Anas η scampered ahead of the group of hungry men, going inside to inform his step-father before they arrived.

"O Umm Sulaym, the Prophet has come with an entire group of his pupils, and what have we to give them!" Abū Ṭalḥah η lamented, as those two loaves of bread Umm Sulaymι had produced prior were the very last scrap of food they had in their house.

"God and His Messenger know best…" Umm Sulaym ι said helplessly.

The Prophet μ entered, and after greeting the household said to Umm Sulaym ι, "O Umm Sulaym, bring me what food you have." So she called her son over and took back the two loaves that she had given him, broke them into pieces in a bowl, squeezed some butter over them, and mixed it all together. The Prophet μ proceeded to say a short supplication over the mixture and, when he had finished, ordered his hosts, "invite ten people to partake."

And in ten people came, as ordered. After they ate their fill, the Prophet µ cheerfully ordered again, "call ten more!" Group after group of ten came, stuffed themselves, and left until eighty people had been satisfied.[167]

As already discussed, prolonged periods of severe hunger were common for the Muslims in Islām's early days. Once, the Prophet µ, driven to restlessness by his famishment left his house and found Abū Bakr and ʿUmar κ right outside. "What are you both doing out at this time?" he asked.

"We're too hungry and have nothing to eat, O Messenger of God, and could think of nothing to do but come out for a walk," they both confessed.

"By God, I came out for the same reason!" the Prophet µ said, smiling weakly. After thinking for a moment, his eyes lit up and he began walking in the direction of the house of one of the more well-to-do *Anṣār*, calling back to his two friends, "follow me!" When they arrived at their destination, they were ushered inside, but this particular Companion's wife informed the trio that her husband was out fetching water and would be back soon. So they began conversing amongst themselves.

"Oh, thank God! There's no more glorious a day, when no better guests could visit me than you, today!" the small gathering heard suddenly from the door, when the master of the house returned and saw who was sitting inside. He quickly went to their small store of food and brought out a branch of dates, offering his three guests therefrom. After having served them their appetizers, he fetched his long knife from its place and started on his way outside.

"Be sure not to slaughter a milking sheep!" the Prophet µ called out after him, aware of what he had in mind. He wouldn't have abided a family going without milk for months to come just so he could have some meat one night.

After their hearty meal had finished, there came a lull in what must have been equally hearty conversation. "I tell you truly, by God, you will be questioned about this grant on the Day of Judgement," the Prophet µ finally advised Abū Bakr η and ʿUmar η, making sure their host heard him as well. "You came out of your houses hungry, but God did not let you return home before granting you this bounty."[168] Aside from being sound spiritual advice about gratitude in general, referring to their host's offering as a bounty from God was a sure way of making him and his wife feel greatly appreciated.

Part of being a noble guest is accepting what is offered by the host – bet it in the form of food or conduct. Once, I went to a studio to film an episode of a live television show. When I arrived, I found that the host, who was a woman, was very upset. The reason, as some of the crew informed me, was that the guest they had just finished filming before me, who was a "*Shaykh*," had offended her with some harsh words; among them was that he refused to be in the same room as her. There are many so-called scholars who practice and preach (at least they're consistent, some of them!) a fabricated, or highly-distorted Islām *not* brought by our noble Prophet, Muḥammad μ.

We know this behaviour is anything but prophetic, as we have on record that when a Companion by the name of Abū Usaydη married, he invited the Prophet μ and some others for a celebratory meal, the one serving guests in their house was none other than his new wife. She took a stone container filled with dates and water around to each of the guests, dipping the date into the water and serving them individually, herself. When the supply of dates was exhausted, she personally gave the Prophet μ the leftover date-water infusion to drink.[169] The Companion who related this event made sure to mention that it was the wife who served the guests because this was not common for Arabs; but the Prophet μ made no objection whatsoever, let alone insisting the affair be conducted as he or others would have it in their own homes. He also enjoyed whatever refreshments were offered without becoming pernickety, as guests – particularly at wedding festivities – often unfortunately do.

On a note slightly tangential to the topic of this chapter, the above incident actually calls to my mind the Gospel story related about Prophet Jesusν who, while ministering and preaching in Bethany, was in the house of one of the Pharisees (who were like the sorts of "*Shaykhs*" mentioned previously, but for the Jews) who had invited him for dinner when a sinful woman entered upon them and began to weep tears of repentance upon seeing her Prophet. Noticing that her tears had begun to wet Jesus' ν feet, the woman knelt and began kissing them and drying them with her long, unbound hair; she proceeded to even break open an expensive jar of perfumed oil and anoint his feet with it.[170] The display was received with indignation and arrogance by the Jewish "Shaykh," but Jesus ν used the moment to illustrate the prophetic precept of God's love for His penitent servants over His puritanical ones. Truly, Jesus ν and Muḥammad μ are two rays shining from the same lamp!

Chapter 13

...as a Host

As aforementioned, hospitality for the Arabs was a jealously-guarded virtue, almost a way of life in and of itself. This was one of the few features of contemporary Arab culture that the Prophet µ actually reinforced, as he has been quoted as having said, "as for those who believe in God and the Day of Judgement, let them treat their guests with esteem and generosity! And those who believe in God and the Day of Judgement should, as well, say good or keep silent!"[171]

By the fifth year of the Prophet's µ mission of calling to the One God in Makkah, the idolatrous Quraysh had made circumstances so unbearable for the earliest Muslims – to the extent of gruesomely torturing several to death for their faith – that the Prophet µ was forced to urge them to flee to safety in far-away Aksum (called Ḥabashahor Abyssinia, located in modern Ethiopia and Eritrea), a land he knew to be under the custodianship of a just and pious Christian ruler, titled "al-Najāshī," or "Negus," whose name was Ashama b. Abjar. This king allowed the small detachment of poor and beleaguered Muslims to settle within his borders, and cared for them as well as the rest of his citizens, to the extent that he refused to extradite them even in exchange for a vast sum offered by two agents of the Quraysh sent to recover the group of "run-away slaves," as they called them.

In fact, it was during the confrontation between these Quraysh and the Muslims, with the Negus sitting in mediation, that he became convinced that Muḥammad µ was in fact a genuine, God-sent Prophet after one of the Muslims recited a small portion of the Qur'ān upon being questioned about Islām's stance on his host-nation's religion of Christianity. Shortly thereafter, he dispatched a delegation to the Prophet µ in Makkah to convey gifts, well-wishes, and a letter stating that he himself had accepted Muḥammad µ and his religion. He would have gone himself had it not been for a spot of political unrest that demanded his personal attention. Sadly, one of the two ships ferrying the delegation across the Red Sea – the one of which the Negus's son and several of his bishops were passengers – sank, but the other arrived safely.

When this delegation finally arrived and was received by the Prophet µ at his home, he began personally serving the members of the party; the Companions who were present rushed up, protesting, "O Messenger of God, please sit! We'll do all this for you!"

"Their countrymen and king have shown the utmost respect in caring for our refugees," the Prophet µ explained, gesturing for his Companions to remain seated as he continued attending to his guests, "and I'd love nothing more than to show them the same welcome."[172]

For a ruler living near the epicentre of Islām to communicate with and eventually find conviction in the Prophet µ was not a singular event. A man named ʿAdī b.

Ḥātim al-Ṭā'īη was, during the Muḥammad's μ mission in the Ḥijāz, the chief (one could say king) of the large and powerful tribe of Banū Ṭāy'. He himself happened to have been a fairly recent convert to Christianity after having travelled to al-Shām, which was then a Byzantine territory. However, he was still wrestling with some questions about reconciling his new religion with the *Ḥanīfah* he had formerly practiced, so his curiosity was piqued by the sudden appearance of this Arabian Prophet μ. So he prepared a list of pertinent questions and journeyed on his own to Muḥammad μ, labouring under the mistaken impression born of his tribal mentality that the office of prophethood should resemble his own, of kingship.

When 'Adī η first met with the Prophet μ, the latter invited the former to his home, so they set off in its direction. On the way, some old lady stopped the Prophet μ and engaged him in a long conversation, asking about this and that. At this 'Adīη thought to himself, "*this guy can't a king!*"

When they finally arrived at the Prophet's μ house, he offered his guest a cushion upon which to sit. There being nothing else of comfort to sit on in the tiny room, and 'Adīη being a polite guest, he refused. The humble accommodations he observed only confirmed 'Adī's η prior assessment, that "*this person is no king!*" But the Prophet μ insisted that 'Adīη have the cushion, so he accepted it and they both sat.

Keen to cut to the chase, the Prophet μ said, "O 'Adī, you take a full quarter of your peoples' wealth. This is not allowed in your religion. Perhaps you've taken notice of our poverty, or the multitude of those who oppose us, and that is why you've refused to accept our religion. But I swear by God, wealth will come to these followers of mine such that none will need any more of it. And I swear by God, security will come to them such that an old woman will be able to travel from Qādsiyyah in Iraq to the Ka'bah without fear of anything but God Himself. I swear by God, you yourself will hear tell of the white citadels of Babylon falling to our forces!"

After the long and involved dialogue that took place after the Prophet's μ preamble, 'Adīŋ finally embraced Islām. He later recounted this story and confirmed the Prophet's μ predictions, saying, "I have already seen the citadels of Babylon fall, as well as an old woman travelling from afar, without fear, to the Ka'bah! And indeed, the third part is coming true as we speak, and a flood of wealth is making its way to the Muslims such that none can ask for more!"[173]

The point of all the aforementioned is to illustrate the Prophet's μ graciousness in playing host, that he always placed his guest above himself – but not because of this particular guest's social status, as the episode also has the Prophet μ stopping along the way and giving his full attention to "some old lady" while the king of a powerful tribe stood silently waiting.

'Alīv once observed that, "people used to visit the Prophet in his house, bringing to him their questions and concerns, and then he wouldn't let them leave until they had not only resolved their issues, but had something to eat as well. Thus fed, his guests would leave with knowledge they could convey to others."[174] As the best host, the Prophet µ insisted on nourishing his guests physically, mentally, and spiritually.

When the Prophet µ knew of a person in need, he would often offer them from the manifold gifts he received from his better-off devotees; he did this so frequently and consistently that he seldom had food enough for himself. In fact, once, Abū Hurayrahη was so aggrieved by the pangs of hunger that he was forced to tie a stone against his stomach (to trick his brain into thinking it was full – this is done in impoverished areas even today). When he could stand it no longer, he went to the Prophet µ to complain, lifting his tunic to demonstrate what drastic measures he had taken. But when he did so, the Prophet µ lifted his own tunic, and what did Abū Hurayrahη see but *two* stones tied against the stomach of God's Messenger µ![175] Such a generous host was he that he had less for himself than the destitute commoners.

Another person once came to the Prophet µ seeking some sustenance, but he had long since cleaned out his stores. The poor man described himself as *majhūd*, which means "completely spent," and must have been on the verge of complete starvation, so the Prophet µ inquired with some of his Companions; one of the *Anṣār* volunteered to host the seeker for the evening.

But when this Companion brought the man to his house and asked his wife if they had anything to offer him, his wife informed him gravely, "all we have is what I made for the kids' dinner tonight."

Taking a moment to strategize, the Companion finally said, "okay... send the kids to bed without dinner, just for tonight. When the Prophet's guest comes in, we'll blow out the candle while he eats. You and I will just pretend to eat along with him, so he's not ashamed." So they enacted their plan and went to sleep hungry.

Now, Islām doesn't obligate neglecting one's own child in favour of their guest, but this was an exceptional circumstance – a man's life was in danger. So the next morning, the Prophet µ met the Companion who had hosted the poor *majhūd* and greeted him, saying, "God is well-pleased with what you've done!"[176] Thus were the Prophet's µ own values implemented by those who were able, even when he himself was not.

Chapter 14

...as a Teacher

In some capacity or another, almost every man acts a teacher to others. The Prophet µ was no exception to this, as his divine calling in particular had as one of its largest components the role of teacher.

Now, there are broadly two ways in which a person can instruct their pupils. The first is to act as nothing more than a postman. He simply carries sealed envelopes containing information of which he hasn't the slightest inkling. Not only is he forbidden from opening these messages, it's just as likely as not that he wouldn't even understand the language or the content, or both, of said messages.

The second manner of teaching is analogous to an ambassador sent with a written message from one head of state to another. This ambassador's responsibility includes, in addition to simply conveying the message, clarifying any and every word if necessary. He is thus made intimately familiar with its holistic meaning and minutest detail – and if he is unsure of something, he is expected to contact his head of state immediately for clarification. And we observe from Muḥammad's µ example of teaching that his methodology followed that of the ambassador.

As Islām's reach widened, its message reached tribes and peoples increasingly far from Makkah and Madīnah, not all of whom spoke with the same accent or even dialect of Arabic. It was thus observed that, any time he addressed a large audience, the Prophet µ tended to repeat himself at least thrice[177] in order to give those present – any number of whom might have spoken a dialect varying widely from the Prophet's µ own Qurayshī variety, or just been hard of hearing – an opportunity to hear and understand him

He also never spoke in long, continuous strings; rather, he had the habit of speaking with pauses[178] long enough for those present to memorize and absorb meanings[179].

Now, the successful teacher should use many different techniques to convey and impart knowledge. We have all, in our primary and secondary school years, had the negative experience of sitting through lessons given by teachers who would simply regurgitate information, commenting dryly on their various points without so much as a single example or anecdote to hold their pupils' attention. These teachers tended to be disliked for their boring delivery and the lack of comprehension in which they aided.

However, another ingenious method of getting the point across consistently employed by the Prophet µ was the use of illustration and analogy. This was perhaps in emulation of the style of the Qur'ān itself, as it heavily relies on vivid imagery to demonstrate its intended idea. For example, we read what may be rendered into English as, "have you not seen how God has formulated the analogy of wholesome speech? It is as a wholesome tree, the roots of which are firmly set; with its branches reaching into the sky, it bears fruit – so long as its Sustainer permits – constantly. Thus does God establish such examples, so that humankind might learn them and bear them ever in mind. And the example of unwholesome speech is as a filthy tree plucked out from above the earth, never to be re-planted."[180]

A few of these illustration-based lessons follow:

In a lesson on the importance of the establishment of one's ritual prayer, the Prophet µ once asked his students, "what do you think; if there flows a river right along and outside your house, and you bathe in it five times a day, would you ever be dirty?" They of course answered in the negative. "Well, this is similar to the case of our five daily prayers. God will purify you from your sins thereby."[181]

In another lesson – this one on the tenacity of greed – the Prophet µ postulated to his students that, "if a human were to be given two valleys full to the brim with gold, he would still long for the next valley over. Nothing can fill the mouth of humankind once and for all but dust."[182]

And in another lesson on the true nature of a Muslim, the Prophet µ asked those gathered to tell him which tree they thought was most like the ideal Muslim. They all called out their answers, naming various desert trees and shrubs. "It is indeed the palm tree, whose leaves offer us shade," the Prophet µ answered finally.[183]

Once, in explaining to his Companions the types of people who would interact with his message, the Prophet µ said, "the similitude of the guidance and knowledge which I bring from God is like a heavy rain falling on the soil. Some of this soil is soft and wholesome, so it absorbs he water and produces much growth. Another type is that which is hard; none of the rainwater is absorbed, so nothing grows, but it at least holds the water on the surface so people and animals can drink from it. However, there is a third type – this neither absorbs water to nourish plants, nor holds it on the surface for the benefit of humans or animals. This is a similar situation to the knowledge which I have brought; some people have taken it in, to their benefit and that of those around them. But some haven't even bothered themselves with it."[184]

On another occasion, the Prophet µ said, "my example with regard to how I am treated by the people is like a person who is standing before a fire at night into which moths and other insects fly. This person rushes to keep the insects away for fear of more falling in, but in they fly to their deaths despite his best efforts. In the same way, I am trying my best to hold people at bay, but they are ignoring me and throwing themselves into Hell."[185]

And to illustrate his own place in the grand scheme of the parade of prophets sent by God throughout human history, the Prophet µ once said, "my example is like a person who has masterfully built a beautiful house. But despite its beauty there was a tiny hole in one of the house's corners, left by a missing brick. So whoever came to visit the house would look at it, amazed, and say, 'this would be the best house I've ever seen if they could just replace the brick in that one corner!' Well, I am that missing brick; I am the final prophet!"[186]

The above seems to have paralleled a prediction made, allegedly, by the Prophet Jesus ν and recorded in Matthew 22:42-43 in which he is purported to have said, "have you never read in the Scriptures: 'the stone the builders rejected has become the cornerstone; the Lord has done this, and it is marvellous in our eyes?' Therefore, I tell you that the Kingdom of God will be taken away from you and given to a people who will produce its fruit."

On the topic of repentance, the Prophet μ once said, "imagine that one of you is travelling through a lifeless desert on his camel. This camel is loaded with your luggage, food, and water. You stop to sleep for a short time, but when you awake, your camel is nowhere to be seen. You get up to search for him, but there isn't a single sign of him anywhere, so you give up hope and decide return to where you had been sleeping to lie back down, resigned to your fate. But as soon as your head settles into the sand, you catch a glimpse of something rather camel-esque from the corner of your eye. So you scramble to your feet and see that it is indeed your camel, still loaded with all of your possessions and provisions! How happy do you except this would make you feel? But God is even more happy with the repentance of His servants than this man in the desert who found his camel!"[187]

A challenge that teachers often face is the need to be able to explain an idea to someone who is having difficulty understanding; simplifying things isn't always easy, but this was something at which the Prophet Muḥammad µ excelled. For example, a Bedouin once came to the mosque and tied his camel to one of the pillars and called out, "who is Muḥammad?"

Someone answered, "that person with bright skin is the one you're looking for."

So the Bedouin betook himself to the Prophet µ and said, "O son of ʿAbd al-Muṭṭalib!" as it was a widespread practice among Arabians to refer to a person by a recent or even more distant grandfather rather than just one's father.

The Prophet µ smiled and acknowledged the gruff desert-dweller, "yes, I'm here – at your service!"

"I'd like to ask you a few frank questions, so don't be offended," the Bedouin began.

Still smiling, the Prophet µ graciously replied, "ask whatever you want." So the Bedouin launched into this impromptu interview of his, asking various questions about the religion the Prophet µ had brought; and for every question, he received a simple answer in good cheer.

Once the Bedouin was satisfied that all of his questions had been answered comprehensively, he stated with finality, "I testify that I accept everything you have brought! I am the ambassador of my tribe; my name is Damām, son of Thaʿlabah, and I was sent by my tribe the Banī Saʿd bin Bakr to ask you what I have asked you!"[188]

There is no doubt, the tribal societies – which are some of the few things growing in the harsh, desertous conditions of Arabia – had a very toughening, blunting effect on the behaviour of those socialised therein. To the otherwise inexperienced, city-raised and city-dwelling sensibilities of the settled, these nomads may have seemed uncouth and severe. But the Prophet μ treated them with gentleness and understanding, as a teacher genuinely concerned with delivering his message effectively.

The above point is made yet more clear by an incident in which a Bedouin came to the mosque in which the Prophet μ and some of his Companions were sat in conversation, entered, stood near on of its walls, and began to urinate. At once shocked and enraged, the Companions shouted immediately for him to stop, but the Prophet μ hushed them and said calmly, "let him finish what he's doing." Once the Bedouin finished relieving himself, the Prophet μ ordered the Companions to fetch a container of water with which to irrigate the affected areas. Then he beckoned for the Bedouin to approach and said evenly, "you know, it's not appropriate to do what you did in the mosques. They're built for performing prayers, remembering God, and reciting Qur'ān."

The Bedouin understood his mistake and, out of appreciation for the Prophet's μ kind and simple words, supplicated loudly, "O God, show mercy to me and to Muḥammad… but not to anyone else!"

Chuckling, the Prophet μ responded, "but God's mercy is much wider than that!" Then he turned to his Companions and chided them gently as well, saying, "you have not been sent to complicate and confuse! Rather, you are sent to simplify and accommodate!"[189]

There is another category of people deserving of kindness and simplicity in teaching besides those raised in ignorance in unforgiving hinterlands – and that is children. The Prophet μ made a habit of speaking to them warmly. Anas η once recounted a time when he was a young teen that the Prophet μ said to him, "my dear boy, if you can spend your days and nights without deceiving anyone, then do so!" After a few moments he added, "my dear boy, that is my Way. Whoever lives according to my Way loves me, and whoever loves me will be with me in Paradise!"[190]

Take note of the Prophet's μ use of terms of endearment to show his love and concern, his waiting between the two statements to allow time for assimilation, and his emphasis on the point by mentioning its reward – three techniques of the best Teacher appointed to humanity μ.

Now, just as there are those who require a softer touch and simpler language, there are those naturally more intelligent students who are quick to understand and absorb information;

for them, a different style is required, and this style was yet another masterfully employed by the Prophet μ.

ʿAbdullāh b. al-ʿAbbās η recounted that once, when he was sitting behind the Prophet μ on a mule, the Prophet μ said to him, "dear boy, do you want me to teach you something that will benefit you?"

"Yes indeed!" the bright young Ibn al-ʿAbbās shouted excitedly.

"Take care of God, and He will take care of you. Take care of Him all the time, and you will find Him next to you. Please Him when you are in ease, and He will see to your needs in times of hardship. If you ever need help, then turn to Him. If you must ask, then ask from Him. Everything has been written. Hence, if all creatures conspire to either help or harm you, they will not be able to do anything but what is written for you. Take heed that patience in the face of adversity brings much good. Take heed, victory comes as a result of patience. Take heed that ease follows hardship and indeed, comfort is attached to discomfort."[191]

Now, such an expansive lesson in such a condensed format would have either remained beyond a more mediocre student's grasp – being possibly even detrimental and confusing – but Ibn al-ʿAbbās η was known to be possessed of a particularly keen intellect even as a child, due possibly in part to the Prophet μ once supplicating, "O God, give him great knowledge of the religion and deep understanding of the

Qur'ān"[192] for him. Indeed, the Prophet µ was an expert educator despite humbly stating, "verily, God is the one who grants… I only distribute."[193]

The success of a teacher depends on many qualities, and the Prophet µ possessed all of them in the most perfect balance; if we continue enumerating and exemplifying each of them, this one short work will grow into several volumes, so only one more shall suffice before moving on to the next chapter.

The ability to keep one's temper while giving instruction is vital, especially when one's pupil's behaviour is disruptive. Once, Muʿāwiyah b. al-Ḥakam η was praying in congregation behind the Prophet µ and someone sneezed. Muʿāwiyah η, as custom dictated, said, "bless you!" At that, those around him turned toward him, casting red-eyed, dagger-like glances his way. "What have I done?" Muʿāwiyah η hissed defensively, feeling embarrassed and offended at the reaction of his peers, "why are you all staring at me?" But this only seemed to make things worse, and the other Companions started hitting their thighs, as if to say *we're supposed to be praying, be quiet!*

After the prayer had concluded, the Prophet µ came to this Muʿāwiyah η and said, "it is unlawful to speak during the prayer, rather one should not but recite from the Qur'ān and remember God." But that was all he did or said; just that warm, friendly advice.

Later on, whenever Muʿāwiyah η would wistfully recount this incident, he would say, "may my father and mother be his ransom, I have never seen a better teacher than the Messenger of God! By God, he neither hit me, nor insulted me, nor even spoke rudely to me!"[194]

Chapter 15

…as a Leader

Leadership ability is an important facet of history's great personalities, and is one which merits close investigation and careful analysis, because this one aspect reveals much about the combined quality and quantity of intelligence, wisdom, and courage (among other things) which constitute a person's character; such things cannot be fully gauged from observation of their performance in other roles. Someone can be a perfect son but fail as a father. Others can be perfect husbands, but not genuine friends, and so on. Similarly, one can be at the pinnacle of all of the above, yet still be a terrible leader, as the ingredients and ratios of different characteristics that result in a great leader are rarely found indeed.

Now, prophethood of the type and at the level to which Muḥammad µ was called had as one its prerequisites for success a high aptitude for leadership, as the scripture he was sent to instruct and implement is a not only a guidebook for the attainment of temporal and heavenly felicity, but also an answer for humanity's major philosophical problems. His position also required that he supervise the Muslims' major undertakings such as their mass migrations, military intervention on behalf of various tribes which requested it, and the defence of Madīnah. His oversight was also required in maintaining the growing Muslims community's peace both within itself and with its neighbours – both of which increasingly included those from different cultural, social, and racial backgrounds than the initial core of Ḥijāzī converts.

One of most momentous and perilous events in Islām's early history was the third and final migration from Makkah to Madīnah; and because it is the one which the Prophet µ personally oversaw and actually participated in, we can get an idea of the efficacy of his leadership from analysing it. Some factors to consider about the undertaking's challenges are as follows.

The distance of the route they had to take, which was along the sea, measures between 500-540/310-335 kilometres/miles. The time during which they conducted the migration was during the months of July to September, when daytime temperatures in the region reach over 40/100 degrees Celsius/Fahrenheit. That distance, in that stifling heat, would have been covered almost exclusively by foot; very few of the migrants, who had to abscond surreptitiously with very little preparation, had the luxury of mounts such as mules, donkeys, camels, or horses. The refugees would have already been worn down by years of persecution by the Quraysh in the form of activities ranging from trade embargos on their tribes or families to imprisonment and torture. And if the heat and exhaustion didn't kill them along the way, dehydration would try *its* hand; and that is to say nothing of the armed search-and-destroy patrols sent out by Makkah's most wealthy.

A person's leadership ability can be judged in part by how effectively they mitigate loss in an endeavour, and how well they facilitate proceedings.

Some time before the aforementioned final migration, the Prophet µ was in need of a temporary solution to the deadly pressure being put on his weaker, less affluent followers by the Quraysh. Negotiation with the heads of Quraysh was a null option; the Prophet's µ own tribe of Banū Hāshim was already under an embargo, and they had been one of the most influential families of the Quraysh clan. So, as we discovered earlier, the Prophet µ sent this first group to safety in Abyssinia. But there was still a large population – growing despite all odds – of Muslims in Makkah, stuck firmly beneath the hard heel of the Quraysh. Muḥammad µ had to do *something*, and all the Muslims who were able had already gone to Abyssinia. So, during the Ḥajj season (which used to last for three months and ten days), when members of various tribes from all over Arabia came as pilgrims to the Kaʿbah, the Prophet µ began seeking out tribal chiefs that might accept this next batch of refugees. Some refused without consideration, either being too committed to their idolatry, or having already fallen prey to the propaganda machine of the Quraysh. Some, on the other hand, did pause for consideration, but stipulated conditions that were simply unacceptable.

This continued until the Prophet µ came upon six members of the Khazraj tribe of Yathrib. When he began his proposal, the Khazraj-men all looked at each-other in surprise.

"So, is this the prophet that those scholars of our Jewish community keep telling us about?" they said amongst themselves. "Our city is going through a hard time right now," they explained to the Prophet μ. "There's a lot of friction between the tribes of Yathrib, but perhaps you – being a prophet – can put an end to it and make peace between us," they continued hopefully. "If you can, you and your followers would be most welcome."

This being the only promising lead, and ever one for promoting reconciliation, the Prophet μ agreed to their terms; they promised to return to Yathrib and speak with their city's notables about the arrangement. The next year rolled around and the Prophet μ was visited again by a contingent from Yathrib, this time composed of men from Khazraj *and* Aws, the tribe with which they had been having the aforementioned friction.

To act as his official representatives and emissaries of Islām itself, the Prophet μ sent Muṣʿab b. ʿUmayrη and ʿAbdullāh b. Umm Maktūmη back with them to Yathrib, where they began spreading the message of Islām (such that, according to the historical narrations, there wasn't a family in the city except that at least one of its members accepted the religion) and laying the groundwork for the reception of the Makkan refugees.[195]

The anticipation these initial representatives built eventually reached the point at which the entire city was desperate to finally meet their prophet – including the three

Jewish tribes who lived in and around Yathrib. This eagerness to welcome the Prophet µ extended even to the common Muslims; groups of them would arrive in their new city with natives practically lying in wait (or literally sitting in trees outside the city limits in some cases) to snatch them away to their houses, keen for the privilege to host these *Muhājirīn* until their own houses could be built. Logistics management and politicking can only be maintained at this level by one with truly exceptional leadership abilities.

Leading from the front is sometimes vital to a project's success; depending on the context, this can translate to the leader actually taking on the most difficult task or doing the most work all-around. In the context of these migrations to Madīnah – as the city came to be known – this meant the Prophet µ putting himself at the most risk to shield his followers.

In order to maximize security, the Prophet µ had migrants depart in small groups including one or two appropriately-equipped, capable fighters (enough to deal with Qurayshī scouts). The leaders of Qurayshī opposition to Muḥammad µ had made a public offer of a reward comprising one hundred camels and a large sum of gold for any who could bring the Prophet µ to them – dead or alive. However, no such bounty was placed on any other migrant's head, so any small caravan he joined for his own safety would have had brought upon it the entire wrath of Arabia's most wealthy clan. This was simply unacceptable.

Further complicating things for the Prophet's µ personal plans for migration was the fact that, while the Muslims did have among them many skilled, brave warriors (such as his own uncle Ḥamzahη, who was known quite literally as "the Lion Hunter"), they did not have *so* many that a sufficient number could be spared to protect the Prophet µ; this too was unacceptable, as the Prophet µ could not countenance even a single caravan making its way unguarded across those treacherous summer sands.

Despite receiving enthusiastic offers of protection from his more martially-inclined Companions, he chose only one man to accompany him – his soft, mild-mannered best friend Abū Bakrη. Since his aim was to divert attention from his followers onto himself, this made his own vector all the more enticing. Which would a merciless, gold-digging opportunist who had no qualms with murder prefer: a risky raid on a caravan guarded by one or two people who could overpower and kill him, and for no promise of reward but perhaps what little he could carry off as spoils, or a couple of unarmed, middle-aged men walking alone through the desert that would fetch him a hundred camels and a heap of gold? The risk to the Prophet's µ other Companions was thus all but completely nullified.

And it was because he was unburdened by worry for his beloved followers, that the Prophet µ made the arduous, perilous trip from Makkah to Madīnah in high spirits; even when one group of mercenaries hot on their trail had caught up with the duo – who were forced to take shelter in craggy cave beneath them – the Prophet µ showed not the faintest sign of apprehension. Abū Bakr η though, being a human like the rest of us, in that moment faced his mortality; he would later recount to others that, "they were right above us! If one of them had so much as looked down at his shoes, he would have seen us!"[196]

In such a situation of sheer panic and terror, Abū Bakr η couldn't help but cry. But Muḥammad µ soothed his best friend, saying calmly so only he could hear, "fear not, for God is with us."[197]

Now, a leader is responsible for the safety of those he leads, and a *good* leader ensures that said safety is maintained, thinking nothing of himself until and unless. An example of this is the cliché of the captain of a sinking ship who, using up every last precious second overseeing the loading of his passengers and crew onto their lifeboats and seeing to their safe dismissal, runs out of time to save himself and goes down with his ship. Prophet Muḥammad µ was just such a captain for the ship of Islām, as evidenced by the fact that as soon as he was satisfied that everything was favourably prepared in Madīnah, he ordered the Muslims to start on their way there in July in the piecemeal fashion discussed above; by September, everyone who was able, had abandoned Makkah. Only two types of Muslim remained: those who were physically unable due to illness or having been detained, and those whose social status protected them from oppression and thus had no need to migrate. Only then did he and his trusted left-hand-man set course for Madīnah to resume control of Islām's helm.

The event of the *Hijrah* was a perfect showcase of yet another important component of leadership possessed in unmatched quantities by the Prophet µ, namely trustworthiness. Before receipt of his first divine revelation and the commencement of his prophetic mission, Muḥammad µ was already famous among the Quraysh for his fidelity, earning him the moniker "*al-Amīn*," meaning "supremely trustworthy/dependable."[198] Thus, people would often consign various articles of their property to his care for safekeeping. Ironically, they continued to do so even after he announced his prophethood – despite tarring him with epithets like madman, magician, and deceiver, every one of them down to the last man knew in his heart of hearts that this Muḥammad µ was still that same old "*al-Amīn*."

So, when the Prophet µ reckoned that the time drew near for his own departure from Makkah, he contacted the people of whose property he yet had possession. He waited for them to collect their belongings until there were only a couple of people's consignments left and he finally contacted the remainder one day to arrange pick-up the next morning. Being fully aware that these activities had about them the scent of finality that would alert those keen-nosed dogs heading the Quraysh that his departure was imminent – and suspecting that these last two or three people whose property he still held would act as informants for them – the Prophet µ had his right-hand-man ʿAlī b. AbīṬālibν stand in for him to see his commitment through. Knowing that his cousin would be safe from the murderous plot hatched by the devilish Quraysh, the Prophet μ slipped out of Makkah with Abū Bakr η that very night, completely undetected.[199]

Notwithstanding the most daunting part of the saga of the Migration nearly drawing to a close with the Muslims' final settlement in the land of freedom and justice established in Madīnah, the end was still some ways off and a firm grip was still needed to steer the nascent Muslim community through the potential complications that still could have been given rise to by the settlement of a large refugee population in a foreign land.

The cultural and social landscape of Madīnah was completely different from that of Makkah; power structures and group dynamics were utterly alien. The substantial and influential presence of a significant Jewish population in Madīnah was perhaps the most striking difference. Makkah was home to some Christians and a handful of native Arab monotheists, but the overwhelming majority religion was Arab paganism – there was no Jewish population to speak of (and why would there be in an epicentre of idolatry), and even the non-Jewish tribes' cultures and customs were different enough from those of Makkah to be a potential source of friction. And even minor friction between Arabs could quickly escalate into bloodshed (as in the previously-cited example of the War of Basūs).

So the Prophet µ could not essentially just drop his people off in Madīnah and put his feet up; a substantial amount of campaigning was still necessary, so he more or less immediately invited every one of Madīnah's tribal chiefs, religious leaders, and persons of influence and with their cooperation drafted a set of by-laws, called the "Wāthiqah al-Madīnah," or "Madīnah Accords," which is preserved until today in the historical record.[200] The main thrust of these accords dealt with citizens' rights, emphasizing equal treatment for all regardless of tribe or religion. There were also provisions obligating upon every citizen the city's defence in case of attack, no matter by whom. Such was the comprehensive, far-sighted nature of the Prophet's µ leadership, that rather than resting on his laurels after getting through the hard bit, he established contingencies for every eventuality.

A final quality that very often *good* leaders lack, keeping them from being *great* leaders, is that of accessibility; open lines of communication between a leader and their followers is a key component of bilaterally building and maintaining trust. The Arab tribes living in and around Makkah implemented this mechanism via something they called the "Dār al-Nadwah," or "Domain of Colloquium," where chieftains would meet one another, and their own followers, for discussion on pressing concerns. Lacking the hierarchical structure (headed by the Quraysh) of Makkah, Madīnah was without such a useful forum, so the Prophet µ had his mosque established partially for filling the same purpose; whenever an issue needed the community-at-large's attention, the *ādhān* (call to prayer) was given and a city council meeting of sorts was held therein.

Chapter 16

...as a Prophet

The duties entailed by the station of prophethood are widely misunderstood, thanks in no small part to popular preachers and myopic "scholars" of religion down through the ages. The matter has become distorted to the point that many are under the impression that prophets came to deliver a script for their followers to parrot, informing them of which words to say and movements to perform, and how many times daily, or which specific clothing all of humanity should wear, or how long the hairs that sprout from one's skin should be allowed to grow. They would never put it in the above terms, but they *are* what their presentations boil down to.

On the contrary, the essential role of prophets was to offer to people solutions, ways of clearing what impediments lay on their respective paths to felicity in both their worldly lives and their lives hereafter. A prophet was meant to practically demonstrate the answers to such existential questions as: just what is a human and why are they on Earth? Where did they come from and where are they going? What is actually good or bad for them, and why do they suffer? These form only the beginning of a long list humanity craves answers for, and the only one who can do so with objective truth is the One χ who created them – and the prophets were the conduits through whom those answers were transmitted from on high.

This pure, crystalline message of the prophets is a divine signal which nevertheless suffers degradation due to human nature – whether it be malicious or benign. But this chapter will explore the ways in which the Final Prophet, Muḥammad µ received and relayed that divine signal via his role as prophet.

The severity of the shame felt by some especially-depraved individuals in Arabia's Era of Ignorance at having a daughter – as this left their family with, as they saw it, one more mouth to feed with one less strong arm on the field of battle or in the marketplace only to be given away years later for the sexual enjoyment of some other man – led them to participate in the ghastly practice of burying them alive in infancy. While this example of *Jāhilī* barbarity is often illustratively cited, it was not actually widespread, but historical records do show that some of those who would later accept Islām as Companions of the Prophet µ regrettably took part. The Prophet µ tenaciously fought every injustice he saw, and this one was no different.

Someone once came to the Prophet µ and confessed, voice taught and crackling with sorrow, "O God's Messenger, we were an oblivious people who used to worship idols and kill our children. I used to have a daughter; she had grown up to the point that she could respond when we called her… oh, how she loved when I used to call her!" Choking back tears, the man continued, "so once I called her and she followed me, all the way to the well not far from my house… and I took her and threw her in. The last thing I remember was her crying out 'daddy, daddy!'"

The Prophet's µ heart could bear it no longer, and the tears that had begun with flooding his eyes finally streamed down his cheeks and off his beard. One of those present in the gathering scolded the man for causing the Prophet µ such distress, but the Prophet µ waved his hand, saying, "leave him be, he's come to ask about that which concerns him." Then he turned to the man who had come and urged him to tell the story again, as the atmosphere of catharsis – a vital psychological ingredient in forgiveness – had been ruined. So he reiterated his account, bringing himself, the Prophet µ, and the rest present to tears once more. After regaining his composure, the Prophet µ said to the man, "God has forgiven the sins of your days of ignorance; go and have a fresh start!"[201]

Now, the Prophet µ was born and raised in the same sick society as these men who gave no second thought to brutally murdering their own flesh and blood, but his socialization never corrupted his heart. And this purity of heart flowed back out to his people – the ones who followed him, anyway – once he held their own actions up to them as a mirror. This man in particular, whose religion and scholars condoned what he did, was awoken to the harsh, gut-wrenching reality of what he had done, like someone waking from a nightmare only to find that they were never really dreaming at all; he was so stricken with grief that he found it impossible to forgive himself and move on. So he sought treatment for his spiritual affliction with the Prophet µ. And as the most perfect doctor for the spirit of both the society and the individual, the Prophet µ heard, diagnosed, and treated his symptoms, healing the man's broken heart, however much it grieved his own to listen to the man's tale. The Prophet µ in this case served as the perfect transmitter of the divine signal, informing the man truly that God forgives the misdeeds of ignorance; and he ensured that this signal was received by essentially giving the man that forgiveness in doing and saying what was needed in order for him to forgive himself.

On another similar occasion, a man came to the Prophet µ, visibly distraught. He admitted that, "I buried seven of my daughters alive in my period of ignorance. What can I ever do to atone?"

"Free one slave for each of them," the Prophet µ answered.

"I have camels, O Prophet," the man suggested, not being one who owned any slaves.

"Then give away for free one camel for each,"[202] the Prophet µ said. Perhaps in this case, the Prophet µ saw something in this man that suggested an imperfection in his sense of contrition – something which true repentance cannot do without. So he suggested this penalty as way to afflict his soul with the necessary measure of remorse, since the hearts of some humans are more attached to their wealth than to even their own children, rather than as any sort of compensation. Again, the divine signal needed to be properly transmitted and received by individuals in full in order to effect positive change in society at large.

In addition to the aforementioned gruesome custom, the Prophet µ (as ridding society of its ills was another principle function of prophethood) successfully abrogated another revolting tradition – that of considering women as chattel, even to the extent of being able to inherit them. For instance, if a father or brother died, his wives were inherited by the remaining relatives; and if one remained whom nobody wanted to marry, she would simply be locked up to live out the rest of her days in isolation.[203] And since limitless polygamy was widely practiced, there could be a staggering number of women all inherited – to be turned into sexual furniture or stowed away – when a wealthy-enough man died.

Apparently, as reported in the historical record, Madīnan culture took a similar approach to its womenfolk. When a man died, his closest friend would go to his widow and wrap her in cloth. She thus became his property, and if she didn't agree to marry him, she had no alternative but to pay him to be freed, or she could simply be locked away as aforementioned if the man had no desire for her.[204]

Another disturbing custom of the Madīnans with regard to the women of the locality was that a husband would badly mistreat his wife until she could bear it no longer and urge him to divorce her, at which point he would marry her off to the highest bidder.

When the Prophet µ encountered these appalling customs – particularly upon hearing of a man dying and his own son wanting to subsequently marry the widow – after his migration, there came down a Qur'ānic verse the rough English meaning of which is, "O you who have committed to belief, it is not lawful that you should forcibly inherit women!" This same verse goes on to prohibit men from instigating divorce in order to recover the wealth spent on dowry, and to obligate living together in harmony and kindness. The verse concludes by reminding the petty and unscrupulous among men that, "if you dislike them (i.e. your wives), then perhaps that which you dislike is that wherein God has placed an abundance of good!"[205]

Yet another misogynistic norm of the pre-Islāmic Arabs was to completely withhold inheritance from the female relatives of the deceased (as well as any below a certain age), reserving it instead for only the strong males.[206] God Himself put a stop to this as well with the revelation of the Qur'ānic verse which equates to, "for the men is a share in what has been left by the parents and near kin, and for the women too is a share in what has been left by the parents and near kin; whether it be little or much, there is a definite share!"[207]

Beside he infanticide some *Jāhilī* Arabs perpetrated against daughters, there was also the infrequent (but still socially acceptable) instance of filicide in times of exceptional scarcity; this was another afront against which the Prophet μ battled armed with his own personal wisdom and divine revelation. ʿAbdullāh b. Masʿūdη once asked the Prophet μ what the three greatest sins were, according to God. The Prophet's μ answer was that, in descending order, they were to put anyone or anything on par with God who created them, to kill one's children out of fear of loss of sustenance because of them, and to engage in adultery with the wife of one's neighbour.[208] This was in confirmation of the Qur'ānic verse God sent down to combat filicide, wherein we find what approximates to, "so do not kill your children fearing poverty, for it is *We* who provide sustenance for yours *and* for you. Indeed, to kill them is an enormity. And do not even approach adultery; it is certainly a foul abomination and an evil path."[209]

The list of oppressions that were acceptable (and even praiseworthy) to the culture of a pre-Islāmic Arab could continue almost ad infinitum – close scrutiny of the subjects addressed by the Qur'ān aids in enumerating them – but Muḥammad's µ filling of the role of prophethood served as a remedy for all of them. However, just as a remedy must be willingly ingested by a patient to have any lasting effect (medicine forced down one's throat will be rejected violently, resented, and never taken again), the Prophet's µ lessons had to be heeded to be implemented. There were of course those who stubbornly refused to even acknowledge the sickness in their society or selves, so they left their cure untouched and remained ill, but enough of a majority received treatment that eventually the wider culture was inoculated against the cancerous injustices which it had once seen as typical, healthy behaviour. With the Prophet's µ fathomless wisdom, he planted in the people's hearts the seeds of hatred for inequality, and as the seeds began to sprout, watered by the Prophet's µ pristine character, the people's hearts were constricted by guilt as they began living in the hell of all those affronts to humanity in which they used to revel. So one-by-one, they queued up for the peace and forgiveness offered by the spiritual and cultural revolution that was Islām.[210]

The attribute of compassion is vital for a medical professional's successful implementation of the treatment plan they have devised for their patient; prophethood, being so readily analogised to the medical field as we have seen above, is no different. God Almighty has stressed the fact of Muḥammad's µ compassion for his people by emphasizing that he was from among them, sending down verses such as what can be translated as, "it is He who has called forth from within an illiterate nation a messenger *fromamong* them…"[211]

Being one of them, Muḥammad µ was prepared to sacrifice whatever was necessary to pry his people from the grasp of ignorance in which they had been so long and firmly held; his first and last concern was for none but them.

On more than one occasion, the Prophet µ was seen offering a particularly lengthy prayer. Surprised and curious, one person approached him afterwards and asked, "O God's Messenger, we've just seen your praying a prayer the like of which we've never seen before…"

"Yes," the Prophet µ explained, standing and dusting himself off, "my prayer was out of fear and hope. You see, I was begging God for three things; He has granted me two, but not the third. I requested that He not destroy my nation with famine [or drowning in another narration], and he has granted that. Then I requested that He not allow them to fall prey to foreign invaders, and this too He granted. But then I requested that He not allow my nation to fight amongst each-other. This, He did not grant."[212] Sadness must have tinged his voice, as he must have had some inkling of the tragic, bloody internecine conflicts that would follow his passing.

On another similar occasion, some Companions saw the Prophet µ offering a ritual prayer, so they drew near; it did their hearts good to observe the Prophet µ in any state, particularly in prayer. But they heard him whispering something other than the prescribed formulae of the ritual prayer with which they were already familiar, so when he finished and stood up they asked him about what he had been saying. "Oh, you noticed?" the Prophet µ said, wryly feigning surprise.

"Yes!" they replied, eager for the Prophet's µ explanation.

"Okay, okay. Well, an incident suddenly occurred to me of a past prophet whose nation had such an army that none could rival it. A time came when he was ordered to choose one of three options for his nation: they could face either a foreign invasion, a famine, or sudden death. So he presented his people with the choices and urged them to decide for themselves; but they insisted he choose for them, being their prophet and leader. So, since it was their habit when faced with a dilemma to offer a prayer, he stood to pray and said, 'O Lord, do not allow barbarians to overrun my people, and do not afflict them with famine. If I must choose one of the three, let it be death!' Thus, within three days seventy-thousand people from his nation were dead. And it was because of this incident which occurred to me that you heard me whispering, 'O Lord, I seek Your protection, and I seek Your strength, for but by You there is neither!'"[213] This was Muḥammad's µ way of communicating to his followers how much compassion and love he had for them, that he would never have been able to make such a grave decision.

As a prophet, Muḥammad µ was blameless, but the thought of his nation – some of whom were particularly virulent and vitriolic in their opposition to him – being subject to divine retribution caused him a great deal of trepidation. A couple of the Prophet's µ closer Companions noticed that he had begun growing some white hairs. Correctly assuming that the impetus or this was distress, they inquired as to the reason. "The chapters of Hūd, Wāqiʿah, Mursalāt, Nabā', and Takwīr in the Qur'ān have turned my hair white,"[214] the Prophet µ informed them sorrowfully. But why would chapters whose subject matters have nothing to do with a prophet's duties or things for which they might be blameworthy cause Prophet µ such *personal* anguish? The reason was nothing other than his compassion and concern for *us*, his nation, as those chapters detail the punishments meted out by God to former nations for disobeying and humiliating their prophets.

In fact, the Prophet µ constantly supplicated for the practical good of his people. He is recorded as once having said, "O people, seek knowledge from the early morning, for I have asked God to bless that time for my nation."

Someone once came to the Prophet µ and asked, knowing that he always asked God for benefit on his nation's behalf, asked why he had never petitioned God for a kingdom comparable to that of Prophet Sulaymān ν. Smiling, the Prophet µ responded, "and how do you know God hasn't given me *better* than the kingdom of Sulaymān? Listen," he explained, "there hasn't been a prophet sent by God except that God granted them some request in their lifetime. Now, many of these prophets were scorned and disobeyed by their people, so their request was for divine punishment; and it was granted. Their nations were destroyed. However, when God presented me with the same opportunity to make a granted request, I asked that He allow me to intercede on my nation's behalf on the Day of Judgement."[215]

Now, the Prophet-King Sulaymānν had, so we believe, the greatest kingdom mankind has ever, and shall never again be, seen. But since such was a worldly kingdom, and even the entire world of good things is as a drop in the bucket of the eternal life hereafter, our Prophet's µ request on our behalf was the most wise and generous possible.

We have also narrated from the Prophet µ in the books of history that he said, "I have been given the choice between two options: half of my nation entering Paradise, or being allowed to intercede for all of them on the Day of Judgement. And I have chosen intercession, because its reach is wider; after all, do you think the righteous will be in need of it? No, rather it would be for those who have fallen into sin."

This chapter on the prophethood of Muḥammad μ can be summarized by relating the conversation that took place – referenced previously – between the Abyssinian Negus and the Makkan refugees, who had fled to him for refuge, when the two Quraysh-men came to forcibly retrieve them. The leader of the group of Muslim refugees, Jaʿfar b. AbīṬālib η (who was the Prophet's μ cousin), was called to plead their case. When the cross-examination reached the point at which the Negus asked Jaʿfar η about the particulars of their new religion, he responded thus:

"O King, we were a people steeped in heedlessness who used to worship idols, eat of the meat of our heathen sacrifices, and commit all manner of sins. We used to sever ties of kinship with impunity, mistreat our neighbours, and the strongest of us freely oppressed the weaker. We continued on this way until God sent to us, from among us, a prophet. We know the prestige of this prophet's lineage, the purity of his character, and the honesty of his speech. He has called us to the worship of the One God and to disown the idols of wood and stone worshipped by our forebears. He has ordered us to speak the truth, faithfully discharge responsibilities, and maintain kinship ties. Likewise, he has forbidden for us social corruption, shedding innocent blood, lying, mistreatment of orphans, and falsely accusing chaste women of indecency. Furthermore, he has ordered us to worship God without associating partners to Him, to perform ritual prayers, to give alms, and to fast.

"We have responded and accepted that call," Jaʿfarη continued after enumerating a handful of other Islāmic injunctions, "obeyed those orders, and desisted from that which has been forbidden. But our tribes opposed and oppressed us for it, and they have attempted to force us to abandon it. But we abandoned our homes instead, hoping to live under your justice in the kingdom wherein we have heard none are tyrannized."

The Negus heard and considered all of this, asking him intently after several moments, "do you have anything that this prophet has brought from God?"

"Yes," Jaʿfar η responded simply.

"Well, do go on, tell me what it is!" the Negus cried, excited at the proposition that this man before him might just be telling the truth – that the man to whom he had pledged his allegiance might just be a genuine prophet of God. So Jaʿfar recited the first portion of the nineteenth chapter of the Qur'ān (titled "Maryam" after the mother of Prophet ʿĪsāν). The Negus and the assembly of his bishops were so moved by Jaʿfar's η recitation that they all began weeping uncontrollably. "I swear by God," the Negus said between sobs, "this message has come from the same source as that of Prophet Mūsā!"[216]

Introduction

Up to this point, our investigation into the Prophet Muḥammad's μ life has focused primarily on the *roles* he as a man filled in society. We scrutinized his performance as a son, father, husband, friend, and relative – most valuable for gauging the intimate features of a person's character and how they behave without the mask we don to show the world. We also looked at him as a teacher, leader, and prophet – best for coming to an understanding of the level of a person's wisdom, knowledge, intellect, and the other relevant skills and attributes. It is hoped thereby that the reader will have derived a bounty of lessons which will benefit them both in this life and the hereafter.

In the coming chapters, I intend to explore another gauge of the unadulterated, essential nature of a person's character, and that is how they conduct themselves while undergoing various involuntary emotional states – for example, in the expression of melancholy, joy, anger, and gratitude. Even the most lauded actors in our times require multiple takes to convincingly express any of the aforementioned (the way they do so is carefully scripted anyway), and the producer still has to choose the best from among them.

Now, if for example a person were to attend a funeral and shed some crocodile tears – putting on the airs of someone greatly bereft of a dearly-loved one – not all, but some in attendance would perceive the ruse for what it was; they would be displeased with the pretender and lose respect for them. Such is the case when anyone is caught in disingenuousness, and even the most Machiavellian sociopath can't maintain a front forever, for everyone.

Were Muḥammad μ such an impostor, some of the more sycophantic simpletons of his followers might have been convinced, but never his intimates – people possessed of keen intellects and unwavering scruples like ʿAlīν, Abū Ṭālibη, Khadījahι, Zayd b. Ḥārithahη, or Abū Bakr η. Khadījah ι for example was not only a business-savvy merchant (who was wealthy enough to send her caravans off on their own – something few other traders could afford to do), but also a twice-married widow before her betrothal to Muḥammad μ. It's simply not reasonable to entertain the possibility that such a shrewd woman could be deceived by some duplicitous conman.

Most of the Prophet's μ closest Companions were similarly sophisticated, experienced, and intelligent, so it is thus similarly unlikely that any of them would have become and remained so fiercely loyal to and zealously loving of Muḥammad μ and his religion.

To that end, let us examine how the Final Prophet μ expressed himself when he was…

Chapter 17

...Oppressed

A person's behaviour changes when they are subjected to oppression, and if we were to carefully observe these changes, we might perceive something of the hidden corners of their character. Some react in an escalatory fashion, becoming even more intensely oppressive in return. Others react in a diffusive manner, managing to drastically decrease or even stop it altogether. Sometimes we are too weak to defend ourselves, while other times we are strong enough but lack the wisdom or experience to do so properly.

The Prophets were all without exception severely oppressed, some even to the point of being murdered, for no other reason than that their divinely-sourced teachings were unpopular with the powers that be – freeing slaves and putting an end to things like exploitation and wanton violence, we can see from history, were always endeavours met with extreme violence. Thus, it is simply the nature of prophethood that its standard-bearers led difficult lives.

When Muḥammad μ was first visited by the Archangel Jibrīlν, Khadījah ι conveyed the former to her cousin Waraqah b. Nawfal, who had become a Christian and thus had some knowledge of revealed scripture. He asked the Prophet μ to tell him what had happened when he met the angel. After the Prophet's μ recounting of the events, Waraqah exclaimed, "that was the angel sent to Prophet Mūsā. Oh, would that I were yet young and energetic when your tribe ejects you from your home!"

"Would they really do such a thing?" Muḥammad μ asked incredulously.

"Yes! None brought what you have brought but were oppressed. If I am still alive when that day comes, I promise to do my utmost to support you!" Waraqah warned the Prophet μ enthusiastically. He did, however, end up passing away before such time as he foretold.[217]

On March 23, 625 CE the Quraysh sent a large contingent from Makkah to Madīnah intent on slaughtering every man and enslaving every woman and child as "revenge" for the Expedition of Badr. Upon receiving intelligence reports on the mobilization of this column, the Prophet μ convened his war council for deliberation on how to proceed. The older, wiser Companions advised the Prophet μ to have their people retreat into the city proper and force the Makkans into laying a protracted siege (something at which tribal Arab armies of the time would have failed miserably), but the younger, more brash Muslims agitated to sally forth and meet the enemy on the field. Public opinion was swayed in their more aggressive suggestion, so out they went. It was during this ill-fated action that the Prophet's μ stalwart, beloved uncle Ḥamzahη was martyred, and when the fray reached its most desperate point, the Prophet μ himself along with his personal bodyguard were engaged, resulting in the Prophet μ sustaining several severe injuries including a laceration on his leg from a passing arrow which bled profusely.

It was this precise moment about which the Prophet was recorded as saying, referring to himself in the third person, "one of the Prophets was assaulted by his tribe until he was bleeding. And as he wiped the blood away, he was saying, 'O Lord, forgive them, for they don't realize what they're doing!'"[218]

Once, during the Prophet's μ time in Makkah before his emigration to Madīnah, he was performing a ritual prayer at the Ḥijr of the Ka'bah when suddenly a man by the name of 'Uqbah b. Abī Mu'ayṭ – one of the heads of Qurayshī opposition to the Prophet μ – came up from behind him, tossed a cloth around his neck, and began strangling him until Abū Bakr η happened upon the scene.

"Would you kill a man for nothing more than his belief in God?" he bellowed indignantly as he shoved 'Uqbah away from the Prophet μ.[219]

On another occasion, Muḥammad μ was beaten so ferociously – and he was a broad, tall, physically strong man – that he fell unconscious. It was the trusty Abū Bakr η who came to the rescue again; as he ran to interject himself between the unconscious Prophet μ and his assailants, he was heard shouting, "what's wrong with you people?! Would you kill him just because he believes in God?!"

"Who's that?" one of the tormenters asked.

"Oh, it's just the son of Quḥāfah, the fool," another of them replied callously.[220]

These were the sorts of things being done to the Prophet μ, who was a rich noble from a prestigious family, so one can only imagine what was being done to the other Muslims, most of whom were from no-account, poor families or even slaves; hence the desperate exodus to Abyssinia on which the Prophet μ sent that first group of pioneers.

When the Prophet μ journeyed with his adopted son Zayd b. Ḥārithah η to proselytize in the city of al-Ṭā'if, he met with the three brothers who held senior positions there.

"Couldn't God find better than you to send?" the first of them crowed disdainfully.

"I refuse to speak with you," squawked the second mockingly, "for if you are a liar in your claim to divine messengership, then you aren't worthy of my attention. But if you truly are sent from God, then I'm not worthy of yours!"

"If God has sent *you*, why, I shall go and rip the very clothes from the Ka'bah!" the third cawed sardonically. And with that, they sent an edict city-wide for every citizen, children included, to pelt the Prophet μ and his companion until they were outside the city limits.

And that they happily did, hurling hunks of gravel at the Prophet μ as Zayd η tried his best to intercept them. They carried on doing this, hot on the duo's heels all the while, until they were beyond the city gate. The Prophet μ, with Zayd's η help, ran into a large garden to tend to their wounds, wash their clothes of the accumulated blood and grime, and rest and recover for their fifty-mile journey back to Makkah.

So the two, supporting each-other's weight, hobbled over to a tree and collapsed beneath its shade gasping for breath through dusty grimaces as the Prophet μ whispered a supplication. The two brothers who owned his particular vineyard happened to see the two men stumble onto their land, as well as the unfortunate circumstances which brought them there, so they took pity and called their young slave – a Christian hailing from Nineveh in Iraq named ʿAddāsη – to take some grapes and a helping hand to the two beleaguered men.

When ʿAddās η offered a grape to the Prophet μ, the latter took the offering, saying "*bismillāh*" before popping it in his mouth. This struck the young Christian as odd, as what the Prophet μ had said meant "with the name of God," and he had only ever known the Arabs of the Ḥijāz to be idolaters.

"People of this land don't say such things!" the boy blurted out.

"And where are you from?" the Prophet μ asked knowingly.

"Nineveh," ʿAddās η replied.

"Ah! The land of Yūnus son of Mattā, that righteous man."

"How do you know about him?" ʿAddās η exclaimed incredulously. After all, these Arabs knew *about* God at least – they even called out to Him on occasion alongside their false deities – but surely not His prophets mentioned in scripture!

"Why should I not? He was a prophet, as am I," the Prophet μ retorted jovially. To prove his point, the Prophet μ continued telling ʿAddās η about the Prophet Yūnus ν, reciting whatever of the Qur'ān had been revealed about him up to that point and answering every last question the bright-eyed young Iraqi had for him. By the end of the encounter, ʿAddās η was no longer a Christian, but a Muslim; he testified in front of his owners that he accepted Muḥammad μ as a true prophet of the One God. They were unhappy with this, but they let him be.

Now, the Prophet μ was a very soft-hearted person by nature and loved children and having the children of al-Ṭā'if participate (rather gleefully, it seems) in the entire city's wholesale violent rejection of his self and his message only added insult to injury – literally. After such a devastating psychological blow on top of all the physical ones, would any of us be prepared immediately thereafter to sit down and engage in a lengthy theological discussion with someone, still bleeding and sore? But this is how Muḥammad behaved after being maximally oppressed.

Furthermore, we who are familiar with them have seen in the various religious scriptures how some of God's Prophets reacted to their people's oppression. But how our prophet, Muḥammad µ, respond? What was that prayer he whispered after collapsing in the cool grass of that garden outside the city which had just bloodied and ejected him? What he is recorded to have said betrays the Prophet's µ profound compassion, sincerity, and sense of accountability:

"O my Lord! To you I complain of my weakness, deficiency in spreading Your message, and inadequacy in the eyes of people! You are the Guardian of the disgraced, so You are my Guardian. To whom have You referred my protection? Have you referred it to the enemy, who will neglect me? Or to those distanced from me? If You are not displeased with me then nothing else matters, yet the tranquillity You bestow is dearer to me still. I seek refuge in You from Your displeasure, and I shall persist in apologizing to You for my failures until I find that You are pleased with me. And save by You, there is neither strength nor protection!"[221] We can see from this that, rather than blaming the citizens of al-Ṭā'if for their arrogant, ignorant rejection of the truth, the Prophet µ blamed himself. He felt a terrible burden of guilt for what had just happened – the level of intrinsic compassion required for such a reaction is staggering and otherwise supernatural – and that it was all due to nothing other than his own inability to convey the message properly. That that message reached its intended audience was truly all that mattered to the Prophet µ, and its rejection pained his heart more than any sticks, stones, or words could.

Further still, we who are familiar with the various religious scriptures know too how God reacted to His Prophets' prayers against their oppressors, how He hastened to answer them obligingly, to cataclysmic effect. And since Muḥammad μ was the last in the line of prophethood, God's consideration was similarly forthcoming. Almost immediately, the Archangel Jibrīl ν came with the news, "O Muḥammad, your Lord has heard what they said to you, has seen what they did to you. I present to you the angel who oversees the mountains, and I place him under your command."

This other angel informed the Prophet μ, "O Muḥammad, you may give me any order. If you wish, I shall bring these two mountains hurtling down upon them!"

"No, not that," the Prophet μ cried, "there may yet be some hope of their descendants obeying God!"[222]

Such was the purity of the Prophet's μ character that even under an intensity of oppression that would drive most of us into a vengeful rage, he not only remained optimistic about those who had just offended him, he even prevented them from being retaliatorily harmed.

When the harried Muslim population began to steadily trickle from Makkah to Madīnah after Muḥammad μ secured a place for them there in his negotiations with the Aws and Khazraj, the chief orchestrators of the opposition to Islām in Makkah reckoned that the Prophet μ might take his leave of their machinations before they could break him and his popular movement. To attempt to trap him and quash Islām once and for all, the heads of obstinate disbelief called to a meeting at their *Dār al-Nadwah* every clever and conniving enemy of Muḥammad µ they could think of. Some suggested simply locking the Prophet µ up and throwing away the key, others suggested summary execution, other suggested this or that; but every proposal was dismissed for one reason or another by a particularly cunning man from Najd. He had hatched a nefarious plot of his own which, when he finally presented it, was accepted happily by all.

"I think we should take one strong man from each and every tribe and give him a spear. They should wait for Muḥammad to exit his house and, as soon as he does, all stick him with their spears at once," the Najdī explained venomously. "That way, his blood will be spread evenly amongst all of us – Banū Hāshim won't have any choice but to accept financial compensation; they can't very well fight all of us, now can they?"

And when the heads of Quraysh caught wind of the Prophet's µ imminent departure from one of the people for whose consignments he had arranged an early-morning collection, they decided to spring their trap on him that very night. But as soon as they confirmed their course of action, the Archangel Jibrīlv informed the Prophet µ of the precarity in which he would soon find himself, the Prophet µ enacted his own plan – mentioned in a previous chapter – and had ʿAlīv sleep in place.

That night, the Prophet μ stepped out of his house, which had by that point been surrounded by spear-wielding young men from every tribe that opposed him, quietly reciting the first few verses of the chapter of the Holy Qur'ān called "Yā-Sīn." As he recited, he sprinkled dust on the heads of the murderous youngsters, causing them to fall miraculously asleep; thus he made his way to meet Abū Bakr η unscathed.

The next morning, one of the agents involved in the assassination plot came to ensure mission success only to find each and every spearman standing outside the house, leaning against their weapons – still asleep! "What are you doing? What happened?" he shouted as he shook them all awake.

"Get out of here and stay quiet, we're waiting for Muḥammad to come out of his house!" one of the boys hissed groggily.

I for one would love to have seen what must have been a most comical mixture of puzzlement and rage that played across the agent's face as he screamed, "you failed! He's gone!"

"I swear to you, we didn't see a thing coming from this house," another of the boys pleaded, brushing the dust out of his hair which had, unbeknownst to him, been placed there by the Prophet μ the night before. After readying themselves, the group of would-be assassins barged into the Prophet's μ house, finding nothing but a still-sleeping 'Alīν.[223]

In this case of one of the worst instances of oppression that can be imposed on a person – attempted murder – the

Prophet's µ reaction was to simply ignore it and carry on with the task at hand rather than breaking down and bemoaning his circumstances or even diverting from his course to offer a riposte.

Now, the incisive student of the Qur'ān will notice that at one place, God describes committed believers by referring to them as "they who, when afflicted with grievous wrong, avenge themselves,"[224] but in another place urges them to "repel misdeeds with those which are better."[225] Rather than being a contradiction, however, this is a valuable reminder for us to be ever-aware of context. Some wrongs require a measured response in order to correct the oppressor, discourage other would-be oppressors, and protect the oppressed; but it is of paramount importance not to allow this response to metamorphose into a brand-new case of oppression of its own. The expeditions undertaken by the Prophet µ are examples of such responses. Conversely, it is in the interest of the greater good that some wrongs be responded to with softness and compassion in order to turn erstwhile oppressors into allies and friends; the aforementioned are examples of such an approach.

Chapter 18

...Victorious

According to Islāmic teachings, the oppressed have recourse to one of two options: they can choose to either forgive and forget, or to retaliate – on the condition that whatever retaliatory action is taken does not exceed the initial offence. It also cannot be a sin in and of itself. For example, a sexual offence may absolutely not be compensated for via a returned sexual offence. The end of the previous chapter briefly synopsized the wisdom behind God's advice to humankind for the treatment of misdeeds, so it should be clear that different contexts require different actions, and different types of people require different types of treatment to bring about the intended goal – which is the same in every case – and that is reformation and restoration.

Half the day is dark, while the other half is bright, but people are seldom so well-balanced. We can observe those who maintain nobility and grace in the face of oppression, dejection, or poverty; but when their circumstances change ostensibly for the better, their attitude transforms into one of harshness, arrogance, and miserliness. And for others, the reverse might be the case – generous and benevolent in times of plenty, but tight-fisted and cold in straightened circumstances. Appraisal of a person's character is thus deficient if made during only one of these two times of day, as it were. So far, we have seen how Prophet Muḥammad µ behaved during the dark night of oppression – he was himself a shining beacon. But how was he during the high times of triumph and jubilation, when he had regained the upper hand over those who had made his life and the lives of those dear to him a veritable hell on earth?

Once, the Prophet µ was travelling with a small group of his Companions through a desertous area, unwittingly being followed by a team of armed Bedouin raiders seeking the reward offered by the heads of Quraysh in return for the Prophet's µ life or person. When the Muslims stopped at midday to rest and find shelter from the bare sun, the team of raiders mirrored them, making sure to remain concealed.

Once they were sure that the Prophet µ was sleeping soundly, with the rest of his travelling companions being scattered about under whatever patches of shade they could find, the raiders sprang into action. Their leader, who had marked Muḥammad µ for himself, silently stalked up to where he lay and noticed that he had hung his sword on a nearby low-hanging branch.

The Prophet µ was stirred awake by the noise the Bedouin made attempting to untangle the sword's baldric from the dry twigs on which it hung, so he sat halfway up, serenely taking in the scene as the Bedouin raised the sword and bellowed, "O Muḥammad, who will protect you from me now?"

"God will," the Prophet µ responded tranquilly without skipping a beat, and very much to the Bedouin's horror. In his shock he dropped the sword in the sand, and in a flash of deft movement the Prophet µ snatched it up and held it aloft. "O Bedouin, who will protect *you* from *me* now?" the Prophet µ bellowed in satire of the Bedouin's previous gloating.

The Bedouin fell back and tried to scramble away, crying out, "O Muḥammad, be gentle with me!"

"Will you accept my message, then?" the Prophet µ said, pursuing the Bedouin with the leisure of a cat pacing before a trapped mouse.

"No. But I promise you that I will never fight against you, or support anyone who does!" With that, the Prophet µ summoned his Companions to his side, told them all that had happened, and released his would-be assassin.

"I have just come to you from the best humankind has to offer!" shouted the Bedouin breathlessly as he re-joined his squad at their hiding place, at once inches from total panic at having seen a man react to a sword in his face as if he had just seen a camel walk past on a Thursday afternoon and in sheer ecstasy at having his life spared. He proceeded to recount the immediately preceding events as they decamped. Not much later, after taking a full bath, this same Bedouin returned to the Prophet µ and presented himself to offer his pledge of allegiance, to become a Muslim.[226]

The Prophet µ would have been well within his rights to strike that man – who was still armed – down the instant he recovered his weapon, but his course of action in the moment of victory added a sincere soul to the ranks of the Muslims rather than adding blood to the sand. This episode repeated it several times during the Prophet's µ life, as history attests, and each time the result was the same.

There was during the Prophet's µ time a certain chief of the large and powerful Banū Ḥanīfah tribe of central Arabia named Thumāmah b. Uthal η, who was also the ruler of the region known as al-Yamāmah (in which the modern Saudi Arabian city of al-Riyāḍ is located). When Muḥammad µ announced his prophethood and initiated the call to Islām, this Thumāmahη was incensed and vowed to kill him at the first opportunity. Being a religious – by Arabian pagan standards – man, Thumāmah η undertook the occasional *'Umrah* (minor pilgrimage) to Makkah, and on one of these occasions, as he was passing the outskirts of Madīnah on his way south to Makkah, he was captured by a Muslim security patrol. They didn't recognize him as the high-status individual he was, but it was clear that he was hostile, so they hauled him back to the city and tied him to a pillar of the Prophet's µ mosque until the Prophet µ – who had been away on a short errand – could return and instruct them further.

When the Prophet µ did return, and was told about the prisoner being held in his mosque, he quickly went to him and, recognizing him immediately, said, "O Thumāmah, what do you have to say for yourself?"

"Nothing but good, O Muḥammad," came the chieftain's snide reply. "Know that if you kill me, it is expensive blood you shed. And if you release me, well… I tend to be a very grateful person! If you want money, then I can give whatever sum you ask." But the Prophet μ turned and left without saying a word.

The next day, the Prophet μ entered again, saying, "O Thumāmah, what do you have to say for yourself?"

"I already told you what I've got," Thumāmah η responded wearily.

The Prophet turned to his Companions disappointedly ordered them, "alright, just let him go."

As soon as they did so, Thumāmah η betook himself to a nearby public garden and bathed in its pool before returning to the mosque, in which Muḥammad μ was still sitting with his Companions. "I bear witness that there is no god but Allāh, and that Muḥammad is His servant and messenger!" Thumāmah η said, jovially addressing all within earshot. He then approached the Prophet μ, saying, "O Muḥammad, there was no face I found more loathsome than yours – until I met you. But today, there is no face dearer to me than yours! And before today, there was no city or town more detestable to me than Madīnah, but now my heart resides here! Your scouts captured me on my way to Makkah for the minor pilgrimage," he explained, perhaps insinuating that his presence would be expected and missed but he could now no longer countenance preforming rituals in honour of the idols he had just forsaken, "so what should I do now?" But the Prophet µ urged him to carry on after congratulating him on his entry into Islām.

When Thumāmah η arrived in Makkah, he made all haste to the Kaʿbah and loudly and proudly proclaimed, "at Your service, O God, at Your service! At Your service unto Whom are no partners, at Your service! All praise and blessing are Yours, and for You is all dominion! You are without partners!" This is a formulaic expression known in Arabic as the *talbiyah.*

One of the horrified onlookers accosted him, gruffly demanding, "have you abandoned your father's religion?"

"What I *have* done," Thumāmah η responded evenly, "was I submitted to the *One True* God at the hands of His messenger, Muḥammad. And by God, you won't get even a single kernel of wheat from my tribe without his permission!"[227]

By this time a crowd had gathered which included some of the heads of Quraysh. When these Qurayshīs overheard the growing number of people murmuring wishes to attack the man, one of them spoke up, saying, "don't you know who this man is? He is the head of the tribe that supplies all of our wheat! Leave him alone!" But despite being left to perform his *ʿUmrah*, now in honour of the One True God, Thumāmah η held true to his word and placed a moratorium on all wheat sales to the Quraysh until, after some negotiators from Makkah pleaded with him, Muḥammad μ permitted Thumāmah η to resume trade.

The above episode highlights two examples of the Prophet's μ conduct as a victor, or one who has the upper hand. The first was his treatment of Thumāmah η. The Prophet μ knew that the Banū Ḥanīfah, of whom Thumāmah η was chief, had a strong hatred – founded on nothing but assumption and rumour, of course – for him and his Companions, so the idea behind keeping him confined to the mosque for two days was to allow him to see what the Muslims and Islām were for himself. This gave him time, as he was an intelligent and perspicacious individual, to analyse and contemplate his own first-hand experiences rather than base a conclusion solely on hearsay. And based on what he saw for himself, history has recorded what conclusion he eventually came to.

The second example was the stance the Prophet μ took with regard to the opportunity this most recently-converted disciple gave him to exploit. He could have taken full advantage of the ability to quite literally starve Makkah to death by cutting off their source of grain; such an approach might have been understandable in light of what horrors Makkah's citizens had visited upon the Muslims. But his impeccable sense of justice precluded such a course of action, and Makkah was allowed to carry on having their daily bread.

Towards the end of the Prophet's μ life, there came a glimmer of light at the end of the tunnel of the tumultuous relations between Makkah and Madīnah in the form of a treaty, known in Arabic as the *Ṣulḥ al-Ḥudaybiyyah*, meaning "the Ḥudaybiyyah Accord." Its signing took place in 6AH/628CE at the eponymous Ḥudaybiyyah, a place near the outskirts of Makkah, and involved not only the Muslims and the Quraysh, but the Banū Khuzāʿah tribe (in support of the Muslims) and the Banū Bakr (in support of the Quraysh) as well.

One of the conditions of the treaty was a strict prohibition of fighting between any of the signatories; however, the ancient enmity between the Banū Bakr and Banū Khuzāʿah flared up into violence two short years after the agreement had been put into effect as a group of raiders from Banū Bakr, supported by Qurayshī forces, invaded a Khuzāʿī village. They slew nearly every man, ravaged their women, and hauled off their property as spoils. But a handful of survivors made their way to the Prophet µ to inform him of this heinous breach of truce (not to mention humanity).

The Prophet µ simply could not brook this magnitude of injustice, so he ordered his Companions to ready themselves for war; as revenge for the battered Banū Khuzāʿah, the Muslims invaded Makkah which surrendered – having been advanced upon from all four of its routes of entry – after almost no fighting (twelve Quraysh and two Muslims were killed in a clash at only one entry point).

When the dust settled, everyone from both sides was gathered together around the Kaʿbah. The people of Makkah, these Quraysh, had subjected the Prophet µ and his sincere followers to torturous oppression and unspeakable atrocities, forcing them to flee the homes and land they loved and usurping their vacated properties, making multiple attempts on the Prophet's µ life, attempting to invade Madīnah – the consequences of which we can only imagine had they succeeded – several times, and formed an entire coalition to stop the spread of justice impelled by Islām.

It was these people at whose faces the Prophet µ now gazed benevolently. He didn't glower impetuously or hurl ego-vindicating taunts at his audience of hostages. What did transpire, however, is a case-in-point of just how chivalrous a man Muḥammad µ was, even in the heady delight of victory.

"O people of Quraysh!" the Prophet µ began his address and cutting mercifully straight to the point, "your transgressions are abrogated! God has forbidden the haughtiness over lineage in which you used to delight during your days of ignorance! All people are from Ādam, and Ādam was made from the same stuff as *dirt*!" Then he recited the Qur'ānic verse which can be rendered as, "O mankind, We have created you from one man and one woman, and caused the situation to be such that you formed nations and tribes – all so that you might recognize each-other. Indeed, the best among you to God is the one who best guards himself from sin. Indeed, God is the All-Knowing, Ever-Aware." And he continued in his own words, "O people of Quraysh, what do you suppose I'm going to do with you?"

"We think that, because you are a noble brother, and the son of a noble brother, you will deal with us kindly," they said;

and they knew this to be true all along, despite their arrogant opposition to the one they had once proudly called "*al-Amīn.*"

"Go then, you're all free!"[228] the Prophet µ finally announced. And this was not only the most supernaturally compassionate thing he could have done to the people who had made the previous thirteen years of his life unbearable (murdering his beloved friends and relatives, and trying on several occasions almost successfully to murder him), but also the most prudent. After all that, he pardoned every offence without so much as harsh word to satisfy even the tiniest shred of vengeance. He understood that with the Muslims now in power, this was the most sensitive, make-or-break time, so he left his people without the slightest opportunity to turn retaliation for valid grievances into cause for yet more grievances on anyone else's part. He needed the people who had hated him most to finally see what it really was to which he called.

That much is enough to conclude that the Prophet's µ grace under fire was matched rather evenly by his magnanimity in victory, but history has saved for us one more example to detail the point further.

About midway between Makkah and Madīnah lived a tribe called Banū al-Muṣṭaliq. Their chief, a man named al-Ḥārith b. Abī Ḍirār, had resolved to launch a raid against Madīnah to which end he had purchased a great many weapons and horses. Such a large appropriation of military equipment naturally drew attention, and word of it eventually reached

Muḥammad µ, who subsequently ordered his Companions to take a column in the direction of Banū al-Muṣṭaliq to reconnoitre and intercept any incoming hostile forces.

This column of Muslims did in fact intercept the Banū al-Muṣṭaliq at a watering hole called al-Muraysī'. They came to grips with each-other, exchanging volleys of arrows and some unenthusiastic melee, with little to no casualties, for about an hour. Seeking a quick conclusion, however, the Muslim commanders ordered a full, rapid advance and envelopment of the entire tribe, which understandably took the Banū al-Muṣṭaliq by surprise, forcing their surrender.

Now, in the days of *Jāhiliyyah*, were an entire tribe taken captive as in this case, they would all be slaughtered, sold into slavery, or some mixture of the two. Islām, however, dictated quite a different code of conduct for a victorious army; options were thus restricted to releasing every captive for God's sake, setting up a prisoner exchange to have Muslim hostages taken by the other side freed, or demanding ransom. In this case the Muslims opted for ransom; when the Prophet µ was informed of the chief's daughter Juwayriyyah bt. Al-Ḥārithı being among the prisoners, he paid her ransom himself, freeing and subsequently marrying her.

When word had spread among the Muslims that the tribe they were holding for ransom was technically now related to their Prophet µ by marriage, every soldier who had taken captives released them immediately. What a shame it is, they must have thought, to hold hostage the tribe of the Prophet's µ father-in-law![229] The consequences of the Prophet's µ manoeuvre were thus as intended – an entire tribe of vehement enemies had been converted into friends, allies, and co-religionists in one fell swoop without so much as a damaged ego.

Chapter 19

...Supportive

Helping one's fellow human in their time of need is one of the most beautiful acts a person can perform. Investigation into the foundational texts of every one of the world's religions makes it clear that they each enjoin on their adherents humanitarian aid for any who seek it, regardless of race, creed, or nationality. As for Islāmic scripture, God has revealed, so we believe, that "piety is not that you turn your face to the east or west, rather piety is to believe in God, the Last Day, the angels, the scripture, and the prophets, and that you give your wealth – for the love of God – to those near of kin and orphans alike, and to the needy, the wayfarer, and whomever asks; and to free slaves, remain observant of worship, and pay alms. And as for those who are true to their word when making a pact, and who persevere in the face of opposition and hardship – they are the pure-hearted; they are the pious!"[230]

So the Qur'ān makes it abundantly clear that a person isn't really righteous until and unless they help those in need. And as a living embodiment of Qur'ānic principles, Muḥammad μ advised his followers constantly along the same lines, making statements such as, "every creature is dependent on God, and the best of them is the most helpful to the others,"[231] and "God will aid anyone who aids his brother."[232] As further emphasis on the Qur'ānic verse referenced above, the Prophet μ is also recorded to have said, "the one who serves widows and orphans is equal to the one struggling for God's sake in fasting by day and praying by night."[233]

Once, on a journey with his Companions, the Prophet µ advised them, "anyone who has an extra mount, let him lend it to the one without. Anyone with extra rations, let him give it to the one with less,"[234]and after listing various other travelling provisions, the companions have assumed that, "no one has the right to keep excess to himself!"[235]

Another time, the Prophet µ was addressing a group and he was recorded as saying, "whoever wishes to be safe from the hardships of the Day of Judgement should either decrease the amount owed to him for debts, or forgive it completely, for those unable to pay."[236]

Elsewhere he said, "there are rooms in Paradise which God has prepared for those who feed people and spread peace."[237]

In another public address, the Prophet µ reminded his people that, "each and every Muslim must pay charity!" But when some objected that they may sometimes be unable due to not having excess funds, the Prophet µ advised them further, "then let such a person find extra work, and give charity from their extra wage." Others raised their concern about being in a situation where there was no work to be found, so the Prophet µ advised further, "then let such a person go and whoever calls for help with anything." Yet again, a similar concern was raised that there may sometimes be no-one who needs help with anything at all. "Let whoever finds himself in such a situation simply avoid doing evil – that would be his charity,"[238] the Prophet µ concluded.

When the Prophet µ was a young man, a merchant came from Yemen to Makkah and sold some of his wares to one of Makkah's elites, a man named al-ʿĀṣ b. Wā'il, under the condition that he would pay for them later. However, al-ʿĀṣ carried on delaying the payment until it became clear to the Yemenī merchant that he intended never to pay, so he petitioned the heads of some of the lesser tribes of Makkah who had made agreements to help members of his own tribe in times of crisis. But due to Ibn Wā'il's status, they all refused to help him.

Distraught and desperate, the man climbed to the top of the hill of Abū Qubays and shouted as loudly as he could in poetic meter,

> *"I beg the family of Fihr* (who was the grandfather of Quraysh) *to help the one whose wares were taken unjustly in Makkah, while he was far from family and home! He is yet in* iḥrām *while his ʿUmrah is incomplete! Respect is for only for the genuine, while the dishonest and impious have none!"*

As soon as these lamentations reached the ears of the people of Makkah, the Prophet's µ uncle al-Zubayr b. ʿAbd al-Muṭṭalib shot to his feet and announced, "this call for help cannot go unanswered!" So he invited the notables from the various prestigious families of Makkah, including his own tribe of Banū Hāshim, for a meal at another Qurayshī notable's house. After they had finished their meal, they got down to the business of what to do about this honour-destroying offence involving the browbeaten merchant from Yemen.

After discussing the matter, and how to go about rectifying the situation, everyone present took an oath to help anyone who was being oppressed – no matter who, nor by whom – and never to ignore any call for help; they called this oath the *Ḥilf al-Fuḍūl*, meaning "Oath of the Virtuous." Immediately after concluding, they all marched to the home of al-ʿĀṣ b. Wā'il, confiscated the Yemenī merchant's goods, and returned them to him.

Some years later, after the Prophet µ had already begun to spread his message, he recounted these events, saying, "I participated in the Oath of the Virtuous, you know, when I was a young man. And even now I'd never break that oath, no matter how much wealth I were offered. Furthermore, if someone called on me to initiate a similar arrangement in Islām, I wouldn't object to it."[239] This is because the principles of justice and support for the needy implemented and protected by the *Ḥilf al-Fuḍūl* were perfectly in line with the spirit of Islām.

During the Battle of Uḥud, a Companion by the name of Qatādah b. al-Nuʿmānη had one of his eyes mangled so badly, a piece of it was hanging down by his cheek. Frantically trying to help him, some of his nearby comrades suggested removing the whole thing, but someone quickly ordered them to take him to the Prophet μ, who at that point in the battle was still well back from the lines in a command post. When they presented Qatādah η to the Prophet μ, the latter took the bits of Qatādah's eye, placed them where they belonged, and supplicated "O my Lord, grant him beauty!" as he held them in place. It was said that when people would see Qatādah η later on, they couldn't even tell which eye had been injured.[240]

Once, the people of Madīnah heard a loud sound out in the distance which caused a great stir, to the point that widespread fear and panic seemed imminent. So the Prophet μ volunteered himself to investigate and report back on whether there was anything to be concerned about. He borrowed Abū Ṭalḥah's η horse and rode off in the direction of the sea. Upon his return, the Prophet μ informed the people, "worry not, I found nothing worth mentioning out there but a sea[storm]."[241] Not only does this illustrate the bravery of the Prophet μ, but also his willingness to offer support to the distressed.

Chapter 20

…Loving

Love is one of the purest feelings and human experiences. By that I do not mean any sort of carnal desire, which often serves as an impetus for nothing but delinquency and corruption; there is a world of difference between the two. Prophet Muḥammad µ was someone whose heart brimmed with this pure love, such that it flowed out unto all of creation. Love also happens to be a central Islāmic principle. God has obligated it upon those who consider themselves His devotees in the Qur'ān in such verses as, "…those who are committed to belief are the most intense in their love of God…,"[242] "convey to them (O Muḥammad µ), 'if you love God, then follow me…,'"[243] and "God loves the noble believers, and they love Him."[244]

The Prophet µ reinforced these verses in his daily, general admonitions. He is recorded as having said such things as:

"None of you shall enter Paradise until you believe! And you will not have believed until you love each-other! So shall I inform you of that which will increase love amongst you? Spread peace amongst yourselves!"[245]

"Almighty God has said, 'My love is for the ones who love one another because of Me, and visit one another because of Me, and give each-other gifts and charity because of Me.'"[246]

"If two people truly love each-other, the most beloved to God among them is the one who loves most."[247]

"God will bestow upon whomever loves for God's sake."[248]

"Whosoever wishes to experience the taste of faith, then let them love for God's sake."[249]

"The one who possesses three things will discover how sweet is the flavour of true faith: that they love God and His Messenger above all else, that they love someone for God's sake, and that they find returning to a state of ungratefulness to God more detestable than being flung into a fire."[250]

"There are those among God's servants who are neither prophets nor martyrs, yet on the day of Judgement will be envied by prophets and martyrs for their proximity to God," the Prophet µ once lectured his Companions while in a gathering in his mosque. When a Bedouin who was sitting in the back corner spoke up to ask just who those people might be, the Prophet's µ face lit up (he tended to be grateful for any teachable moment that presented itself), and he replied, "they are God's servants from different cities and different tribes; they've no blood relation between them, no connection to speak of – not even any business relationship. Yet still, they love each-other solely for God's sake. God shall illuminate their faces, and will place them on pedestals of pearl before the people, and they shall know no fear when fear is all that will be known by the rest."[251]

Because love is such a dominant theme in the proper implementation of Islām, the verses and authenticated statements of the Prophet µ are enough to fill their own tomes. But it should suffice the purpose of this work to provide an example from the Prophet's µ life of how he expressed his love.

Once, the Prophet µ visited a graveyard and said, "peace be upon you, O people at rest in the courtyard of believers! Verily, we will soon join you." Then he paused, thinking for a moment before pensively saying, "If only I could stay alive to see my brothers."

Those who had accompanied him on his visit to the graves were confused by this. "Are we not your brothers, O Messenger of God?"

"No, rather you are my Companions," the Prophet µ explained softly, "my brothers, you see, are those who have yet to come."

"How would you recognize members of your nation whom you've not yet met?"

"If one of you had a black horse whose limbs were all white, would you not recognize it?" the Prophet µ asked, setting up the sort of illustration for which his teaching style is so well-known. They all affirmed. "Well, that's how my brothers will come to me on the Last Day, limbs shining white from their ablutions. And I will be waiting for them next to the spring."[252]

The Companions sacrificed life and limb for the Prophet µ and his message, and he loved them dearly. But the love he felt for later generations of Muslims to come – love purely for God's sake – is what led him to refer to us as "brothers" rather than his own Companions – may God be pleased with them.

Chapter 21

...Loved

There are two qualities which typically engender love in people for others. Well-known historical personalities and other sorts of celebrity are loved by their fans for their virtues. For example, Leonardo DaVinci is loved for his brilliance in the arts and sciences. Albert Einstein is loved for his mastery in the field of physics, breaking ground in ways which continue to benefit us even today. Nelson Mandela is loved because of his wise leadership and uncompromising stand for justice. Every famous personality has some particular thing about them which compels us to love them.

Now, it is wholly plausible that despite your love for someone's academic genius, for example, spending time with them might actually cause you to hate them due to their having a noxious character. Similar is the case of some actor, or whatever-else, in the top of their field; they might be the absolute worst spouse, parent, or friend, and if people knew the person behind the public reputation, their excellence in one arena could no longer garner the love it otherwise would. They are loveable only from a distance – upon moving closer, the heat of their bad qualities evaporates what love you had for them to the extent that you become unsure if you even liked them all that much in the first place.

The Prophet µ, however, after reviewing all of the preceding, can be placed safely outside of this category of celebrity. The closer his followers got, the *more* they fell in love with him – and what has been mentioned in this humble work is but a scratch on the surface of Muḥammad's µ virtue. In fact, I have become convinced that God alone knows the true extent of the Prophet's µ quality; after all, he is reported to have said, "God has taken care that I was brought up in the best way."[253] This is similar to the case of a teacher and student – none but the teacher can accurately assess the abilities of their pupil, not even the student (they may yet have hidden abilities or knowledge which they never even realized their teacher gifted them with, waiting for the opportunity to be utilized).

There is no other human being who is loved for their whole being but the Prophet Muḥammad µ, even by we who have never met him. Every aspect of his life and personality – known and well-documented as they are – is a new flame attracting us moth-like to love of him. In the words of Imām ʿAlī b. AbīṬālibv, "the one who did not know him would yet glorify him, but the one who did know him would love him!"[254]

The next few pages shall serve to represent a few drops in the ocean of love people had for Muḥammad µ.

ʿAlī v was once asked the way in which he and his fellows used to love the Prophet µ, and he answered, "I swear by God – we used to love him more than we loved our children, fathers, mothers, wealth… we loved him more than a sip of cold water when thirsty!"[255] Now, ʿAlī was one of the most eloquent Arabs of his time, but he was never one for exaggeration. Though his statement may have waxed poetic, it was nevertheless frank and honest.

In Islām's earliest days, the Prophet μ kept his preaching quiet, only calling to people individually or in small groups. When the ranks of Muslims had swelled to thirty-nine, Abū Bakr η suggested to the Prophet μ that they begin proclaiming their message openly. The Prophet μ warned him of the disadvantage their small numbers gave them, but Abū Bakr η insisted. So the Prophet μ gave him permission, and they all marched to the Kaʿbah to give a public sermon.

But when Abū Bakr η stood and started calling the people to stop their oppression of the less-fortunate, and to be good to their relatives and neighbours, the gathering mass of pagans descended upon the Muslims and began beating them and trampling them underfoot. Abū Bakr η himself was so savagely attacked that his nose was indistinguishable from the rest of his face, and when word had gotten to some other members of Banū Taym – his tribe – they hurried to where the commotion was in front of the Kaʿbah, dove in and repelled his attackers, hauling him from beneath the heaving throng. He was so badly bloodied, and by this point unconscious, that they feared he had been killed; so they placed his body on a long piece of cloth and used it as a stretcher to bear him home. The members of Banū Taym who had rescued their kinsman were furious, vowing to kill ʿUtbah as revenge as he was the one who was beating their cousin most ferociously when they had happened upon the scene. So they surrounded Abū Bakr η and tried to awaken him, talking to him and calling his name until his senses returned.

"What has happened to Muḥammad?" were the first words out of his mouth as he snapped back to consciousness. Satisfied that their kinsman hadn't been killed, but caring little for the movement he had joined – or its leader – the gathered Taym-men filed one-by-one from Abū Bakr's η house, leaving him alone with his mother Umm Khayr ι. "What has happened to the Prophet," he asked her desperately.

"I don't know *what* happened to your friend," she said tersely.

"Go to Umm Jamīl, daughter of al-Khaṭṭāb, and find out from her," he requested weakly.

So off she went in search of news about her son's best friend. When she arrived at Umm Jamīl's ι house, she said to its occupant, "Abū Bakr wanted me to ask you about Muḥammad, son of ʿAbdullāh."

Abū Bakr's η mother hadn't yet embraced Islām by this point, and Umm Jamīl ι, who *had* embraced Islām and wanted to avoid trouble for it, eyed her with some suspicion. "I don't know either of those people," she said cagily. "But… if you want me to come help you with your son, I'm willing to do so." She must have heard about the incident by the Kaʿbah earlier that day, and would have been very worried about their movement's senior personalities.

"Yes," Abū Bakr's η mother said, probably relieved to have a hand, as her son was in such a bad state, "please do come with me."

But when the two ladies arrived at Abū Bakr's η home, and Umm Jamīl ι saw Abū Bakr η lying on the ground in a bloody heap, she dropped all pretence and cried out, "the people who did this to you are the people of sin! I ask God to punish them for what they've done to you!"

"What… has happened… to the Prophet μ?" was all Abū Bakr η could manage to say in response.

"But your mother is here," Umm Jamīl ι said cautiously after regaining her composure, resuming the charade.

"There'll be no harm on you from her," Abū Bakr η said weakly.

"He's safe and sound," Umm Jamīl ι said, dropping her guard finally.

"Where is he?"

"He went to Arqam's house," she said. Arqam b. Abī Arqamη was the seventh person to embrace Islām, and he had opened his home to the relatively few Muslims at that point to use as a secret meeting hall wherein the Prophet μ would gather his Companions, teaching them newly revealed verses of the Qur'ān as they came.

"By God, I swear I shan't eat or drink until I have gone to see the Prophet myself!" Abū Bakr η said. And he kept his promise until that night. Under cover of darkness, Umm Jamīlι and Umm Khayrι, with Abū Bakr η propped up between them, made their way through the deserted streets of Makkah to Arqam's η house. As soon as they entered the room in which Muḥammad μ sat resting, Abū Bakr η threw himself upon his beloved companion and started kissing his cheeks and shoulders.

The Prophet μ hugged Abū Bakr η in return, trying his best to restrain his friend – who had mere hours before been beaten to within an inch of his life, mind – to protect him from over-exertion and further injury. All the commotion gave the other Muslims who were already there, nursing each-other's wounds and praying, quite a start. But when they got up and saw that it was Abū Bakr η, alive and well (mostly), they all pounced on *him*, hugging him and voicing their relief and praises to God.

"How are you feeling then, O Abū Bakr?" the Prophet μ finally asked after things had settled back down.

"May my mother and father be your ransom, O Messenger of God," Abū Bakr η exclaimed, "they could do nothing to me but what that evil man did to my face." After remembering that his mother had brought him, and that she was still in the room, he gestured toward her, saying, "here is my mother. Please call her to God and pray for her. It may be that God saves her from punishment by you." So the Prophet μ did just that, conversing with Abū Bakr's η mother and praying for her until she finally accepted Islām there in the house of Arqam b. Abī Arqamη (wherein they stayed, recovering for the next month).[256]

The above episode is a poignant illustration of the depth of love the Prophet's μ followers and friends had for him. If something similar had happened to one of us, it's as likely as not that instead of "where is the Prophet?" our response to such tribulations would be, "this all happened to me because of him, let me never see his face again!" or perhaps, "yeah I'll see if he's alright as soon as *I'm* better." But Abū Bakr η became so obsessed with finding out about the Prophet μ after their ambush at the Ka'bah that he remained unsatisfied until he could see with his own two eyes that his Prophet μ was safe. And this sort of compulsive worry over Muḥammad's μ well-being, while disregarding one's own, was a trait shared by his sincere Companions.

A woman of the Banū Dinār tribe had lost her husband, father, *and* brother in the Battle of Uḥud; she was brought this grave news after the battle's conclusion as the Muslim soldiers filtered back into Madīnah to head home. But, as if she hadn't even heard that her life had just been a bit torn apart, she nervously asked the group of men who had come, "but what happened to the Prophet?"

They looked at each-other briefly, probably a bit puzzled. "He is fine, thank God."

"Show him to me, I want to see for myself," she said, now bordering on frantic.

They turned to look through a loosely-grouped body of men walking slowly by, saw the Prophet µ among them, and pointed him out for the lady. With that, she deflated with a sigh of relief and called out, "any other suffering is pittance compared to the suffering of losing you!"[257]

Another rather grisly but nonetheless illustrative episode from early Islāmic history is that known famously as the "Incident of Rajīʿ," named for the well at which it took place in 3AH/625CE. A delegation came to the Prophet µ representing the tribes of ʿUdhal and Qarrah requesting that he send some of his Companions to stay with them in order to tutor them in the particulars of Islām – which they had purportedly just accepted. But on the way back, escorted by six of Muḥammad's µ most well-learned Companions, the tribesmen turned on their guests with swords drawn and called for allies who had been lying in ambush. They informed the Muslims that they only wanted to take them hostage in exchange for ransom, but four of them were killed resisting capture anyway. Thus the two remaining Companions, Zayd b. al-Dathinnahη and Khubayb b. ʿAdīη, were bound and hauled to Makkah for sale as slaves to the Quraysh (who were, of course, their mortal enemies).

Upon being purchased, Zayd b. al-Dathinnah η was dragged to a spot beneath the Kaʿbah whereupon he was gruesomely tortured by having bits of flesh sliced from his arms and legs. Abū Sufyān b. Ḥarb, seeing an opportunity to get hold of his arch nemesis Muḥammad μ at last, dangled this opportunity in front of Zayd η. "I ask you by God, O Zayd. Wouldn't you prefer that Muḥammad were in your place, going through this instead of you, and you were back home with your family, safe and sound?" he asked, perversely mocking Zayd ν as he bled in the sand before the shade of the Kaʿbah.

"By God," Zayd η groaned defiantly through gritted teeth, "I wouldn't prefer that he be struck with a wooden stick where he is now, even if *that* meant I could be back with my family!"

"I've never seen another person loved as Muḥammad is by his Companions" Abū Sufyān intoned, dejected and defeated. With his plan dismantled, Abū Sufyān sold Zayd η along to Ṣafwān b. Umayyah, who quickly had him killed as revenge for his father's death at Badr.[258]

During ʿUmar b. al-Khaṭṭāb's η stewardship of the Muslim nation, he had a habit of walking the streets of Madīnah (which was still the Muslims' capitol at that point) in search of problems needing solutions. On one of these patrols during the late night, he saw one house with a light in the window. As he approached – his first thought was probably that the occupants were being kept awake by hunger – he could hear the voice of an old woman wholeheartedly singing the following verses as she worked at some wool:

"May the prayers of the righteous be upon Muḥammad!

May the noble and good pray over him!

You used to remain awake, crying, while praying at dawn.

I wish for different ways to die to be in the same place as my beloved!"

These words landed heavily on ʿUmar's η heart; he sat down in the street where he stood and wept for several minutes, reminiscing sorrowfully. After composing himself, he got up, went to the house from whence he had heard the singing, and tapped on the door.

"Who is it?" asked the woman.

"It is only ʿUmar, son of al-Khaṭṭāb."

"And what might this ʿUmar want at such an hour?"

"May God have mercy on you, it's nothing to worry about," ʿUmar η chuckled, probably still rubbing the tears from his long beard. She opened the door and bade him enter. As soon as he stepped inside, he said, "please, would you repeat the poem you were reciting before?" She obliged and recited it again. "Please, include me with the two of you!" he said when she finished.

"And 'Umar as well; forgive him, O Ever-Forgiving God!" the woman recited in a style to match the poem. Pleased with her extra verse, 'Umar η saw himself out of the woman's house and resumed his patrol.[259] History never recorded this lady's name, but the name of God's Final Prophet μ was recorded on her heart – and history bears witness to that much, at least!

Love is expressed in varying ways by different people. Some express theirs as highlighted in the above examples, while for others, the smallest things show the greatest care. 'Abdullāh b. Mas'ūdη used to accompany the Prophet μ frequently. Whenever they went to a house together and the Prophet μ removed his shoes or sandals to enter, Ibn Mas'ūd η would, without fail, pick them up and wear them on his arm until such time as the Prophet μ needed them again – at which point he would personally see to fitting them back on the Prophet's μ blessed feet. He also insisted on pouring the water for the Prophet's μ ablutions and picking and preparing his *miswak* (a tooth-brushing stick taken from the *arāk* tree, the use of which the Prophet μ had a particular fondness).[260]

When the Prophet μ became seriously ill shortly before his passing and became bed-ridden with fever, Abū Bakr η and 'Abbāsη walked past a group of *Anṣār* in the mosque and noticed that the lot of them were crying. When 'Abbās η inquired as to why, they replied mournfully that "we were just thinking about how the Prophet used to sit with us…"

These *Anṣār*, who had vowed to protect the Prophet µ and support his message and followers by whatever means necessary, were well aware of the illness which had afflicted their Prophet µ; they took note of its severity and came to the conclusion that it would be his last, that death was soon to follow. With that thought came recollections of all the Prophet's µ beautiful stories and blessing-filled conversations, and the realization that they would all soon be nothing but a memory. What else could they do under the weight of that stark reality but sit and cry?

Unable to abide the sadness he saw on these men's faces and heard in their voices, ʿAbbāsη immediately betook himself to the Prophet's µ bed and recounted what had just transpired. Without a word, the Prophet µ stood, wrapped his head up, exited his house into the mosque, and climbed its pulpit – for the final time. After voicing the customary praises and thanks to God, the Prophet µ advised all who could hear his voice, "I order you to take care of my *Anṣār*, because they are my closest supporters! They have fulfilled every promise, and left nothing on their end of the bargain but the reward God has promised and prepared for them. So accept the good they do, and forgive their shortcomings."[261]

During this same address, the Prophet µ also said, "God has given a choice to some of his servants – a choice between this world and the world hereafter. One servant has chosen the hereafter."

At that, Abū Bakr η began to weep uncontrollably. "But we have sacrificed our mothers and fathers for you, O Messenger of God!" he cried out.

Why is this old man crying, Abū Sa'īd al-Khudrīη wondered in puzzlement. He grabbed Abū Bakr's η attention and said gruffly, "so God gave a choice to someone and he chose the hereafter… so what?" But as soon as he had said the words, a terrible realization dawned on him and the import of the Prophet's μ words stunned him into an awful silence. Besides serving as another reminder of how far above the rest of theirs Abū Bakr's η perception and intelligence were, this was also an indication that the Prophet μ was speaking about himself. Dying.[262]

Once, a Companion by the name of 'Abdullāh b. Zayd al-Anṣārī came to the Prophet μ lamenting, "O Messenger of God, when we die, you will be in the highest level of Paradise. We'll never get the chance to see you!"

To assuage the poor man's sadness, the Prophet μ recited the verse of the Qur'ān which we have mentioned once before, "whomsoever obeyed God and His Messenger are *with* those upon whom God bestowed His favours from among the Prophets, the steadfast affirmers of truth, the martyrs, and the righteous; what excellent associates are they!"

Later on, after the Prophet's μ death, this particular Companion – so great was his love for the Prophet μ – would supplicate to God in his grief, "O my Lord, make me blind so that I do not see anyone after my beloved until I meet him again!" His prayer was answered, and he did indeed lose his sight.[263]

A common symptom of the one stricken by love is eagerness to gather up anything that serves as a reminder of them, particularly personal effects. Anas b. Mālik η has been cited as saying that, "once, a barber was giving the Prophet a haircut, and I noticed the Companions who were around him hurrying to catch the hairs as they fell."[264] He himself had collected three of the Prophet's μ hairs himself, incidentally, and when he died he willed that they be placed over his eyes before being buried.[265]

The thought of one's truly-beloved may even be the last that plays through their mind. After the conclusion of one of the Muslims' battles, the Prophet – concerned for an individual whom he had not seen among the survivors – asked those gathered around him, "who will go and ascertain the condition of Saʿd, son of Rabīʿ?" One of the *Anṣār* volunteered and scampered off in search of his comrade.

When he finally came across Saʿd η, the Companion who had gone in search of him knelt where he lay and informed him, "the Prophet sent me to find you, to see if you're alive or dead."

"I'm as good as dead," Saʿd η strained to say. "Go back to Prophet and convey my greetings, and tell him I said, 'may God reward you with the best a prophet can receive.' And also, tell my tribe I said, 'you have no excuse in God's sight if the Prophet suffers injury so long as you are alive!'" And as soon as his final concern – which was the Prophet η – was voiced, he promptly died.[266]

The Prophet μ was recorded as once saying, "those who have the strongest love for me will be a people who come after me. They will sacrifice everything they have for but a glimpse of me."[267] A case in point of the fulfilment of this prophecy was the *tābiʿī* (one who personally met and studied at the feet of a Companion of the Prophet μ) named Khālid b. Maʿdān al-Ḥimṣī whose primary instructor from among the Companions was Thawbānη, the Prophet's μ freed-slave.

Now, we met this Thawbān η in a previous chapter, and saw his intense devotion to the Prophet μ; this love flowed from Thawbān η like a spring from which his student Khālid was one of those fortunate enough to drink. In fact, ʿAbdah bt. Khālid b. Maʿdān once said, "when my father lay in bed, he would lament of how sorely he missed the Prophet – peace and blessings of God be upon him – and he would mention various Migrants and Helpers by name, calling out, 'these are my forebears, my roots… my heart longs for none but them! O my Lord, I have missed them for so long now, so please take me to you!' And he would keep repeating this until he fell asleep."[268]

Chapter 22

...Smiling

Smiling is one of the more endearing activities in which humans engage; when done at a particular time or in just the right way, it becomes nothing short of contagious. Unpleasant situations can be diffused with nothing more than a well-timed smile. But smiling isn't appropriate for every situation and place; smiling, for example, in the faces of the deceased's family-members at a funeral would have none of the usually-desired effects.

With regard to smiling, the Prophet μ has been purported to have said such words of encouragement as, "you will be unable to include all people in your financial support, so at least include them in your smile and good behaviour,"[269] "your smile in the face of your brother is even a form of charity!"[270] and "do not disparage any good deed, no matter how small, even if it's just meeting your brother with a smile!"[271]

Jarīr b. ʿAbdullāhη once recounted that, "the Prophet never kept me from visiting him, not once since I embraced Islām; in fact, he smiled every time he saw me!"[272]

Another Companion by the name of Abū al-Dardā'η was once reproached by his wife for smiling every time he spoke. "Stop doing that, people will think you're a simpleton!" she said.

"Oh, is that so?" Abū al-Dardā'η retorted, probably a bit smug. "It just so happens that I never saw our Prophet speaking except that *he* had a smile on *his* face!" [273]

Muḥammad μ, as a result of his divine mission, was the object of abundant abuse – as we have seen in previous chapters – both verbal and physical. The Prophet's μ open enemies were the most overtly hostile, but he had a more insidious form of opposition from within the ranks of those who called themselves "Muslims" as well – God named them "*Munāfiqūn*," or "Hypocrites" in the Qur'ān – and they took every chance they got to covertly attack the Prophet μ; the more gutless among them took to insulting the members of the Prophet's μ Household. Their mockery and attacks on the Prophet μ were as vile and crude as can be imagined, and included spreading such rumours as, "he has lost his mind and fallen into sexual impotency due to the effects of black magic," "that son-in-law of his ʿAlī is feminine," "he has no sons so his lineage is severed," "he gets his messages from evil spirits, even Satan himself," and other such mendacious vulgarities.

Now, Zayd b. Ḥārithahη, the adopted son of the Prophet μ whom we met in a previous chapter, was married to Thuwaybahι the Abyssinian freed-slave who had looked after the Prophet μ as a child; they had a son together named Usāmah η. As we saw previously, the Prophet's μ love for this Zayd η*and* his son Usāmahη was such that he nicknamed them together "Beloved, son of the Beloved."[274] And since the dastardly tactics of the Hypocrites rose not much higher than besmirching the honour of those whom the Prophet µ loved – as a way of hurting him – they spread the rumour that Usāmahη was not truly the son of Zaydη, but had been born of adultery. They "knew" this, they alleged, because Usāmah's complexion was so much closer to his darker Abyssinian mother's than his lighter Arabian father's.

But a delegation from the Banū Mudlij tribe, whom we know now were renowned for their ability to deduce an individual's details by examining their feet, came to visit the Prophet µ in his home, and it so happened that Zayd η and Usāmah η were both asleep on the same mat, feet protruding from beneath the short blanket which covered them. Catching sight of the two pairs of appendages, one of the Mudlij-men exclaimed, "these feet are from one another!" This caused the Prophet to smile all the way to his wife ʿĀ'ishah'sι house. When she asked why he was beaming so, he Prophet µ recounted the aforementioned events.[275] Even though the Hypocrites had grieved the Prophet's µ heart with their abominable slander, just that smile of his served as a devastating riposte.

People after the Prophet's µ death were starving for even the slightest bit of information about him. Once, Jābir b. Samurah η was asked by someone if he ever sat with the Prophet µ, to which he replied, "yes, quite often in fact. He would remain in his place after praying his pre-dawn prayer until sunrise. After sunrise, he would get up to leave. He would often pass his Companions as they told stories of their lives from before they had embraced Islām. But when they would laugh, the Prophet would just smile."[276]

In a similar vein, ʿĀ'ishah ι was once asked how the Prophet μ used to behave. Her simple response was that the Prophet μ "was the softest of men, and even more generous, smiling, and laughing."[277] She also said; "I have never seen any men more smiling than the Prophet μ"[278] This is actually an important point – many men are all smiles and jokes with friends and colleagues, but stone-faced and harsh with their wives. But here the Prophet's μ wife disclosed that Muḥammad μ was as jovial at home as he was anywhere else.

Chapter 23

...Laughing

It is possible to examine why and how a person laughs to ascertain some of their characteristics. For example, if we see that a person laughs upon seeing another person slip and fall down, or laughing at others failing in some endeavour (like having a job application refused), it can be deduced that the personality being observed is not a positive one. Furthermore, if a person guffaws or laughs uproariously, even in the presence of elderly or otherwise-respected people, it can be deduced that the personality being observed is one lacking in respect and decorum. So, how and why did our beloved Muḥammad μ laugh?

As a Companion by the name of ʿAbdullāh b. al-Ḥārithη tells it, "the Prophet didn't really used to laugh, rather he simply smiled."[279]

Even the Mother of the Believers ʿĀ'ishah ι is on record as saying, "I have never seen the Prophet laugh to the point of showing his uvula; he did, however, used to smile."[280] These two reports – one from outside and the other from behind closed doors – confirm that the manner of the Prophet's μ laughter was one of refinement and dignity, something that would qualify as more of a chuckle than a bona fide belly-laugh. But what were some of the things that used to elicit such laughter from the Seal of Prophethood μ?

Once, the people of Madīnah came to the Prophet µ to seek his assistance during a time of famine and drought. So the Prophet µ ordered a few of his Companions to haul his pulpit to the field outside the city designated for large prayer gatherings and had the word spread for everyone to congregate there at a certain time.

When the time came, and everyone had gathered as requested, the Prophet µ ascended the steps of his pulpit, sat down, and called out, "O people! You have complained to me of dearth and drought. God has advised that if you pray to Him, He has promised to accept." He then stood, faced away from the congregation, raised his hands, and proceeded to pray two units (*rakaʿāt*) of ritual prayer (*ṣalāh*). No sooner had he finished, then heavy grey clouds rushed in above the city, flashing with lightning and rumbling with thunder; and by God's leave, it began to rain so heavily that rivulets had begun forming in the valleys around the city even before the Prophet µ was able to seek shelter back at his mosque.

Tickled at seeing how abundantly water now flowed in the previously parched Madīnah, the Prophet µ laughed through a grin so wide his molars were visible, calling out above the din of the storm, "I bear witness to God's omnipotence, and that I am His servant and messenger!"[281] Being so delighted at blessings being bestowed upon others that it forces one into a fit of laughter is a sure sign of a genuine character.

Once, an ambassador from the Byzantine Emperor came to the Prophet µ with a message. During the course of their conversation, the Prophet µ began to explain Islām's principles to the man, and eventually offered for him to accept it. But the man politely refused, saying, "I follow the religion of the nation on whose behalf I came to you. I will not change my religion until I go return to them."

In response, the Prophet µ simply chuckled and recited the Qur'ānic verse, "surely, you do not guide those whom you love, rather God grants guidance to whomever wants it; and He knows better about the guided ones."[282] This reaction to having his message refused was one of nobility; not only did his light mood put the Byzantine ambassador at ease in what could easily have been a rather tense situation – reassuring him that his rejection of Islām would bear no immediate consequences – but the Prophet µ also made it clear with his choice of verse that his attitude toward the Christian ambassador was yet one of love. If only modern callers to Islām took this single lesson from the Prophet's µ life!

Arabs during the time of *Jāhiliyyah* had many strange traditions, some of which have been mentioned already; one of them was the practice known as *ẓihār*. This took place when a husband wanted to divorce his wife in the most insulting way possible – perhaps after a catastrophic argument – to emphasize the finality of their separation. They would do this by making such rude remarks as, "you're as good to me as my mother's back!" which in other words meant, "as I cannot marry my mother, neither will I ever re-marry you!" This divorce was eternally binding, forever precluding any possibility of reconciliation or re-marrying.

Islām, however, abolished this unjust and emotionally abusive practice with the revelation of the verse in the Qur'ān the meaning of which is, "as for those among you who enact *ẓihār* against their wives – they are not their mothers! Their mothers are they who bore them; what they say is an atrocious falsehood. However, God is Ever-Pardoning and Forgiving."[283] The Qur'ān goes on in the next verse to establish a reversal to this sort of divorce by way of penalizing the husband with the mandatory manumission of a slave for tarnishing his wife's honour.

Once, during the Prophet's µ life, a man divorced his wife via *ẓihār* and re-married her, but consummated the marriage without having paid the penalty of freeing a slave. Hoping to make amends, he went to the Prophet µ and informed him of what had happened. "Why, oh why, did you do such a thing?" the Prophet µ asked the man.

"I saw the bright skin of her legs under the moonlight and was unable to control myself!" the man howled with regret. Noting the man's earnestness, the Prophet µ just chuckled and advised him against doing anything similar in the future.[284]

The Prophet µ once, in a gathering of his Companions, was relating a parable to highlight God's all-encompassing compassion and the ideal manner of one of His truly repentant devotees. "I know of the person who will leave the fire and enter Paradise last," the Prophet µ began wryly. "He will be brought on the Day of Judgement and told to offer up his minor sins to cover his major ones. So they will present his minor sins, saying, 'you have committed such-and-such a sin on such-and-such a day.' Unable to deny and fearful of having his major sins revealed, he will reply, 'yes!' Then he will be told, 'now for every sin, you will be rewarded!' Then he will say, 'O God, I have so many other sins to show you!'" By the end of the story, the Prophet µ was laughing through a smile that showed the whiteness of his teeth.[285]

Once, the Prophet µ was walking with Anasη. He was wearing a type of overcoat, made in Yemen at the time, with heavily embroidered borders. Suddenly, a Bedouin approached them from behind, yanking on the Prophet's µ cloak to get his attention so hard that the roughness of the garment's border left a red mark on the Prophet's µ neck. Being a Bedouin, the man thought nothing of the harshness of his behaviour, and proceeded to address the Prophet µ rather gruffly, "O Muḥammad, let them give me something that belongs to God and not to you!" At that, all the Prophet µ could do was chuckle and order his Companions to give the Bedouin some wealth.[286]

The Prophet µ enjoyed a good practical joke as much as the next man, and one his Companions, a man by the name of Nuʿaymān b. ʿAmr η, was a prolific trickster infamous among the Companions for his antics. Once, Abū Bakr η took a trip to Buṣrā (the city in modern-day Syria, not to be confused with

Baṣrah in Iraq) with this Nuʿaymānη and one Suwaybiṭ b. Ḥarmalahη, whom Abū Bakr η made responsible for provisions.

At one point during the journey, Abū Bakr η had separated from the group for one reason or another, and Nuʿaymānη said to Suwaybiṭη, "hey, give me some food," probably in the endearingly annoying way with which those of us with friends possessed of a similar disposition are painfully familiar.

"Not until Abū Bakr comes back," Suwaybiṭ replied, perhaps taking his responsibilities a bit too seriously for Nuʿaymān's η liking. At this, he resolved to make Suwaybiṭη pay for his grave offence.

When a couple of travellers on their own way passed between them, Nuʿaymān η called them over and said quietly, but not enough to arouse suspicion, "will you buy my slave?"

"Of course!" the travellers said, probably in need of an extra pair of hands.

Setting his trap with the suaveness of used goat salesman, Nuʿaymān η explained in his most professional voice, "alright, the thing is, my slave is a joker and loves to pretend that he's actually free. So if he starts telling you he's free, I don't want you to offend him by leaving!"

"Don't worry, we'll buy him," the travellers said. They must have thought the situation was a bit odd, but they needed the help. So they agreed on a price of ten camels, and threw a rope around Suwaybiṭ's η neck.

At that, Suwaybiṭη jumped and shouted in protest, "hey, he's having you on! I'm no slave, I'm a free man!"

"Yeah, yeah, we know all about that," the travellers said patronizingly as they hauled Suwaybiṭη away.

Abū Bakr η returned not long after and asked Nuʿaymānη where Suwaybiṭη had gone, and he was regaled with the tale of Nuʿaymān's η most recent masterwork. Wasting no time, though, Abū Bakr η promptly set off to retrieve Suwaybiṭη and refund the travellers their camels.

When the trio got back to Madīnah and told the Prophet μ about the shenanigans, he laughed with them about it for the entire following year.[287]

Another prank for which Nuʿaymān η was infamous was the "gifts" he often gave the Prophet μ. Whenever he would enter Madīnah's market, he would find something nice, take it after arranging to pay later, and present it to the Prophet μ, exclaiming, "this is a gift for you!" When the merchant would eventually come to Nuʿaymān η, expecting to be paid, Nuʿaymānμ would lead him to the Prophet μ and say, "O Messenger of God, please can you pay him for his wares?"

"Didn't you give it to me as a gift" the Prophet μ would ask knowingly.

"You know... I didn't have the money on me at the time, but I still wanted you to have it," Nuʿaymān η would say solemnly. And every time, the Prophet μ would simply laugh and pay the merchant.[288]

The Prophet μ himself loved to joke and banter with his Companions as well. There was once a villager by the name of Ẓāhirη who had a habit of bringing a gift to the Prophet μ from his village every time he visited Madīnah. To show his appreciation, the Prophet μ would send him back to his village with a camel loaded with provisions. This Ẓāhir η was actually quite an ugly man, but he was very dear to the Prophet's μ heart, such that he used to say, "Ẓāhir is out village, and we are his city!" Once, when Ẓāhir η was in Madīnah's marketplace selling his commodities, the Prophet μ snuck up behind him and threw his arms around him, squeezing him in a great bear hug.

"Who is that! Let go of me!" Ẓāhir η screeched. But when he caught on that it was the Prophet μ, he back up into him and wouldn't allow him to let go.

"Who will buy this slave of mine!" the Prophet μ called out jovially.

"O Messenger of God, if you try to sell me I'm afraid you'll find me too cheap!" Ẓāhir η laughed.

"Ah, but you are precious in the eyes of God!" the Prophet μ retorted, joining in his laughter.[289]

Chapter 24

...Angry

Anger is as natural in a human as laughter. Everyone is affected by it, and we differ only in what provokes it. Some are angered over race issues, others over religious issues, others over financial issues, et cetera. We also differ in the intensity of our anger. Some of us have such a defective temper that anger causes us to lose sight of the very notion of right and wrong, while others remain firmly in control. Our expressions also vary across a spectrum ranging from violence against other people or inanimate objects, to a mild sarcastic comment, to no overt reaction at all. And similar to the case of laughter, an analysis of the how and the why of a person's expression of their anger is a good gauge of their character, as anger has the added effect of exposing what most of us tend to keep otherwise hidden; some who merely pretend at nobility by donning a mask of magnanimity end up revealing their true grotesquery when pushed to do so by anger. And because anger has the potential to cause irreparable damage, the Prophet µ advised those who count themselves among his followers to monitor it closely.

Someone came to the Prophet µ seeking some general counsel once, and the Prophet's µ only instruction was, "do not become angry!" The person repeated his request for advice several times, hoping for a list of things to take home, but each time the Prophet's µ answer came back the same, "do not become angry!"[290]

The Prophet µ is recorded as once advising another of his Companions that, "when you become angry, then do not speak; just stay quiet!"[291] Yet another Companion related that the Prophet µ told him, "teach people in a way which is easy for them, never difficult. And if you become angry, stay quiet. If you become angry, stay quiet. If you become angry, stay quiet!"[292] The Prophet µ had a habit of emphasizing particularly important concepts by repeating them thrice.

Hind b. Abī Hālahη, a step-son of the Prophet µ, once described his step-father thusly: "His anger was never provoked by worldly things; but if someone's rights were violated, he became unrecognizable and his anger would not abate until things were rectified. He never became angry or took revenge on his own behalf."[293] An example of the Prophet µ remaining ireless for his own sake presented itself in the previous chapter; a person would typically express some level of irritation – rightfully so – upon being injured and accosted in the way the Prophet µ was by the Bedouin who grabbed his cloak. But the Prophet µ just laughed and acquiesced to his boorish demands.[294] But if the dignity or rights of someone else were ever offended in the Prophet's µ presence, his anger was immediate and intense.

Someone once came to the Prophet µ, complaining, "O Messenger of God, I do not pray the pre-dawn prayer in the mosque because so-and-so makes it too long for me to bear."

"I have never seen the Prophet angrier while delivering a sermon than he was that day," Abū Masʿūdη, the Companion who was present, commented when he related the episode years later.

In that address, the Prophet μ stood and said, "O people! There are some among you who turn the prayer into a burden! When one of you leads the prayer, then make it as short as possible – think of the ill and elderly behind you, as well as those with pressing engagements!"[295] An *imām* (prayer leader) lengthening the congregational prayer creates an opportunity to trample on many people's many rights. Notwithstanding, the Prophet μ may have delivered this speech passionately – more angrily than some had ever seen, in fact – but look at its content; there is no harsh or abusive language. He refrained from even mentioning anyone by name so as to spare their feelings despite the wrong they did. Conversely, when we reach heights of rage that even those familiar with us have never seen, insulting and humiliating the cause (human or otherwise) are the bare minimum.

In fact, anger never impacted the pristine, candid, truthful manner of the Prophet's μ speech. ʿAbdullāh b. ʿAmrη, who had a habit of writing down things the Prophet μ would say, was reproached by some of the senior Companions for doing so. The reason they cited was that perhaps the Prophet μ – being of course a human being – might become angry and say something he did not mean. But when ʿAbdullāh η complained to the Prophet μ of this, the Prophet μ simply pointed to his mouth and said, "carry on writing… by God, nothing but the truth exits here."[296]

Once, Usāmah b. Zaydη went off in pursuit of some enemies with a group of *Anṣār*. When at last one was overtaken and surrounded, he quickly cried out, "I submit!" In the original Arabic, he would have essentially been calling himself Muslim. But, assuming this sudden change of heart in a fleeing combatant to be merely a ploy, Usāmah η dispatched him anyway.

Upon returning home after the battle's conclusion, the Prophet µ was informed of the above, so he summoned Usāmah η. "Did you kill him after he submitted?" the Prophet µ gloweringly inquired.

"He only did it to save his skin!" Usāmah η pleaded.

"Did you *kill* him? *After* he *submitted*?" the Prophet µ repeated witheringly. And he carried on, asking things like, "well, why not cut out his heart to read his intentions," his voice intensifying on each repetition, until Usāmah η wished he hadn't become Muslim until that very day (to hence be free of his sins).[297] Such was the anger of the Muḥammad µ, sparked only by injustice perpetrated against others.

Chapter 25

...Sadness

The Prophet's µ care and compassion for others made not only the fire of the fury he felt at their oppression especially intense, but also the depth of the sorrow he felt at their wilful misguidance, virulent opposition to his message, and the punishment that awaited such obstinacy. His dejection at times became such that Allāh χ sent down verses specifically for his encouragement, such as "so persevere; there is no steadfastness except with God. Neither grieve on their account, nor trepidate over their stratagems!"

The Prophet's µ immeasurable love for people like his wife Khadījah ι, uncle Abū Ṭālib η, and uncle Ḥamzah η was proportional to the anguish with which their deaths afflicted him.

Walking the field in search of Ḥamzahη in the aftermath of the Battle of Uḥud, the Prophet µ eventually found the corpse of his beloved uncle; there he lay in the middle of the valley, disembowelled with his liver (Hind, the wife of Abū Sufyān b. Ḥarb and mother of Muʿāwiyah, had taken and fulfilled an oath to eat Ḥamzah's η liver as compensation for the members of her own family he had killed at Badr), nose, and ears missing. The ghastly sight and heavy loss devastated the Prophet µ for some time.[298]

Another incident which history purports to have left the Prophet µ particularly broken-hearted was the tragic loss of *forty* of his most scholarly Companions in the "Incident of Bi'r Maʿūnah," named for the well at which it took place.

Abū Barā' b. Mālik, a notable personality from Najd, came to visit the Prophet µ in Madīnah, inquiring about Islām. The Prophet µ obliged him and explained his message, but Abū Barā' neither accepted nor rejected it, nevertheless suggesting that his message might be well-received in Najd if the Prophet µ sent some of his learned Companions to preach there. He even went as far as to pledge his personal protection to whomever the Prophet µ sent after he voiced his concerns for their safety, so the Prophet µ sent forty (Najd is a large area) of his best students.

When the party made camp at the well called Bi'r Maʿūnah, they sent someone ahead to ʿĀmir b. al-Ṭufayl (who was the nephew of Abū Barā' and the head of their tribe) with a letter from the Prophet µ. This ʿĀmir, who was zealously hostile to Muḥammad µ and Islām, received the letter and promptly, without even reading it, called for a contingent of horsemen from the Banū Sulaym – who were stationed nearby – and led them in a raid on the encamped Muslims, massacring them to all but the last man, Kaʿb b. Zaydη. This incident so distraught the Prophet µ that for thirty days after, he invoked curses on its perpetrators in the pre-dawn ritual prayer.[299]

Chapter 27

...Crying

Humans are moved to tears by various stimuli, and each of us has our own. What does move us to tears can disclose our emotional inclinations. In my own opinion, crying is one of the most intimate ways we express our feelings, and I feel this is evinced by the fact that we tend to attempt to hide ourselves away during bouts of weeping, only allowing others to see when it's completely unavoidable. Examining what moved the Prophet µ to tears will allow us an extremely close look at his heart and soul.

History has recorded that the Prophet µ shed tears over his Companions' illnesses. When he visited Saʿd b. ʿUbādahη when he was seriously ill, several of his other close Companions accompanied him. When they saw the Prophet µ reduced to tears by Saʿd's η deteriorated state, they too began crying. "Listen!" the Prophet µ advised them, "God does not punish for what falls from eyes or the sadness which afflicts the hearts, rather He either punishes or shows compassion based on the action of this," and he pointed to his tongue.[300]

If grave ailments in his Companions caused the Prophet µ enough grief to shed tears, their deaths did even more so. As we saw in a previous chapter, the Prophet µ kissed and cried over the dead body of ʿUthmān b. Maẓʿūn.[301] We also saw that the Prophet µ cried upon hearing the lamentations of some of the *Anṣārī* ladies over their martyred menfolk.

Usāmah b. Zaydη stopped visiting the Prophet µ for a while after his father Zayd b. Ḥārithahη was martyred. However, when Usāmah η did finally go and see the Prophet µ again, the Prophet µ began crying immediately. "Why have you not come to me before now? Have you come only to sadden me?" the Prophet µ asked Usāmah η upon seeing him, re-opening the wound of losing his beloved Zayd η.

The next day, as Usāmah η was making his way to the Prophet's µ house for another visit, the Prophet µ happened to be outside and saw Usāmah η approaching from afar. "You're going to do to me again what you did yesterday!" the Prophet µ called out to him, only half in jest; when Usāmah arrived before the Prophet µ, he could see that his tears had already begun to fall.[302]

Once, Umm Faḍl bt. Ḥārithι came to the Prophet µ seeking solace after having a disturbing dream. "I saw something terrible last night," she said the next morning, unable to shake the memory.

"Go on, what was it?" the Prophet µ inquired.

"It was… really bad," she said hesitantly, looking away but still seeing the nightmarish images in her mind's eye.

"Just tell me," the Prophet μ said tenderly, wishing for nothing more than to relieve his Companion of her distress.

"Okay. I saw… it was something like pieces of your body falling into my lap," she began, cringing.

But paradoxically (considering the grisly nature of the dream's visuals), the Prophet's μ face brightened as his posture relaxed noticeably. "This is a good dream!" he explained. "It means that my daughter Fāṭimah will give birth to a baby boy whom you will look after." And the interpretation of Umm Faḍl's ι dream was what came to pass; Fāṭimah ο gave birth to Ḥusayn ν and often asked Umm Faḍl η to babysit him.

But once, while watching the young Ḥusayn ν, she brought him to see his grandfather. When she went to place the boy on the Prophet's μ lap, she saw that his eyes were full of tears. "Oh, what's happened? What's the matter?" she asked, surprised.

"The angel Jibrīl has just come to me with news," the Prophet μ explained gravely. "He said that my nation will kill my son…"

"Kill… him?" Umm Faḍl ι gestured toward baby Ḥusayn ν, a look of horror spreading across her face.

"Yes," the Prophet μ confirmed as he hugged his grandson tighter, "Jibrīl even brought me a handful of the red sand from the ground upon which he shall be felled."[303]

The reminder of death in general often brought the Prophet µ to tears. Once, he was walking down a road with a few of his Companions when they were passed by several men bearing a corpse to its final resting place on a bier. Seeing this, the Prophet µ sat and began to cry, saying through his streaming tears, "O my brothers, prepare yourselves for this!"[304]

Sorrow wasn't the only thing that tugged at the strings of the Prophet's µ heart enough to bring tears to his eyes. He was also known, out of his fathomless compassion, known to worry so fervently for his people's proper guidance and success in the life hereafter that he would cry when being reminded of the possibility of their going astray. Once, the Prophet µ was reciting the supplication of Prophet Ibrāhīm ν captured in the verse of Qur'ān which translates, "My Lord, indeed these (idols) have misguided a great many from among humankind. So whoever obeys me is with me; but as for whoever disobeys me, then You are the Ever-Forgiving, Most Merciful," after which he proceeded to recite another Qur'ānic verse which relates a prayer once made by the Prophet ʿĪsāν, translated as, "if You punish them, they are Your slaves (to do with as You please); but if You forgive them, then You are Most Exalted in Might, Most Wise."

After reciting these verses, the Prophet µ raised his hands and called out in desperation, "Oh, my Lord! My nation, my nation!" and began to weep.

But at that moment, the Archangel Jibrīl ν descended with glad tidings from Allāh χ for the Prophet μ: "O Muḥammad, you will not be displeased regarding your nation!"[305]

The Qur'ān often moved the Prophet μ to tears – either when he recited from it himself, or when listening to others. The Prophet μ once requested that the famous ʿAbdullāh b. Masʿūdη to recite some Qur'ān for him.

"You want *me* to recite for you, when *you* are the one who received it?" he asked, humbled but incredulous.

"Yes, I enjoy listening to others," the Prophet μ replied frankly. So he commenced to reciting the chapter entitled "*al-Nisā'*."

When he reached the verse whose meaning is, "so how about when We bring forth from every nation a witness, and against these (your nation) We bring you?" the Prophet μ could bear it no longer.

"That's enough!" he called, eyes brimming with tears.[306]

What caused the Prophet μ to have such a reaction? A review of *Sūrah al-Nisā''s* contents is called for in order to discover the reason. The verse upon which Ibn Masʿūdη had been ordered to halt is the forty-first verse of its chapter. However, he had started his recitation from the first verse. The chapter begins with reminding its reader that Gad has caused every human to be ultimately the offspring of the same two mother and father, and orders us to guard ourselves from the punishment of the life hereafter by maintaining ties of kinship. The chapter then moves on to order us to care well for orphans and not usurp what wealth or property they have been left with. Orphans, so the exhortation continues, should be treated as one's own family; failing that, the Qur'ān advises those who find themselves in such a situation to marry the orphan's mothers as a way to endear their children to them and coax them into treating them equitably.

Having now broached the subject of marriage, the chapter goes on to enumerate some spousal duties (such as not surreptitiously consuming one another's wealth and husbands maintaining their wives well and not overburdening them), after which it goes into some detail on how to justly calculate inheritance. God then warns people against avarice and encouraging miserliness, emphasizing the importance of giving charity. And finally, by the point at which Ibn Masʿūd η was told to stop his recitation, God informs us that Muḥammad μ is going to be called on the Day of Judgement to stand as a witness against his nation – us.

It seems most likely that as Ibn Masʿūdη recited in the particularly efficacious and powerful way for which he was known, the Prophet μ was being reminded of all of his people's most infernal qualities. Perhaps the thought of all those innocent little daughters buried alive, downtrodden destitute left to die in affluent Makkah's streets, and mistreated orphans left with nothing by greedy relatives – and that he, personally, would be the one bearing witness to their blame for all of it on the Day of Judgement – was too much for the Prophet μ to cope with at once. No doubt he could still see the faces of people he knew himself who had been affected by the issues raised in those verses; recall in a previous chapter how copiously the Prophet's μ tears fell while listening to one of his Companions recount how he threw his baby girl into a well during the days of *Jāhiliyyah.* And no doubt, he cried over the punishment he knew some of his tribe – who were kin, after all – would receive despite all of the effort he and his devoted followers had expended in trying to drag them from darkness to light.

The sheer emotional and spiritual load placed upon an individual while engrossed in sincere remembrance of God – particularly during the ritual prayer – also brings tears to the eyes, and the Prophet μ was no exception. ʿAlī b. AbīṬālibν once spied the Prophet μ praying beneath a tree at night, crying profusely, when they were on a journey together with several other Companions (the rest of whom were asleep).[307]

Another Companion has reported once seeing the Prophet μ in prayer, crying so heavily that the breaths beating out of his chest sounded like a windmill.[308]

Once, the Mother of Believers ʿĀ'ishahι was asked about the most astonishing thing she had ever seen vis-à-vis the Prophet μ, to which she replied, "in the middle of the night one time, he roused me and asked if I minded if he got up to pray. I told him I would have loved to just be with him, but since what made him happy also made me happy, I encouraged him to do as he wished. So he got up, performed his ablution, and began praying. After some time, his crying was such that his beard, the front of his tunic, and the ground around his feet had become wet with tears. He must have been in that state all the way up until the time for our pre-dawn prayers, because Bilāl came to summon him and was surprised to see him in such a state, saying, 'O Messenger of God, why are you crying when you are faultless before God?' But the Prophet just answered, 'should even I not be a grateful servant?'"[309]

The strong emotionality of certain other solemn Islāmic rituals naturally brought tears to the Prophet's µ eyes. For example, he was once observed approaching the gate of the *ḥaram* (the sacred area surrounding the Kaʿbah), setting his camel down before entering, and touching the black stone at the Kaʿbah's corner. As he did so, his eyes filled with tears and he wept, proceeding to perform seven circuits of circumambulation (*ṭawāf*), completing them by approaching the black stone and kissing it.

Before moving on to the final chapter, we need to explore one more thing which elicited the Prophet's µ tears.[310]

When he began to spread the message, Arabian society was – as we have seen – steeped in a culture of oppressive and harmful traditions. One of Muḥammad's µ principle duties as divine prophet and messenger was the eradication of these activities; this duty was the one for which he received some of his most severe abuse, as every societal ill was seen – rather perversely – as being a sacred duty, particularly because of their popularisation by what could be considered the scholars, saints, and celebrities of the Quraysh.

Despite the hardship this momentous task entailed, the Prophet µ gave his utmost to make what little headway he did in Makkah, but the tension it placed the heads of the Quraysh in – even relatively soon after the Prophet µ began his preaching – forced them to eventually approach Abū Ṭālibη, who was Muḥammad's µ most adamant and powerful defender.

"O Abā Ṭālib," began their disingenuously sycophantic address, "we respect you or your age and your status. We asked you to put a stop to your nephew's activities, but you've yet to do anything about it. By God, we cannot bear any more of the insults he slings on our forefathers, the humiliation he heaps on our saints, and the challenges he makes against our intelligence! So, either you stop him, or you'll have to let our two groups fight until only one remains!"

After the Qurayshī bigwigs said their piece and left, Abū Ṭālib η called Muḥammad µ to his house and said, "O my nephew! Your tribe came to me and said such-and-such. Do yourself a favour, do me a favour… don't put me in a position I can't handle!"

Assuming by such a statement that his uncle would no longer support or protect him, the Prophet µ declared vehemently, "I swear by God, O uncle, that if they were to give me the Sun in my right hand and the Moon in my left to deter me from this path, I would not leave it until and unless death came to me!" Overcome by his emotions, the Prophet μ stood and made for the door, tear-filled eyes overflowing.

But Abū Ṭālib's η words were meant only as a precaution, and his beloved nephew μ had misconstrued them. "O my nephew!" he called after the Prophet μ, "go and do what you must, for I will never disown you!"[311]

Chapter 27

...Facing his Mortality

Death and dying are inherently emotional subjects, and stories involving them can, and often are, fabricated to manipulate the emotions of a given audience. Purported narrations about the Prophet's μ death are no exception – storytellers and orators contrived many tales about the circumstances surrounding the Prophet's μ passing, the falsehood of which are made manifest by (sometimes obvious) disagreement with the Qur'ān. An example of such follows:

Ibn ʿAbbāsη has been alleged to have reported that the Angel of Death came to the Prophet μ during the illness he suffered shortly before passing away. The Angel asked permission to enter the chamber in which the Prophet μ lay, his head resting in the lap of his son-in-law and cousin ʿAlīν. In response to the Angel's customary greeting Muslims offer one another (that is to say, "may peace, God's mercy, and His blessing be upon you"), ʿAlīν rather tersely responded, "go away, we're busy right now."

"O Abā al-Ḥasan, don't you know who this is?" the Prophet μ chided ʿAlīν. "This is the Angel of Death. Come in!" the Prophet invited cheerily.

Upon entering, the Angel said, "your Lord has sent you a greeting."

"Where is Jibrīl?" the Prophet µ inquired, accustomed as he was to his interactions with the Archangel ν.

"He is rather far away at the moment, but he is on his way," said the Angel of Death, heading outside to stand awaiting Jibrīl's ν arrival.

"O Angel of Death, why have you come outside to wait?" Jibrīl ν inquired of his colleague, surprised that he had delayed performing his duty.

"Muḥammad asked about you, that is why," was the Angel's reply. So, they both proceeded inside and sat before the Prophet µ.

"Peace be upon you, O Abā al-Qāsim," began Jibrīl, "this shall be our last meeting."

After all of this, the one who fabricated this *ḥadīth* added, "I have been told that the Angel of Death has not greeted anyone before nor after," probably to add yet more flavour to his story. Forgeries of this sort abound, and they tend to serve their purpose of enflaming emotions and coaxing tears, and they are shared by well-intentioned laymen, preachers, and even academics despite the stark impermissibility of doing so. The dangers inherent to spreading these fairy-tales outweighs any fleeting benefit, and such is unbefitting of the true believer (*mu'min*).[312]

The above tradition must have been used at some point as an ad hoc answer to the question of whether the Prophet μknew his death was imminent, and how if so. In my own understanding, the Prophet μ never received such a concrete pronouncement; rather, there were a few key events which must have alerted his intuition to the proximity of his death, and these indications of his suspicion were hinted at to his Companions.

The first of them was that the Archangel Jibrīl ν, who normally revised the entirety of the Qur'ān with the Prophet μ once every year, did so *twice* in the year during which he died.

Once, Fāṭimaho entered upon the Prophet μ, walking in a manner which resembled her father μ exactly. When the Prophet μ noticed her, he called her over and welcomed her joyfully. After he bade her sit next to him, he leaned in close to her and whispered something in her ear which caused her to begin crying. But he immediately whispered something else which caused her to begin laughing. ʿĀ'ishahι, who was an audience to this strange interaction, was consumed with curiosity; she had, after all, never seen sorrow followed so quickly by joy. So after the Prophet μ got up to leave, she approached Fāṭimah o and asked what the Prophet μ had been whispering to her, but her inquiry was met with Fāṭimah's o refusal to disclose her father's μ secret.

However, after the Prophet's μ death, ʿĀ'ishah ι asked again, and Fāṭimah o agreed to tell her. "The first thing he told me," she explained, "as that Jibrīl used to revise the Qur'ān with him once a year, but this year he did so twice. He said that he thought it might be because he would be dying soon, so he advised me to be patient. But it saddened me so, that I couldn't help but cry. But then he said that I would be the first person in his family to join him. And that overjoyed me so, that I couldn't help but laugh."[313]

Another indirect indication of the Prophet's µ approaching fate was that he himself referred to what ended up being his final pilgrimage *as* his "*Ḥijjah al-Widā*ʿ," or "Farewell Pilgrimage." This caused the Prophet's µ Companions quite a bit of consternation, as they had no idea at that point why the Prophet µ had referred to it thusly. A Companion named Jābir η recounted later that he had noticed that, "the Prophet performed the rituals of the pilgrimage with great tranquillity, ordering us to do the same, and also to carry on performing them. What he said was, 'learn how to perform these rituals from me, because I am unsure if I will see you again after this year.' And he died two months later."[314]

Because tribes from all over the Arabian Peninsula had begun to accept Islām and place themselves under the political influence of Muḥammad's µ Madīnah, it became necessary to dispatch religiously-learned members of his core following to distant localities. One such person chosen for such a mission was one Muʿādh b. Jabalη, whom the Prophet µ sent to Yemen in 10AH, but not before giving some final instructions which happened to make reference to his own death.

As the Prophet µ walked next to Muʿādh η on his mount, accompanying him to Madīnah's city limits, he said, "O Muʿādh, you may not see me after this year. It just may be that when you come back here, you will be visiting my mosque and my grave." Then he stopped and turned to face Madīnah, saying, "you know… my family thinks that they are closer to me than any other people. But they're not quite right. The closest to me are the ones who guard themselves against sins and grave errors, regardless of where they reside. O my Lord, I have not permitted them to destroy what I have established! By God, my nation will flow out of their religion as water flows from its container when poured."[315]

According to a great number of our scholars, the revelation of the chapter of the Qur'ān entitled "*al-Naṣr*" was yet another sign that the Prophet's µ death was soon to come.

The stalwart ʿUmar b. al-Khaṭṭāb η used to attend the reunions which were held for the veterans of the Expedition of Badr, and on a few occasions he brought with him one ʿAbdullāh b. al-ʿAbbāsη, who was at that time still very young. To this some of the more senior veterans objected, saying, "why is it that you're including someone as young as our own children?"

"But he's still someone you know!" ʿUmar η replied, defending his decision. To illustrate why he thought it prudent to bring a child to a gathering of much older, battle-hardened men – ultimately because he recognized Ibn al-ʿAbbās's wisdom and maturity – he brought him again to one of these veterans' meetings an addressed all of the men present. "What do you think about the verse, 'when comes the conquest and God's support?'" he asked, citing the first verse of *Sūrah al-Naṣr.*

Some simply remained silent, while others offered their explanations, variously along the lines of, "it means that we have been ordered to praise God and ask him for forgiveness once we gain support and conquest is granted us."

"Do you agree with them, O son of al-ʿAbbās?" ʿUmar η asked knowingly.

"No," the boy replied simply, probably much to the crowd's surprise.

"Well then, what do you say?" ʿUmar η questioned, as an attorney questions a witness on the stand.

"The first verse is a sign of the Prophet's coming death. And the verse, 'so glorify your Lord with praises and seek His forgiveness; indeed He is most accepting of repentance,' is a reminder of what to do when it comes."

"What you have said is all I know, and nothing more!" ʿUmar η said triumphantly.[316] And if these two knew, how could the Prophet μ remain yet unaware?

The Prophet μ had a habit of paying a visit to the plot of land beneath which were buried the martyrs of the Battle of Uḥud in order to pray for them. In the final year of his life, he did so as normal, but afterward ascended his pulpit in his mosque and gave a short address, saying, "I am both your asset and a witness over you. I see before me the basin promised to me in the hereafter. I have been granted the keys to the treasures of the Earth; and while I am not afraid that you fall back into idolatry, I *am* afraid that you will fall into fighting each-other over that wealth." [317]

Several days later, the Prophet μ, who had by this time become seriously ill, felt the need to address his followers, so he called upon ʿĀ'ishah ι and Ḥafṣah to fill seven vessels with water from seven different wells and drench him with each of them. Having done this, he sent for Faḍl b. al-ʿAbbāsη to help him – with joints stiff and head bandaged – walk to and mount his pulpit. The Prophet μ then had Faḍl η gather the people together to listen to what he had to say.

"O people," said the Prophet μ after commencing with customary praises and thanksgiving to God, "my time has come! If I have beaten any of you – here I am, come and avenge yourself. If I have offended your honour – then here is my honour, take it for yourself. If I have usurped any of your property – then my property is here, compensate yourselves. Let none of you think I will think negatively of whomever takes revenge on me; you know that it's not my way to think badly of anyone.

"The most beloved among you, to me, is the one who either takes his revenge or forgives – so that I meet my Lord with an unburdened heart. Thus, I have no choice but to keep asking you." Then he descended the pulpit in order to lead the congregation in their midday prayers, but afterward climbed back up and continued his appeal. "O people, if any of you has anything – anything at all – to say, then say it. Do not think that you will be exposed, for to be exposed in this life is easier than in the life hereafter."

Then someone stood out of the crowd and called out, "O Messenger of God, you owe me three coins of silver!"

"I do not claim you are lying, so I won't ask you to take an oath, but please remind me because I've forgotten… why do I owe you that?" the Prophet µ responded.

"Do you remember, once some poor person came when I was with you, and you asked me to give him three silver coins?"

Remembering indeed, the Prophet µ turned to Faḍlη and said, "compensate him." Then he again resumed his appeal, saying, "O people, if any of you is in need of prayer, let me know now so that I may pray for you."

"O Messenger of God," another man said as he stood, "I am a liar and hypocrite; and I sleep too much!"

The Prophet µ immediately raised his hands and supplicated, "O my Lord, give this man truthfulness and certainty, and remove his laziness!"

Another man stood and shouted, "O Messenger of God! I too am a liar and a hypocrite – there isn't a single sin which I haven't committed!"

ʿUmar b. al-Khaṭṭāb η could resist no longer and spoke up, "hey! You've exposed yourself!"

"Let him be, O ʿUmar," the Prophet μ said, "as I said, being exposed in this life is better than in the next life!" And again, he raised his hands and supplicated, "O my Lord, give him truthfulness and certainty, and improve his good standing!"[318] It must be said at this juncture that, as far as Islāmic norms are concerned, exposing one's sins is actually highly discouraged (something ʿUmar η knew, hence his outburst; this also explains why it took so much coaxing from the Prophet μ). However, the point of this narration – if it is indeed authentic – was to show people being granted solace from the psychological burden placed upon them by their sins, much akin to a person going to a psychiatrist or therapist, or even a physician, exposing symptoms to have them diagnosed and cured.

Now, a matter of grave national concern needed to be addressed despite the Prophet's μ infirmity. After the conclusion of the Treaty of Ḥudaybiyyah with the Quraysh, the Prophet μ set about dispatching emissaries to the various heads of state surrounding the Arabian Peninsula, such as those of Egypt, Bahrain, and the Byzantine and Sassanid Empires. The messenger who had been sent to the Byzantines was captured by a patrol and taken to the commander of their Syria province.

When it was revealed that he was a messenger sent by the Arabian Prophet μ, the commander had him killed.

For this, the Prophet μ demanded justice from the Emperor. However, his demand was not only brushed aside, it provoked military action on the Byzantines' part, and they dispatched a punitive force straight to Madīnah. This all, incidentally, took place concurrently with the Prophet μ falling terminally ill, but he still ordered his Companions to prepare to meet the threat head-on, appointing Usāmah b. Zaydη as the head of the column.

But this defensive force was delayed; even though the Prophet μ continued giving orders for its preparation, it was prevented from leaving until after the Prophet's μ death. However, the dire consequences had it never been mustered, prepared, and sent off at all would have been immeasurable, and the Prophet's μ dedication to the responsibility of leadership he still bore – despite his crippling illness – saved the Muslims from utter destruction.

Knowing he was going to die soon, facing his own mortality, Muḥammad's μ primary concern was still for nothing but us.

Chapter 29

Death of the Prophet Muḥammad µ

The Prophet µ fell ill towards the month of the lunar Islāmic calendar called Ṣafar in the eleventh year after his migrated from Makkah to Madīnah, and he remained so for approximately thirteen days. Now, even when he was ill, it was his habit to spend one night in each of his wives' houses, but when he became bed-ridden he sought permission from all of them to remain in one wife's house; they agreed. But his illness had so depleted him that the services of ʿAlīν and Faḍl b. al-ʿAbbāsη were required to convey the Prophet µ, feet dragging from exhaustion, to his final place of residence, the house of ʿĀ'ishah ι.

Even on death's doorstep, we can see how the Prophet µ honoured his wives. Polygamy was widely accepted as a norm in those days, but Arabians unfortunately had a culture of misogyny to go along with it, and their many wives were often badly oppressed. Contrary to that norm, the Prophet µ – who had been sent with the divine light of a message of justice and equality – was concerned even until the end of his life with treating them all well. Even in his dying days, the Prophet µ was the epitome of Islām's most cardinal ideal, living and breathing the Qur'ānic verse which can be translated as, "surely We have dispatched Our messengers with clear arguments, and sent with them a covenant and a set of scales wherewith mankind should establish justice."[319]

Despite the severity of his body aches and fever, the Prophet μ insisted on leading congregational prayers in his mosque until, on Thursday the 8th of the month of Rabīʿ al-Awwal, Bilālη came to summon him to lead the night prayer. The Prophet μ tried to stand, but fell unconscious. When he awoke a short time later, he asked, "have the people prayed yet?"

"No, O Prophet, they are waiting for you," Bilāl η said. So the Prophet μ sent someone to fetch cool water so that he could douse himself and lower his temperature enough to lead the prayer.

Having done so, the Prophet μ tried again to stand, but again fell unconscious. This happened several times, and each time the Prophet μ came around, he would ask if the people had prayed yet. "Let Abū Bakr lead the prayer, then," the Prophet μ ordered when it became clear that he would simply be unable to lead himself.

"But he is too soft-hearted," ʿĀ'ishah ι objected, "he'll be crying too much to lead." But the Prophet μ insisted, and eventually Abū Bakr η did lead that night's congregational prayer.[320]

Every prayer thereafter, in fact, was led by Abū Bakr η except for on one occasion. It was on a Sunday afternoon during which the Prophet µ felt within himself a slight improvement; he asked two of his kinsmen to support him as he made his way to the front of the mosque to assume leadership of that day's midday prayer, but the Companions were already standing in prayer behind Abū Bakr. Some of them, however, caught a glimpse of him out of the corners of their eyes and would have jumped for joy had such a thing not constituted an invalidation of their ritual.

Subtly, the congregation made Abū Bakr aware that the Prophet µ had come out of his chambers, but the Prophet µ signalled for them to carry on as they were, making his way to stand in front of Abū Bakr and commence to leading *him* while he led the rest.

Assuming that the Prophet µ had now made a full recovery, the Companions all gathered for the late afternoon prayer and waited for the Prophet µ to come out and lead as he would normally have before this latest affliction. But his condition had deteriorated even further, and he was unable to come out again.

The next day, Monday the 12th of Rabīʿ al-Awwal, the Prophet µ stood during the morning prayer and, pushing aside the curtains which partitioned his chambers from the rest of the mosque, he looked out at his Companions, smiling warmly. Those who saw this made as if to stop praying, but the Prophet µ motioned for them to carry on. He dropped the curtain back in its place, lay back down – never to stand again. Umm Salamahı came to see the Prophet µ (as she had every day of his final illness) later that day, and he asked her laboriously, "has ʿAlī come back yet?"

When ʿAlī ν did finally come, the women stood and left the room, letting them speak in private. Sitting nearest the door, Umm Salamah ι couldn't make out any of what the Prophet µ whispered through his pain to ʿAlīν, but it seemed to her to have been orders and advice. After their conversation, ʿAlīν, who was the last person to whom the Prophet µ spoke, left the room, immediately setting about the tasks given him by the Prophet µ.[321]

Some time later in the day, ʿAbd al-Raḥmān b. Abī Bakrκ entered the room holding a *miswak* in his hand. ʿĀ'ishah ι, upon whose chest the Prophet's µ head now rested, noticed him eyeing the stick longingly – its use in cleaning his mouth, after all, was one of the few worldly pleasures the Prophet µ indulged in – and took it from him, preparing it for him as she always used to. She handed it to the Prophet µ and he used it more thoroughly than she had ever seen; thereafter he lifted his hands, repeating the words, "the highest companion" thrice. With that, he left this world.[322]

May the peace and blessings of God be upon His final Prophet and Messenger Muḥammad, and upon his Kin, his Wives, and his Companions altogether.

Index

Personalities

Abā Ṭālib 35
ʿAbbās .... passim
ʿAbd al-Muṭṭalib .... passim
ʿAbd al-Raḥmān 100
ʿAbd al-Raḥmān b. Abī Bakr 225
ʿAbd al-Raḥmān b. ʿAwf 47, 99
ʿAbd al-ʿUzzah 40
ʿAbd Manāf 40
ʿAbdah bt. Khālid b. Maʿdān 185
ʿAbdullāh .... passim
ʿAbdullāh b. al-ʿAbbās 217
ʿAbdullāh b. al-Ḥārith 60, 190
ʿAbdullāh b. ʿAmr 200
ʿAbdullāh b. Jaʿfar 50
ʿAbdullāh b. Masʿūd .... passim
ʿAbdullāh b. Salām 63
ʿAbdullāh b. Umm Maktūm 124
ʿAbdullāh b. Zayd al-Anṣārī 183
Abū ʿAbdillāh Thawbān b. Bajdud 85
Abū al-Dardā' 186, 187
Abū Bakr .... passim
Abū Barā' b. Mālik 203
Abū Bark 17
Abū Dharr al-Ghifārī 79

Abū Hurayrah 55, 63, 116
Abū Lahab 9, 60
Abū Mas'ūd 199
Abū Salamah 58, 60
Abū Salamah 'Abdullāh b. 'Abd al-Asad al-Makhzūmī 58
Abū Sayf 47
Abū Sufyān 179
Abū Sufyān b. Ḥarb 179
Abū Ṭalḥah 107, 108, 167
Abū Ṭalḥah b. Thābit 89
Abū Ṭālib .... passim
Abū Ṭufayl 15
Abū Usayd 110
'Addās 148
'Adī 114, 115
'Adī b. Ḥātim al-Ṭā'ī 113
'Ā'ishah .... passim
'Ā'ishah bt. Abī Bakr 41
'Ā'ishah's 188
al-Aqrā' b. Ḥābis 53
al-'Āṣ b. Wā'il 165
al-Ḥārith b. Abī Ḍirār 162
'Alī .... passim
'Alīv, Abū Ṭālib 143
'Alī b. Abī Ṭālib .... passim
al-Muṭṭalib 31, 32
al-Najāshī 112

al-Zubayr b. ʿAbd al-Muṭṭalib.. 166
Āminah.. passim
Āminah bt. Wahb... 28
ʿĀmir b. al-Ṭufayl... 203
ʿĀmir b. Fuhayrah... 95
Anas 89, 90, 193
Anas b. Mālik.. passim
Arqam b. Abī Arqam.. 176, 177
ʿĀṣ b. Wā'il 167
Ashama b. Abjar 112
Asmā 67
Asmā' bt. ʿUmays... 66
ʿAwn b. Jaʿfar b. AbīṬālib 50
Barakah 16, 35
Barrah bt. ʿAbd al-ʿUzzah 31
Bilāl 223
Faḍl 219
Faḍl b. al-ʿAbbās.. 218, 222
Fāṭimah .... passim
Fāṭimah al-Zahrā' 38
Fāṭimah bt. ʿAmr 31
Fāṭimah bt. Asad.. 18, 28
Gabriel 21
Ḥafṣah 218
Ḥalīmah .... passim
Ḥalīmah al-Saʿdiyyah 60
Ḥalīmah's.. 15

Ḥamzah 64, 125, 145, 202
Ḥamzah b. ʿAbd al-Muṭṭalib 60
Ḥarb 51
Ḥārith 11, 13
Ḥārithah..81, 82, 84
Hārūn's... 51
Ḥasan .... passim
Hāshim... 32
Hind b. Abī Hālah... 199
Hind, the wife of Abū Sufyān b. Ḥarb 202
Husain 54
Ḥusayn.. passim
Ḥuyayy b. Akhṭab.. 75
Ibn ʿAbbās 213
Ibn Masʿūd 208, 209
Ibn Wā'il 166
Ibrāhīm... passim
ʿĪsā 140, 207
Ismāʿīl 23
Jābir... 106
Jābir b. ʿAbdillāh.. 105
Jaʿfar 140
Jarīr b. ʿAbdullāh 186
Jesus 111
Jibrīl 144, 151, 214
Juwayriyyah bt. Al-Ḥārith 163
Kaʿb b. Zayd 203

Khadījah .... passim
Khālid 100, 185
Khālid b. al-Walīd 99
Khālid b. Maʿdān al-Ḥimṣī 184
Khubayb b. ʿAdī 179
Mālik b. Naḍr 89
Māryah 39
Maryam 140
Muʿādh b. Jabal 216
Muʿāwiyah 202
Muḥammad .... passim
Muḥammad b. Jaʿfar 50
Muḥammad, son of ʿAbdullāh 175
Muḥsin 49
Muqawqis 40
Mūsā 140, 144
Muṣʿab b. ʿUmayr 124
Mushabbir 51
Muṭahhar 39
Muṭayyab 39
Negus 112, 113, 139, 140
Negus of Abyssinia 56
Nuʿaymān 194, 195, 196
Prophet-King Sulaymān 138
Qāsim 37
Qatādah b. al-Nuʿmān 167
Quḥafah 146

Ruqayyah 39, 46, 50
Sa'd b. Abī Waqqāṣ 66, 92
Sa'd b. 'Ubādah 92, 204
Sa'd, son of Rabī' 184
Ṣafiyyah 75
Ṣafiyyah bt. Ḥuyayy 76
Ṣafwān b. Umayyah 179
Sā'ib b. Abī Sā'ib 96
Salamah 58
Salmān 87, 88
Salmān al-Fārisī 80, 86, 105
Shabīr 51
Shabr 51
Shaybah b. Hāshim 31
Shaymā' 61
Shaymā' bt. al-Ḥārith 60
Suwaybiṭ 194
Suwaybiṭ b. Ḥarmalah 194
Ṭāhir 39
Ṭayyib 39
Thawbān 44, 80, 85, 184
the Angel of Death 213
Thumāmah 157
Thuwaybah 9, 60, 187
Umāmah 49, 56
Umāmah bt. Abī al-'Āṣ 52
'Umar .... passim

ʿUmar b. Abī Salamah 59
ʿUmar b. al-Khaṭṭāb .... passim
Umm Ayman 16, 17, 34, 35
Umm Faḍl 206
Umm Faḍl bt. Ḥārith 205
Umm Jamīl 176
Umm Jamīl, daughter of al-Khaṭṭāb 175
Umm Khayr 176
Umm Kulthūm 37, 38, 39, 50
Umm Maʿbad 95
Umm Salamah 224
Umm Salamah Hind bt. Suhayl al-Makhzūmiyyah 58
Umm Sulaym 89, 108
Unaysah bt. al-Ḥārith 60
ʿUqbah b. Abī Muʿayṭ 146
Usāmah 187, 188
Usāmah b. Zayd 200, 205, 221
ʿUtaybah 38
ʿUtaybah b. Abī Lahab 38
ʿUtbah 174
ʿUtbah b. Abī Lahab. 39
ʿUthmān b. ʿAffān 38, 39, 103
ʿUthmān b. Maẓʿūn 93, 204
ʿUthmān son of Maẓʿūn, ... 46
ʿUyaynah 54
ʿUyaynah b. Badr 54
Wahb b. ʿAbd Manāf 31

Waraqah 145
Waraqah b. Nawfal... 144
Yūnus son of Mattā... 148
Ẓāhir.. 196
Zayd .... passim
Zayd b. al-Dathinnah 179
Zayd b. Ḥārithah .... passim
Zayd b. Muḥammad.. 83
Zaynab .... passim

Places

Abyssinia .... passim
al-Ḥudaybiyyah 29
al-Riyāḍ 156
al-Sārah 85
al-Shām 8, 27, 86, 114
Arabia 10, 14, 88
Arabian Peninsula 220
Asia 14
Babylon 115
Badr 39, 45
Bahrain 220
Baqīʿ 94
Baṣrah 194
Bethany 111
Buṣrā 194
Byzantine 114, 220
Egypt 220
Eritrea 112
Ethiopia 112
Gaza 31
Ḥabashah 112
Ḥijāz 11, 34
Hisarköy 87
Ḥudaybiyyah 160
Ḥunayn 61
Īran 86

Iraq....49, 87, 148, 194
Iṣfahān....86
Jaʿfar b. Abī Ṭālib....66
Jiʿrānah....15
Jordan....8
Kaʿbah....passim
Kaʿbah's....23, 34
Karbalā'....49
Khaybar....66
Lebanon....8
Madīnah....passim
Makkah....passim
Makkah's....22
Makkan....26
Mawṣil....87
Mosul....87
Mount ʿArafah at....80
Najaf....49
Nusaybin....87
Palestine....8
Qādsiyyah....114
Sassanid....221
Saudi Arabian....156
Syria....8, 194, 221
the hill of Abū Qubays....166
Turkey....87
Yarmūk....49

Bibliography

AL-ADAB AL-MUFRAD by Muhammad b. Ismael Al-Bukhari Al-Ju'fi (d. 870 AD, Uzbekistan), Publisher; DAR AL-SADIQ, Jabal, KSA, second edition 2000.

AL-ADAB AL-MUFRAD, by Abu Abdullah Muhammad b. Ismael Al-Bukhari (d. 870 AD, Uzbekistan), Publisher AL-MATBA'AH AL-SALAFIYYAH, Cairo, Egypt,1956.

AL-AHADITH AL-MUKHTARAH, by Diauddin Muhammad b. Abdul-Wahid Al-Maqdisi (d. 1245 AD, Syria), Publisher; DAR AL-KHIDR, Beirut, Lebanon, third edition 2000.

AL-AMALI, by Yahya b. Al-Husain Al-Shajari Al-Jurjani Al-Husaini (d. 1105 AD), Publisher; Dar Al-Kutub Al-Ilmiyyah, Beirut, Lebanon, first edition 2001.

AL-ANWAR FI SHAMAIL AL-MUKHTAR SALLALLAHU ALAIHI WA SALLAM, by Husain b. Masud Al-Baghawi (d. 1122 AD, Iran), Publisher; DAR AL-MAKTABI, Damascus, Syria, first edition 1995.

AL-ANWAR FI SHAMAIL AL-MUKHTAR, by Abu Muhammad Husain b. Masud Al-Farra Al-Baghawi (d. 1122 AD, Iran), Publisher; DAR AL-MAKTABI, Damascus, Syria, first edition 1995.

AL-BAHR AL-MUHIT, by Abu Hayyan Muhammad b. Yusuf Al-Gharnati (d. 1344 AD, Spain/Egypt), Publisher; DAR AL-KUTUB AL-ILMIYYAH, Beirut, Lebanon, first edition 1993.

AL-BAHR AL-ZAKHKHAR Abu Bakr Ahmad b. Amr Al-Bazzar (d. 905 AD, Iraq), Publisher; MAKTABAH AL-ULUM WA AL-HIKAM, Madinah, KSA, first edition 1988.

AL-BAHR AL-ZAKHKHAR Abu Bakr Ahmad b. Amr Al-Bazzar (d. 905 AD, Iraq), Publisher; MAKTABAH AL-ULUM WA AL-HIKAM, Madinah, KSA, first edition 2005.

AL-BAHR AL-ZAKHKHAR Abu Bakr Ahmad b. Amr Al-Bazzar (d. 905 AD, Iraq), Publisher; MAKTABAH AL-ULUM WA AL-HIKAM, Madinah, KSA, first edition 1995.

AL-BAHR AL-ZAKHKHAR Abu Bakr Ahmad b. Amr Al-Bazzar (d. 905 AD, Iraq),Publisher; MAKTABAH AL-ULUM WA AL-HIKAM, Madinah, KSA, first edition 2003.

AL-BAHR AL-ZAKHKHAR Abu Bakr Ahmad b. Amr Al-Bazzar (d. 905 AD, Iraq), Publisher; MAKTABAH AL-ULUM WA AL-HIKAM, Madinah, KSA, first edition 1988.

AL-IHSAN FI TAQRIB SAHIH IBN HIBBAN, by Abu Hatim Muhammad b. Faisal Al-Busti (d. 965 AD, Afghanistan), Publisher; DAR AL-TA'SIL MARKAZ AL-BUHUTH WA TIQANIYYAH AL-MA'LUMAT, Cairo, Egypt, first edition 2014.

AL-IHSAN FI TAQRIB SAHIH IBN HIBBAN, by Abu Hatim Muhammad b. Faisal Al-Busti (d. 965 AD, Afghanistan), Publisher; DAR AL-KUTUB AL-ISLAMIYYAH, Beirut, Lebanon,1987.

AL-IHSAN FI TAQRIB SAHIH IBN HIBBAN, by Abu Hatim Muhammad b. Faisal Al-Busti (d. 965 AD, Afghanistan), Publisher; MUASSASAH AL-RISALAH, Beirut, Lebanon, first edition edition 1988.

AL-IHSAN FI TAQRIB SAHIH IBN HIBBAN, by Abu Hatim Muhammad b. Faisal Al-Busti (d. 965 AD, Afghanistan), Publisher; MUASSASAH AL-RISALAH, Beirut, Lebanon, second edition 1993.

AL-IHSAN FI TAQRIB SAHIH IBN HIBBAN, by Abu Hatim Muhammad b. Faisal Al-Busti (d. 965 AD, Afghanistan), Publisher; DAR AL-TA'SIL MARKAZ AL-BUHUTH WA TIQANIYYAH AL-MA'LUMAT, Cairo, Egypt, first edition 2014.

AL-ISABAH FI TAMYEEZ AL-SAHABAH, by Shihabuddin Ahmad b. Nuriddin Ibn Hajar Al-Asqallani (d. 1449 AD, Egypt), Publisher; MAKTABAH IBN TAIMIYYAH, Cairo, Egypt, 1993

AL-ISABAH FI TAMYEEZ AL-SAHABAH, by Shihabuddin Ahmad b. Nuriddin Ibn Hajar Al-Asqallani (d. 1449 AD, Egypt), p 495 V 2, Publisher; DAR AL-KUTUB AL-ILMIYYAH, Beirut, Lebanon, first edition 1995.

AL-JAME' AL-SAHIH, by Abu Abdullah Muhammad b. Ismael Al-Bukhari (d. 870 AD, Uzbekistan), Publisher DAR IBN KATHIR, Damascus, Syria, first edition 2002.

AL-JAME' LI AHKAM AL-QURAN, by Abu Abdullah Muhammad b. Ahmad Al-Ansari Al-Qurtubi (d. 1273 AD, Spain/Egypt), Publisher; MUASSASAT AL-RISALAH, Beirut, Lebanon, first edtion 2006.

AL-KAMIL FI AL-DHU'AFAA, by Abu Ahmad b. Adi Al-Jurjani, (d. 976 AD, Iran), Publisher DAR AL-FIKAR LI AL-TIBA'AH WA AL-NASHR WA AL-TAWZI', Berut, Lebanon, second edition 1985.

AL-KAMIL FI AL-TARIKH, by Abu Al-Hasan Ali b. Muhammad Al-Jazari Ibn Al-Athir (d. 1233 AD, Turkey/Iraq), Publisher; DAR AL-KUTUB AL-ILMIYYAH, Beirut, Lebanon, first edition 1987.

AL-KHASAIS AL-KUBRA, by Jalaluddin Abdul-Rahman b. Abu Bakr Al-Suyuti (d. 1505 AD, Egypt), Publisher; DAR AL-KUTUB AL-HADITHAH, Cairo, Egypt.

AL-MAGHAZI AL-NABAWIYYAH, by Abu Abdullah Muhammad b. Umar Al-Waqidi (d. 823 AD, Iraq), Publisher; Oxford University Press, London, UK, 1965, (Re-prented; third edition 1984).

AL-MAQASID AL-HASANA FI BAYAN KATHIR MIN AL-AHADITH AL-MUSHTAHIRA ALA AL-ALSINA, by Muhammad Abdul-Rahman Al-Skhawi (d. 1497 AD, Egypt), Publisher; DAR AL-KITAB AL-ARABI, first edition 1985.

AL-MU'JAM AL-AWSAT, by Abu Al-Qasim Sulaiman b. Ayub Al-Tabarani (d. 918 AD, Iran), Publisher; DAR AL-HARAMAIN, Cairo, Egypt, 1995.

AL-MU'JAM AL-KABIR, by Abu Al-Qasim Sulaiman b. Ayub Al-Tabarani (d. 918 AD, Iran), Publisher; MAKTABAH IBN TAIMIYYAH, Cairo, Egypt, 1983.

AL-MUNTADHAM FI TARIKH AL-MULUK WA AL-UMAM, by Abu Al-Faraj Abdul-Rahman b. Ali Ibn Al-Jawzi (d. 1200 AD, Iraq), Publisher; DAR AL-KUTUB AL-ILMIYYAH, Beirut, Lebanon, first edition 1992.

AL-MUNTAKHAB MIN MUSNAD by Abd b. Humaid Al-Keshi (d. 863 AD, Shahrisabz, Uzbekistan), Publisher; DAR BALNASIYYAH, Riyadh, KSA, second edition 2002.

AL-MUSANNAF, by Abdul-Razzaq b. Hammam Al-San'ani (d. 828 AD, Yemen), Publisher; DAR AL-TASIL, Cairo, Egypt, first edition 2015.

AL-MUSNAD AL-JAME', by Abdullah b. Abdul-Rahaman Al-Darimi (d 869 AD, Uzbekistan), Publisher; DAR AL-BASHAIR AL-ISLAMIYYAH, Beirut, Lebanon, first edition 2013.

AL-MUWATTA, by Abu Abdullah Malik b. Anas Al-Asbahi Al-Himyari (d. 795, Madinah), Publisher; MUSTAFA AL-BABI AL-HALABI, (DAR IHYA AL-TURATH), Cairo, Egypt, 1985.

AL-SHIFA BI TA'RIF HUQUQ AL-MUSTAFA, by Ayad b. Musa (d. 1149 AD, Morocco), Publisher; JAIZAT DUBAI AL-DAWLIYYAH LI AL-QURAN AL-KARIM, Dubai, UAE, first edition 2013.

AL-SIRAH AL-NABAWIYYAH, by Abu Bakr Muhammad b. Ishaq Al-Madani (d. 768 AD, Madinah/Iraq), Publisher; DAR AL-KUTUB AL-ILMIYYAH, Beirut, Lebanon, first edition 2004.

AL-SIRAH AL-NABAWIYYAH, by Abu Bakr Muhammad b. Ishaq Al-Madani (d. 768 AD, Madinah/Iraq), Publisher; DAR AL-KUTUB AL-ILMIYYAH, Beirut, Lebanon, third edition 2003.

AL-SIRAH AL-NABAWIYYAH, by Abu Muhammad Abdulmalik b. Hisham Al-Himyari (d. 833 AD, Egypt), Publisher DAR AL-KITAB AL-ARABI, Beirut, Lebanon, third edition 1990.

AL-SUNAN AL-KUBRA, by Abu Abdul-Rahman Ahmad b. Shuaib Al-Nasai (d. 915 AD Mecca/Turkmenistan), Publisher; MUASSASAT AL-RISALAH, Beirut, Lebanon, first edition 2001.

AL-SUNAN AL-KUBRA, by Abu Bakr Ahmad b. Husain Al-Baihaqi (d. 1066 AD, Iran), Publisher; DAR AL-KUTUB AL-ILMIYYAH, Beirut, Lebanon, third edition 2003.

AL-TABAQAT AL-KABIR, by Muhammad b. Sa'd Al-Baghdadi (d. 845 AD, Iraq), Publisher; MAKTABAH AL-KHANJI, Cairo, Egypt, year 2001.

AL-TABAQAT AL-KABIR, by Muhammad b. Sa'd Al-Baghdadi (d. 845 AD, Iraq), Publisher; DAR AL-KUTUB AL-ILMIYYAH, Beirut, Lebanon, first edition 1990.

AL-TABAQAT AL-KABIR, by Muhammad b. Sa'd Al-Baghdadi (d. 845 AD, Iraq), Publisher; DAR AL-KUTUB AL-ILMIYYAH, Cairo, Egypt, third edition 2017.

AL-TAFSIR, by Abdul-Razzaq b. Hammam Al-San'ani (d. 828 AD, Yemen), Publisher; DAR KUTUB AL-ILMIYYAH, Beirut, Lebanon, first edition 1999.

AMAL AL-YAWM WA AL-LAYLAH, by Ibn Al-Sunniy Abu Bakr Ahmad b. Muhammad Al-Ja'fari Al-Hashimi (d. 974 AD, Iran), Publisher; DAR AL-ARQAM, Beirut, Lebanon, first edition 1998.

ASBAB AL-NUZUL, by Abu Al-Hasan Ali b. Ahmad Al-Nisapuri Al-Wahidi (d. 1076 AD, Iran), Publisher; DAR AL-KUTUB AL-ILMIYYAH, Beirut, Lebanon, first edition 1991.

AYYAM AL-ARABIYYAH, by Muhammad Ahmad Jaad, Ali Muhammad Al-Bijawi and Muhammad Abu Al-Fadl Ibrahim, Publisher; ISA AL-BABI AL-HALABI, Cairo, Egypt 1942.

DALAIL AL-NUBUWWAH, by Abu Bakr Ahmad b. Husain Al-Baihaqi (d. 1066 AD, Iran), Publisher; DAR AL-KUTUB AL-ILMIYYAH, Beirut, Lebanon, and DAR AL-RAYYAN LI AL-TURATH, Cairo, Egypt, first edition 1988.

DIWAN ABU TALIB, by Dr. Muhammad Al-Tunji, Publisher; DAR AL-KITAB AL-ARABI, Beirut, Lebanon, first edition 1994.

FAWAID IBN SHAHIN, by Abu Hafs Umar b. Ahmad Al-Baghdadi (d. 995 AD, Iraq), Publisher; DAR IBN ATHIR, Kuwait, first edition 1994.

HILYAT AL-AWLIA WA TABAQAT AL-ASFIA, by Abu Nuaim Ahmad b. Abdullah Al-Asbahani (d. 1038 AD, Iran), Publisher; MAKTABAH AL-KHANJI, Cairo, Egypt, and DARK AL-FIKAR, Beirut, Lebanon, 1996.

HILYAT AL-AWLIA WA TABAQAT AL-ASFIA, by Abu Nuaim Ahmad b. Abdullah Al-Asbahani (d. 1038 AD, Iran), Publisher; DAR AL-KUTUB AL-ILMIYYAH, Beirut, Lebanon, 1988.

IMTA' AL-ASMA' BIMA LI AL-NABIYYI MIN AL-AHWAL WA AL-AMWAL WA AL-HAFADAT WA AL-MATA', by Ahmad b. Ali Al-Maqrizi (d. 1442 AD, Cairo), Publisher, DAR AL-KUTUB AL-ILMIYYAH, Beirut, Lebanon, first edition 1999.

JAME' AL-BAYAN 'AN TA'WIL AYI AL-QURAN, by Muhammad b. Jarir Al-Tabari (d. 923 AD, Iraq), Publisher; DAR HAJR, Cairo, Egypt, first edition 2001.

JAMHARAT ANSAB AL-ARAB, by Abu Muhammad Ali b. Ahmad Ibn Hazm Al-Andalusi (d. 1064 AD, Spain), Publisher; DAR AL-MA'ARIF, Cairo, Egypt, 1982.

JAWAME' AL-SIRAH AL-NABAWIYYAH, by Abu Muhammad Ali b. Ahmad Ibn Hazm Al-Andalusi (d. 1064 AD, Spain), DAR KUTUB AL-ILMIYYAH, Beirut, Lebanon, first edition 2003.

KITAB AL-AMALI, by Yahya b. Al-Husain Al-Shajari Al-Jurjani (d.1105 AD, Iran), Publisher; DAR AL-KUTUB AL-ILMIYYAH, Beirut, Lebanon, first edition 2001.

KITAB AL-DU'A, by Abu Al-Qasim Sulaiman b. Ayub Al-Tabarani (d. 918 AD, Iran), Publisher; DAR AL-BASHAIR AL-ISLAMIYYAH, Beirut, Lebanon, first edition 1987.

KITAB AL-ZUHD WA AL-RAQAIQ, by Abdullah b. Mubarak Al-Marwazi (d. 797 AD, Turkemnistan/Iraq), Publisher; DAR AL-ME'RAJ AL-DAWLIYYAH, Riyad, KSA, first edition 1995.

MA'ALIM AL-TANZIL, by Abu Muhammad Husain b. Masud Al-Baghawi (d. 1122 AD, Iran), Publisher; DAR TAYBAH, Riyadh, KSA, 1992.

MA'RIFAT AL-SAHABA, by Abu Nuaim Abdullah b. Ahmad Al-Asbahani (d. 1038 AD, Iran), Publisher; DAR AL-WATAN, Riyadh, KSA, first edition 1998.

MAFATIH AL-GHAIB, by Fakhruddin Abu Abdullah Muhammad b. Umar Al-Razi (d. 1210 AD, Iran/Afghanistan), Publisher; DAR AL-FIKAR, Beirut, Lebanon, 1981.

MAJMA' AL-AMTHAL, by Abu Al-Fadl Ahmad b. Muhammad Al-Midani (d. 1124 AD, Iran), p 374, V 1, Publisher; MATBA'AH AL-SUNNAH AL-MUHAMMADIYYAH, Cairo, Egypt, 1955.

MUSANNAF IBN ABU SHAYBAH, by Abu Bakr Muhammad b. Abdullah Ibn Abu Shaybah (d. 849 AD, Iraq), Publisher; DAR AL-QIBLAH LI AL-THAQAFAH AL-ISLAMIYYAH, Jeddah, KSA, first edition 2006.

MUSANNAF IBN ABU SHAYBAH, by Abu Bakr Muhammad b. Abdullah Ibn Abu Shaybah (d. 849 AD, Iraq), Publisher; AL-FARUQ AL-HADITHAH, Cairo, Egypt, first edition 2008.

MUSANNAF IBN ABU SHAYBAH, by Abu Bakr Muhammad b. Abdullah Ibn Abu Shaybah (d. 849 AD, Iraq), Publisher; MAKTABAT AL-RUSHD NARHIRUN, Riyadh, KSA, first edition 2004.

MUSNAD ABU AWANAH, by Abu Awanah Yaqub b. Ibrahim Al-Isfaraini (d. 928 AD, Iran), Publisher; DAR AL-MA'RIFAH, Beirut, Lebanon, first edition 1998.

MUSNAD ABU HANIFAH, by Sadruddin Musa b. Zakariya Al-Haskafi (d. 1252 AD, Turkey), with its commentary AL-MAWAHIB AL-LATIFAH SHARH MUSNAD ABI HANIFAH, by Muhammad Abid b. Ahmad Al-Ansari (d. 1841 AD, India/Madinah), Publisher; DAR AL-NAWADIR, Damascus, Syria, first edition 2013.

MUSNAD ABU YA'LA, by Abu Ya'la Ahmad b. Ali Al-Mausilli (d. 919 AD Iraq), Publisher; DAR AL-MA'MUN, Damascus, Syria, second edition 1989.

MUSNAD ABU YA'LA, by Abu Ya'la Ahmad b. Ali Al-Mausilli (d. 919 AD Iraq), Publisher; DAR AL-MA'MUN, Damascus, Syria, first edition 1988.

MUSNAD AHMAD, by Abu Abdullah Ahmad b. Muhammad b. Hanbal Al-Marwazi (d.855, Iraq), Publisher; MUASSASAH AL-RISALAH, Beirut, Lebanon, first edition 2001.

MUSNAD AHMAD, by Abu Abdullah Ahmad b. Muhammad b. Hanbal Al-Marwazi (d.855, Iraq), Publisher; Publisher; DAR AL-HADITH, Cairo, Egypt, first edition 1995.

MUSNAD AL-SHIHAB AL-QUDA'I, by Abu Abdullah Muhammad b. Salamah Al-Quda'i (d. 1062 AD, Egypt), Published; MUASSASAH AL-RISALAH, Beirut, Lebanon, first edition 1985.

MUSNAD IBN ABU SHAYBAH, by Abu Bakr Muhammad b. Abdullah Ibn Abu Shaybah (d. 849 AD, Iraq), Publisher; DAR AL-WATAN, Riyadh, KSA, first edition 1997.

MUSTARDAK ALA AL-SAHIHAIN, by Abu Abdullah Muhammad b. Abdullah Al-Nisapuri (d 1012 AD, Iran), Publisher; DAR AL-KUTUB AL-ILMIYYAH, second edition 2002.

MUSTARDAK ALA AL-SAHIHAIN, by Abu Abdullah Muhammad b. Abdullah Al-Nisapuri (d 1012 AD, Iran), Publisher; DAR AL-HARAMAIN, Cairo, Egypt, first edition 1997

MUSTARDAK ALA AL-SAHIHAIN, by Abu Abdullah Muhammad b. Abdullah Al-Nisapuri (d 1012 AD, Iran), Publisher; DAR AL-KUTUB AL-ILMIYYAH, second edition 2002.

SAHIH IBN KHUZAIMA, by Abu Bakr Muhammad bin Ishaq Ibn Khuzaimah (d. 923 AD, Iran), Publisher; AL-MAKTAB AL-ISLAMI, Beirut, Lebanon, 2003.

SAHIH MUSLIM, by Abu Al-Husain Muslim b. Hajjaj Al-Nisapuri (d. 875 AD, Iran), Publisher; DAR TAYBAH, Riyadh, KSA, first edition 2006.

SAHIH TIRMIDHI, by Abu Isa Muhammad b. Isa Al-Tirmidhi (d. 892 AD, Uzbekistan), Publisher; DAR AL-GHARB AL-ISLAMI, Beirut, Lebanon, first edition 1996.

SHAMAIL MUHAMMADIYAH, by Abu Isa Muhammad b. Isa Al-Tirmidhi (d. 892 AD, Uzbekistan), Publisher; DAR AL-HADITH, Beirut, Lebanon, third edition 1998.

SHAMAIL MUHAMMADIYYAH, by Abu Isa Muhammad b. Isa Al-Tirmidhi (d. 892 AD, Uzbekistan), Publisher; MAKTABAH AL-ULUM WA AL-HIKAM, Cairo, Egypt, first edition 2008.

SHARH USUL I'TIQAD AHL AL-SUNNAH WA AL-JAMA'AH, by Abu Al-Qasim Hibatullah b. Hasan Al-Razi Al-Lalikai (d. 1027 AD, Iran), Publisher; Umm Al-Qura University, Mecca, KSA.

SHUAB AL-IMAN, by Abu Bakr Ahmad b. Husain Al-Baihaqi (d. 1066 AD, Iran), Publisher; MAKTABAH AL-RUSHD LI AL-NASHR WA AL-TAWZEA, Riyadh, KSA, first edition 2003.

SIAR A'LAAM AL-NUBALA, by Shamsuddin Al-Dhahabi (d. 1348 AD, Syria), Publisher; DAR AL-KUTUB AL-ISLAMI, Beirut, Lebanon, 2010.

SUNAN ABU DAWUD, by Abu Dawud Sulaiman b. Al-Ash'ath Al-Sijistani (d. 889 AD, Iraq), Publisher; DAR AL-RISALAH AL-ALAMIYYAH, Damascus, Syria, first edition 2009.

SUNAN ABU DAWUD, by Abu Dawud Sulaiman b. Al-Ash'ath Al-Sijistani (d. 889 AD, Iraq), Publisher; DAR AL-RISALAH AL-ALAMIYYAH, Damascus, Syria, first edition 2009.

SUNAN AL-NASAI, by Abu Abdul-Rahman Ahmad b. Shuaib Al-Nasai (d. 915 AD Mecca/Turkmenistan), Publisher; Ministry of religious affairs, KSA, 1999.

SUNAN DARIMI, by Abdullah b. Abdul-Rahaman Al-Darimi (d 869 AD, Uzbekistan), Publisher; DAR AL-BASHAIR AL-ISLAMIYYAH, Beirut, Lebanon, first edition 2013.

SUNAN IBN MAJAH, by Abu Abdullah Muhammad b. Yazid Al-Qazwini (d 887 AD, Iran), Publisher; DAR IHYAA AL-KUTUB AL- ARABIYYAH, Cairo, Egypt, year 1952.

SUNAN IBN MAJAH, by Abu Abdullah Muhammad b. Yazid Al-Qazwini (d 887 AD, Iran), Publisher; DAR IHYAA AL-KUTUB AL- ARABIYYAH, Cairo, Egypt, year 1952.

TARIKH AL-MULUK WA AL-RUSUL,by Muhammad b. Jarir Al-Tabari (d. 923 AD, Iraq), Publisher; DAR AL-MA'ARIF, Cairo, Egypt, second edition 1967.

TARIKH AL-MULUK WA AL-RUSUL,by Muhammad b. Jarir Al-Tabari (d. 923 AD, Iraq), Publisher; DAR AL-MA'ARIF, Cairo, Egypt, second edition 1967.

TARIKH MADINAT DIMISHQ, by Abu Al-Qasim Ali b. Hasan Ibn Asakir Al-Dimishqi (d. 1176 AD, Syria), Publisher; DAR AL-FIKAR, Beirut, Lebanon, 1995.
USUD AL-GHABAH FI MA'RIFAT AL-SAHABAH, by Abu Al-Hasan Ali b. Muhammad Al-Jazari (d. 1233 AD, Iraq) Publisher; DAR AL-KUTUB AL-ILMIYYAH, Beirut, Lebanon, first edition 1996.

USUD AL-GHABAH FI MA'RIFAT AL-SAHABAH, by Abu Al-Hasan Ali b. Muhammad Al-Jazari (d. 1233 AD, Iraq), Publisher; DAR AL-KUTUB AL-ILMIYYAH, Beirut, Lebanon, first edition 1996.

References

[1]AL-MUSNAD AL-JAME', by Abdullah b. Abdul-Rahaman Al-Darimi (d 869 AD, Uzbekistan), chapter; HUSN MU'ASHARAH AL-NISA, N; 2439, Narrator; Aisha RA p 539, published by DAR AL-BASHAIR AL-ISLAMIYYAH, Beirut, Lebanon, first edition 2013.

SAHIH TIRMIDHI, by Abu Isa Muhammad b. Isa Al-Tirmidhi (d 892 AD, Uzbekistan), chapter; FI FADHL AZWAJ AL-NABI, N; 3895, Narrator; Aisha RA, p 188 V 6, published by DAR AL-GHARB AL-ISLAMI, Beirut, Lebanon, First edition 1996.

SUNAN DARIMI, by Abdullah b. Abdul-Rahaman Al-Darimi (d 869 AD, Uzbekistan), chapter; HUSN MU'ASHARAH AL-NISA, N; 2439, Narrator; Aisha RA p 539, published by DAR AL-BASHAIR AL-ISLAMIYYAH, Beirut, Lebanon, first edition 2013.

SUNAN IBN MAJAH, by Abu Abdullah Muhammad b. Yazid Al-Qazwini (d 887 AD, Iran), chapter; KITAB AL-NIKAH, BAAB HUSN MU'ASHARAH AL-NISA, Narrator; Abdullah b. Abbas, p 636 V 1, publisher; DAR IHYAA AL-KUTUB AL- ARABIYYAH, Cairo, Egypt, year 1952.

MUSTARDAK ALA AL-SAHIHAIN, by Abu Abdullah Muhammad b. Abdullah Al-Nisapuri (d 1012 AD, Iran), chapter; KITAB AL-BIRR WA AL-SILAH, N; 7327/88, Narrator; Abdullah b. Abbas, p 191 V 4, publisher; DAR AL-KUTUB AL-ILMIYYAH, second edition 2002.

[2]USUD AL-GHABAH FI MA'RIFAT AL-SAHABAH, by Abu Al-Hasan Ali b. Muhammad Al-Jazari (d. 1233 AD, Iraq), p 123 V 1, Publisher; DAR AL-KUTUB AL-ILMIYYAH, Beirut, Lebanon, first edition 1996.

[3]JAMHARAT ANSAB AL-ARAB, by Abu Muhammad Ali b. Ahmad Ibn Hazm Al-Andalusi (d. 1064 AD, Spain), p 16, Chapter; NASAB ABDULLAH BIN ABDUL-MUTTALIB, Publisher; DAR AL-MA'ARIF, Cairo, Egypt, 1982.

JAWAME' AL-SIRAH AL-NABAWIYYAH, by Abu Muhammad Ali b. Ahmad Ibn Hazm Al-Andalusi (d. 1064 AD, Spain), p 128, Narrator; Urwah b. Zubair, Narrator; DAR KUTUB AL-ILMIYYAH, Beirut, Lebanon, first edition 2003.

TARIKH MADINAT DIMISHQ, by Abu Al-Qasim Ali b. Hasan Ibn Asakir Al-Dimishqi (d. 1176 AD, Syria), Narrator; Urwah RA, p 172 V 3, Publisher; DAR AL-FIKAR, Beirut, Lebanon, 1995.

[4]AL-SIRAH AL-NABAWIYYAH, by Abu Muhammad Abdulmalik b. Hisham Al-Himyari (d. 833 AD, Egypt), Narrator; Halimah, p 189 V 1, Publisher DAR AL-KITAB AL-ARABI, Beirut, Lebanon, third edition 1990.

[5] - DALAIL AL-NUBUWWAH, by Abu Bakr Ahmad b. Husain Al-Baihaqi (d. 1066 AD, Iran), chapter; BAAB DHIKR RIDA' AL-NABI SALLALLAHU ALAIHI WA SALLAM WA MURDI'ATUHU WA HADINATUHU, Narrator; Halimah bt. Al-Harith Al-S''diyyah, p 134, V 1, publisher; DAR AL-KUTUB

AL-ILMIYYAH, Beirut, Lebanon, and DAR AL-RAYYAN LI AL-TURATH, Cairo, Egypt, first edition 1988.

- AL-IHSAN FI TAQRIB SAHIH IBN HIBBAN, by Abu Hatim Muhammad b. Faisal Al-Busti (d. 965 AD, Afghanistan), N; 6335, Chapter; DHIKR SHAQQ JIBRIL ALAHISSALAM SADRA AL-MUSTAFA SALLALLAHU ALAIHI WA SALLAM FI SIBAHU, p 246 V 14, Publisher; MUASSASAH AL-RISALAH, Beirut, Lebanon, second edition 1993.

- MUSNAD ABU YA'LA, by Abu Ya'la Ahmad b. Ali Al-Mausilli (d. 919 AD Iraq), Narrator; Halimah Al-Sa'diyyah, N; 7163, p 93 V 13, Publisher; DAR AL-MA'MUN, Damascus, Syria, first edition 1988.

- AL-SIRAH AL-NABAWIYYAH, by Abu Muhammad Abdulmalik b. Hisham Al-Himyari (d. 833 AD, Egypt), Narrator; Halimah, p 189 V 1, Publisher DAR AL-KITAB AL-ARABI, Beirut, Lebanon, third edition 1990.

[6] ibid

[7]AL-TABAQAT AL-KABIR, by Muhammad b. Sa'd Al-Baghdadi (d. 845 AD, Iraq), p 92 V 1, Publisher; DAR AL-KUTUB AL-ILMIYYAH, Beirut, Lebanon, first edition 1990.

[8]SUNAN ABU DAWUD, by Abu Dawud Sulaiman b. Al-Ash'ath Al-Sijistani (d. 889 AD, Iraq), Narrator; Abu Tufail, p 457 V 7, Publisher; DAR AL-RISALAH AL-ALAMIYYAH, Damascus, Syria, first edition 2009.

AL-BAHR AL-ZAKHKHAR Abu Bakr Ahmad b. Amr Al-Bazzar (d. 905 AD, Iraq), Narrator; Abu Al-Tufail Aamir b. Wathilah, N; 2781, p 208 V 7, publisher; MAKTABAH AL-ULUM WA AL-HIKAM, Madinah, KSA, first edition 1995.

AL-ADAB AL-MUFRAD, by Abu Abdullah Muhammad b. Ismael Al-Bukhari (d. 870 AD, Uzbekistan), Narrator; Abu Al-Tufail, p 473, Publisher DAR AL-SIDDIQ, Al-Jubail, KSA, second edition 2000.

[9]SUNAN ABU DAWUD, by Abu Dawud Sulaiman b. Al-Ash'ath Al-Sijistani (d. 889 AD, Iraq), Narrator; Umar b. Al-Saeb, p 457 V 7, Publisher; DAR AL-RISALAH AL-ALAMIYYAH, Damascus, Syria, first edition 2009.

DALAIL AL-NUBUWWAH, by Abu Bakr Ahmad b. Husain Al-Baihaqi (d. 1066 AD, Iran), chapter; BAAB WUFUD WAFD HAWAZAN ALA AL-NABI SALLALLAHU ALAIHI WA SALLAM WA HUWA BI AL-JEIRRANAH MUSLIMIN WA RADD AL-NABI SALLALLAHU ALAIHI WA SALLAM ALAIHIM SABAYAHUM, Narrator; Umar b. Al-Saib, p 200, V 5, publisher; DAR AL-KUTUB AL-ILMIYYAH, Beirut, Lebanon, and DAR AL-RAYYAN LI AL-TURATH, Cairo, Egypt, first edition 1988.

[10]USUD AL-GHABAH FI MA'RIFAT AL-SAHABAH, by Abu Al-Hasan Ali b. Muhammad Al-Jazari (d. 1233 AD, Iraq), p 291 V 7, Publisher; DAR AL-KUTUB AL-ILMIYYAH, Beirut, Lebanon, first edition 1996.

AL-ISABAH FI TAMYEEZ AL-SAHABAH, by Shihabuddin Ahmad b. Nuriddin Ibn Hajar Al-Asqallani (d. 1449 AD, Egypt), p 178 V 13, Publisher; MAKTABAH IBN TAIMIYYAH, Cairo, Egypt, 1993.

AL-TABAQAT AL-KABIR, by Muhammad b. Sa'd Al-Baghdadi (d. 845 AD, Iraq), p 212 V 10, Publisher; MAKTABAH AL-KHANJI, Cairo, Egypt, year 2001.

[11]AL-ISABAH FI TAMYEEZ AL-SAHABAH, by Shihabuddin Ahmad b. Nuriddin Ibn Hajar Al-Asqallani (d. 1449 AD, Egypt), p 178 V 13, Publisher; MAKTABAH IBN TAIMIYYAH, Cairo, Egypt, 1993.

AL-TABAQAT AL-KABIR, by Muhammad b. Sa'd Al-Baghdadi (d. 845 AD, Iraq), p 212 V 10, Publisher; MAKTABAH AL-KHANJI, Cairo, Egypt, year 2001.

[12]AL-ISABAH FI TAMYEEZ AL-SAHABAH, by Shihabuddin Ahmad b. Nuriddin Ibn Hajar Al-Asqallani (d. 1449 AD, Egypt), p 178 V 13, Publisher; MAKTABAH IBN TAIMIYYAH, Cairo, Egypt, 1993

AL-TABAQAT AL-KABIR, by Muhammad b. Sa'd Al-Baghdadi (d. 845 AD, Iraq), p 213 V 10, Publisher; MAKTABAH AL-KHANJI, Cairo, Egypt, year 2001.

[13]AL-ISABAH FI TAMYEEZ AL-SAHABAH, by Shihabuddin Ahmad b. Nuriddin Ibn Hajar Al-Asqallani (d. 1449 AD, Egypt), p 179 V 13, Publisher; MAKTABAH IBN TAIMIYYAH, Cairo, Egypt, 1993

SAHIH MUSLIM, by Abu Al-Husain Muslim b. Hajjaj Al-Nisapuri (d. 875 AD, Iran), Narrator; Anas RA, p1147 V 2, Publisher; DAR TAYBAH, Riyadh, KSA, first edition 2006.

[14]SAHIH MUSLIM, by Abu Al-Husain Muslim b. Hajjaj Al-Nisapuri (d. 875 AD, Iran), Narrator; Anas RA, p 1147 V 2, Publisher; DAR TAYBAH, Riyadh, KSA, first edition 2006.

SUNAN IBN MAJAH, by Abu Abdullah Muhammad b. Yazid Al-Qazwini (d 887 AD, Iran), chapter; KITAB AL-JANAIZ, N; 1635 Narrator; Anas, p 573 V 1, publisher; DAR IHYAA AL-KUTUB AL-ARABIYYAH, Cairo, Egypt, year 1952.

AL-TABAQAT AL-KABIR, by Muhammad b. Sa'd Al-Baghdadi (d. 845 AD, Iraq), p 215 V 10, Publisher; MAKTABAH AL-KHANJI, Cairo, Egypt, year 2001.

AL-ISABAH FI TAMYEEZ AL-SAHABAH, by Shihabuddin Ahmad b. Nuriddin Ibn Hajar Al-Asqallani (d. 1449 AD, Egypt), p 179 V 13, Publisher; MAKTABAH IBN TAIMIYYAH, Cairo, Egypt, 1993.

[15]AL-TABAQAT AL-KABIR, by Muhammad b. Sa'd Al-Baghdadi (d. 845 AD, Iraq), Narrator; Abdullah b. Abbas, p 98 V 1, Publisher; MAKTABAH AL-KHANJI, Cairo, Egypt, year 2001.

[16]HILYAT AL-AWLIA WA TABAQAT AL-ASFIA, by Abu Nuaim Ahmad b. Abdullah Al-Asbahani (d. 1038 AD, Iran), Narrator Anas RA, p 121 V 3, Publisher; MAKTABAH AL-KHANJI, Cairo, Egypt, and DARK AL-FIKAR, Beirut, Lebanon, 1996.

AL-MU'JAM AL-AWSAT, by Abu Al-Qasim Sulaiman b. Ayub Al-Tabarani (d. 918 AD, Iran), Narrator; Anas, p 189 V 1, Publisher; DAR AL-HARAMAIN, Cairo, Egypt, 1995.

[17]MA'RIFAT AL-SAHABA, by Abu Nuaim Abdullah b. Ahmad Al-Asbahani (d. 1038 AD, Iran), Narrator; Abdullah b. Abbas, p 77 V 1, Publisher; DAR AL-WATAN, Riyadh, KSA, first edition 1998.

AL-MU'JAM AL-AWSAT, by Abu Al-Qasim Sulaiman b. Ayub Al-Tabarani (d. 918 AD, Iran), Narrator; Abdullah b. Abbas, p 87 V 7, Publisher; DAR AL-HARAMAIN, Cairo, Egypt, 1995.

[18] MUSTARDAK ALA AL-SAHIHAIN, by Abu Abdullah Muhammad b. Abdullah Al-Nisapuri (d 1012 AD, Iran), chapter; MANAQIB AMIR AL-MUMININ ALI BIN ABI TALIB RADIYALLAHU ANHU, N;4572/170, Narrator; Ali, p 116 V 3, publisher; DAR AL-KUTUB AL-ILMIYYAH, second edition 2002.

HILYAT AL-AWLIA WA TABAQAT AL-ASFIA, by Abu Nuaim Ahmad b. Abdullah Al-Asbahani (d. 1038 AD, Iran), Narrator Anas RA, p 121 V 3, Publisher; MAKTABAH AL-KHANJI, Cairo, Egypt, and DARK AL-FIKAR, Beirut, Lebanon, 1996.

[19]AL-TABAQAT AL-KABIR, by Muhammad b. Sa'd Al-Baghdadi (d. 845 AD, Iraq), Narrator; Abdullah b. Abbas, p 98 V 1, Publisher; MAKTABAH AL-KHANJI, Cairo, Egypt, year 2001.

[20] Ibid

[21]AL-KHASAIS AL-KUBRA, by Jalaluddin Abdul-Rahman b. Abu Bakr Al-Suyuti (d. 1505 AD, Egypt), Narrator; Jalhamah b. Arfatah, p 310 V 1, Publisher; DAR AL-KUTUB AL-HADITHAH, Cairo, Egypt.

The poem is attributed to Abu Talib in few other sources such as;

AL-JAME' AL-SAHIH, by Abu Abdullah Muhammad b. Ismael Al-Bukhari (d. 870 AD, Uzbekistan), p 245, Publisher DAR IBN KATHIR, Damascus, Syria, first edition 2002.

MUSANNAF IBN ABU SHAYBAH, by Abu Bakr Muhammad b. Abdullah Ibn Abu Shaybah (d. 849 AD, Iraq), Narrator; Aisha RA, p 310 V 14, Publisher; DAR AL-QIBLAH LI AL-THAQAFAH AL-ISLAMIYYAH, Jeddah, KSA, first edition 2006

[22]AL-TABAQAT AL-KABIR, by Muhammad b. Sa'd Al-Baghdadi (d. 845 AD, Iraq), Narrator; Abu Mujliz, p 99 V 1, Publisher; MAKTABAH AL-KHANJI, Cairo, Egypt, year 2001.

AL-SIRAH AL-NABAWIYYAH, by Abu Muhammad Abdulmalik b. Hisham Al-Himyari (d. 833 AD, Egypt), p 207 V 1, Publisher DAR AL-KITAB AL-ARABI, Beirut, Lebanon, third edition 1990.

AL-TABAQAT AL-KABIR, by Muhammad b. Sa'd Al-Baghdadi (d. 845 AD, Iraq), Narrator; Dawud b. Al-Husain, p 99 V 1, Publisher; MAKTABAH AL-KHANJI, Cairo, Egypt, year 2001.

[23]AL-JAME' AL-SAHIH, by Abu Abdullah Muhammad b. Ismael Al-Bukhari (d. 870 AD, Uzbekistan), Narrator; Abu Hurairah, p 539, Publisher DAR IBN KATHIR, Damascus, Syria, first edition 2002.

AL-SIRAH AL-NABAWIYYAH, by Abu Muhammad Abdulmalik b. Hisham Al-Himyari (d. 833 AD, Egypt), p 191 V 1, Publisher DAR AL-KITAB AL-ARABI, Beirut, Lebanon, third edition 1990.

AL-TABAQAT AL-KABIR, by Muhammad b. Sa'd Al-Baghdadi (d. 845 AD, Iraq), p 103 V 1, Publisher; MAKTABAH AL-KHANJI, Cairo, Egypt, year 2001

[24] MUSTARDAK ALA AL-SAHIHAIN, by Abu Abdullah Muhammad b. Abdullah Al-Nisapuri (d 1012 AD, Iran), chapter; KITAB MA'RIFAT AL-SAHABAH, N; 4424, Narrator; Mujahid b Jabr, p 709 V 3, publisher; DAR AL-HARAMAIN, Cairo, Egypt, first edition 1997

DALAIL AL-NUBUWWAH, by Abu Bakr Ahmad b. Husain Al-Baihaqi (d. 1066 AD, Iran), Narrator; Mujahid b. Jabr, p 162, V 2, publisher; DAR AL-KUTUB AL-ILMIYYAH, Beirut, Lebanon, and DAR AL-RAYYAN LI AL-TURATH, Cairo, Egypt, first edition 1988.

[25] MUSNAD AL-SHIHAB AL-QUDA'I, by Abu Abdullah Muhammad b. Salamah Al-Quda'i (d. 1062 AD, Egypt), Narrator; Anas b. Malik, p. 103 V 1, Published; MUASSASAH AL-RISALAH, Beirut, Lebanon, first edition 1985.
AL-SUNAN AL-KUBRA, by Abu Abdul-Rahman Ahmad b. Shuaib Al-Nasai (d. 915 AD Mecca/Turkmenistan), Narrator; Abu Mu'awiyah Jahimah Al-Sulami RA, p 489 V 2, Publisher; MUASSASAT AL-RISALAH, Beirut, Lebanon, first edition 2001.
[26] Surah 31- Luqman; 14
[27] DALAIL AL-NUBUWWAH, by Abu Bakr Ahmad b. Husain Al-Baihaqi (d. 1066 AD, Iran), chapter;BAAB WAFAT ABDULLAH ABI RASULULLAH WA WAFAT AMINA BINT WAHB WA WAFAT JADDIHI ABDUL-MUTTALIB BIN HASHIM, p 189, V 1, publisher; DAR AL-KUTUB AL-ILMIYYAH, Beirut, Lebanon, and DAR AL-RAYYAN LI AL-TURATH, Cairo, Egypt, first edition 1988.

[28] DALAIL AL-NUBUWWAH, by Abu Bakr Ahmad b. Husain Al-Baihaqi (d. 1066 AD, Iran), chapter;BAAB WAFAT ABDULLAH ABI RASULULLAH WA WAFAT AMINA BINT WAHB WA WAFAT JADDIHI ABDUL-MUTTALIB BIN HASHIM, Narrator; Abdullah b. Masud, p 189, V 1, publisher; DAR AL-KUTUB AL-ILMIYYAH, Beirut, Lebanon, and DAR AL-RAYYAN LI AL-TURATH, Cairo, Egypt, first edition 1988.

AL-AMALI, by Yahya b. Al-Husain Al-Shajari Al-Jurjani Al-Husaini (d. 1105 AD), N; 2946, p 414 V 2, publisher; Dar Al-Kutub Al-Ilmiyyah, Beirut, Lebanon, first edition 2001.

[29] MUSTARDAK ALA AL-SAHIHAIN, by Abu Abdullah Muhammad b. Abdullah Al-Nisapuri (d. 1012 AD, Iran), chapter; KITAB AL-JANAIZ, N; 1389/125, Narrator; Abdullah b. Abbas, p 531 V 1, publisher; DAR AL-KUTUB AL-ILMIYYAH, second edition 2002.

DALAIL AL-NUBUWWAH, by Abu Bakr Ahmad b. Husain Al-Baihaqi (d. 1066 AD, Iran), chapter; WAFAT ABDULLAH ABI RASULULLAH, WA WAFAT AMINAH BINT WAHB, WA WAFAT JADDIHI ABDUL-MUTTALIB BIN HASHIM, p 190, V 1, publisher; DAR AL-KUTUB AL-ILMIYYAH, Beirut, Lebanon, and DAR AL-RAYYAN LI AL-TURATH, Cairo, Egypt, first edition 1988.

SHUAB AL-IMAN, by Abu Bakr Ahmad b. Husain Al-Baihaqi (d. 1066 AD, Iran), chapter; ZIYARAT AL-QUBUR, p 470, V 11, publisher; MAKTABAH AL-RUSHD LI AL-NASHR WA AL-TAWZEA, Riyadh, KSA, first edition 2003.

[30] MUSTARDAK ALA AL-SAHIHAIN, by Abu Abdullah Muhammad b. Abdullah Al-Nisapuri (d 1012 AD, Iran), chapter; KITAB AL-JANAIZ, N; 1389/125, Narrator; Buraidah, p 531 V 1, publisher; DAR AL-KUTUB AL-ILMIYYAH, second edition 2002.

AL-KAMIL FI AL-DHU'AFAA, by Abu Ahmad b. Adi Al-Jurjani, (d. 976 AD, Iran), chapter; TARJUMAT YAYHA BIN AL-YAMAN AL-IJLI AL-KUFI, p 236 V 7, publisher DAR AL-FIKAR LI AL-TIBA'AH WA AL-NASHR WA AL-TAWZI', Berut, Lebanon, second edition 1985.

AL-BAHR AL-ZAKHKHAR Abu Bakr Ahmad b. Amr Al-Bazzar (d. 905 AD, Iraq), Narrator; Buraidah b. Al-Hasib, N; 4373, p 272 V 10, publisher; MAKTABAH AL-ULUM WA AL-HIKAM, Madinah, KSA, first edition 2003.

[31]AL-SIRAH AL-NABAWIYYAH, by Abu Muhammad Abdulmalik b. Hisham Al-Himyari (d. 833 AD, Egypt), p 127 V 1, Publisher DAR AL-KITAB AL-ARABI, Beirut, Lebanon, third edition 1990.

AL-MUNTADHAM FI TARIKH AL-MULUK WA AL-UMAM, by Abu Al-Faraj Abdul-Rahman b. Ali Ibn Al-Jawzi (d. 1200 AD, Iraq), p 237 V 2, Publisher; DAR AL-KUTUB AL-ILMIYYAH, Beirut, Lebanon, first edition 1992.

[32]AL-SIRAH AL-NABAWIYYAH, by Abu Muhammad Abdulmalik b. Hisham Al-Himyari (d. 833 AD, Egypt), p 127 V 1, Publisher DAR AL-KITAB AL-ARABI, Beirut, Lebanon, third edition 1990.

[33]AL-SIRAH AL-NABAWIYYAH, by Abu Muhammad Abdulmalik b. Hisham Al-Himyari (d. 833 AD, Egypt), p 126 V 1, Publisher DAR AL-KITAB AL-ARABI, Beirut, Lebanon, third edition 1990.

AL-MUNTADHAM FI TARIKH AL-MULUK WA AL-UMAM, by Abu Al-Faraj Abdul-Rahman b. Ali Ibn Al-Jawzi (d. 1200 AD, Iraq), p 198 V 2, Publisher; DAR AL-KUTUB AL-ILMIYYAH, Beirut, Lebanon, first edition 1992.

[34]JAWAME' AL-SIRAH AL-NABAWIYYAH, by Abu Muhammad Ali b. Ahmad Ibn Hazm Al-Andalusi (d. 1064 AD, Spain), p 9, DAR KUTUB AL-ILMIYYAH, Beirut, Lebanon, first edition 2003.

AL-MUNTADHAM FI TARIKH AL-MULUK WA AL-UMAM, by Abu Al-Faraj Abdul-Rahman b. Ali Ibn Al-Jawzi (d. 1200 AD, Iraq), p 204 V 2, Publisher; DAR AL-KUTUB AL-ILMIYYAH, Beirut, Lebanon, first edition 1992.

[35]AL-MUNTADHAM FI TARIKH AL-MULUK WA AL-UMAM, by Abu Al-Faraj Abdul-Rahman b. Ali Ibn Al-Jawzi (d. 1200 AD, Iraq), p 205 V 2, Publisher; DAR AL-KUTUB AL-ILMIYYAH, Beirut, Lebanon, first edition 1992.

[36]AL-TABAQAT AL-KABIR, by Muhammad b. Sa'd Al-Baghdadi (d. 845 AD, Iraq), p 96 V 1, Publisher; MAKTABAH AL-KHANJI, Cairo, Egypt, year 2001.

[37] DALAIL AL-NUBUWWAH, by Abu Bakr Ahmad b. Husain Al-Baihaqi (d. 1066 AD, Iran), chapter; BAAB MA JAA FI SHAFAQAT ABDUL-MUTTALIB BIN HASHIM ALA RASULILLAH SALLALLAHU ALAIHI WA SALLAM, Narrator; Kandir b. Said p 20, V 2, publisher; DAR AL-KUTUB AL-ILMIYYAH, Beirut, Lebanon, and DAR AL-RAYYAN LI AL-TURATH, Cairo, Egypt, first edition 1988.

[38]AL-SIRAH AL-NABAWIYYAH, by Abu Muhammad Abdulmalik b. Hisham Al-Himyari (d. 833 AD, Egypt), p 194 V 1, Publisher DAR AL-KITAB AL-ARABI, Beirut, Lebanon, third edition 1990.

AL-TABAQAT AL-KABIR, by Muhammad b. Sa'd Al-Baghdadi (d. 845 AD, Iraq), p 96 V 1, Publisher; MAKTABAH AL-KHANJI, Cairo, Egypt, year 2001.

AL-SIRAH AL-NABAWIYYAH, by Abu Bakr Muhammad b. Ishaq Al-Madani (d. 768 AD, Madinah/Iraq), p 116 V 1, Publisher; DAR AL-KUTUB AL-ILMIYYAH, Beirut, Lebanon, first edition 2004.

[39]AL-TABAQAT AL-KABIR, by Muhammad b. Sa'd Al-Baghdadi (d. 845 AD, Iraq), p 97 V 1, Publisher; MAKTABAH AL-KHANJI, Cairo, Egypt, year 2001.

[40]AL-SIRAH AL-NABAWIYYAH, by Abu Muhammad Abdulmalik b. Hisham Al-Himyari (d. 833 AD, Egypt), p 194 V 1, Publisher DAR AL-KITAB AL-ARABI, Beirut, Lebanon, third edition 1990.

AL-SIRAH AL-NABAWIYYAH, by Abu Bakr Muhammad b. Ishaq Al-Madani (d. 768 AD, Madinah/Iraq), p 116 V 1, Publisher; DAR AL-KUTUB AL-ILMIYYAH, Beirut, Lebanon, first edition 2004.

[41]AL-SIRAH AL-NABAWIYYAH, by Abu Muhammad Abdulmalik b. Hisham Al-Himyari (d. 833 AD, Egypt), p 194 V 1, Publisher DAR AL-KITAB AL-ARABI, Beirut, Lebanon, third edition 1990.

AL-SIRAH AL-NABAWIYYAH, by Abu Bakr Muhammad b. Ishaq Al-Madani (d. 768 AD, Madinah/Iraq), p 116 V 1, Publisher; DAR AL-KUTUB AL-ILMIYYAH, Beirut, Lebanon, first edition 2004.

[42]AL-TABAQAT AL-KABIR, by Muhammad b. Sa'd Al-Baghdadi (d. 845 AD, Iraq), p 96 V 1, Publisher; MAKTABAH AL-KHANJI, Cairo, Egypt, year 2001.

[43]AL-TABAQAT AL-KABIR, by Muhammad b. Sa'd Al-Baghdadi (d. 845 AD, Iraq), p 97 V 1, Publisher; MAKTABAH AL-KHANJI, Cairo, Egypt, year 2001.

[44]AL-TABAQAT AL-KABIR, by Muhammad b. Sa'd Al-Baghdadi (d. 845 AD, Iraq), p 97 V 1, Publisher; MAKTABAH AL-KHANJI, Cairo, Egypt, year 2001.

AL-SIRAH AL-NABAWIYYAH, by Abu Bakr Muhammad b. Ishaq Al-Madani (d. 768 AD, Madinah/Iraq), p 120 V 1, Publisher; DAR AL-KUTUB AL-ILMIYYAH, Beirut, Lebanon, first edition 2004.

[45]AL-TABAQAT AL-KABIR, by Muhammad b. Sa'd Al-Baghdadi (d. 845 AD, Iraq), p 97 V 1, Publisher; MAKTABAH AL-KHANJI, Cairo, Egypt, year 2001.

AL-MUNTADHAM FI TARIKH AL-MULUK WA AL-UMAM, by Abu Al-Faraj Abdul-Rahman b. Ali Ibn Al-Jawzi (d. 1200 AD, Iraq), p 282 V 2, Publisher; DAR AL-KUTUB AL-ILMIYYAH, Beirut, Lebanon, first edition 1992.

[46]AL-SIRAH AL-NABAWIYYAH, by Abu Muhammad Abdulmalik b. Hisham Al-Himyari (d. 833 AD, Egypt), p 194 V 1, Publisher DAR AL-KITAB AL-ARABI, Beirut, Lebanon, third edition 1990.

AL-TABAQAT AL-KABIR, by Muhammad b. Sa'd Al-Baghdadi (d. 845 AD, Iraq), p 97 V 1, Publisher; MAKTABAH AL-KHANJI, Cairo, Egypt, year 2001.

AL-MUNTADHAM FI TARIKH AL-MULUK WA AL-UMAM, by Abu Al-Faraj Abdul-Rahman b. Ali Ibn Al-Jawzi (d. 1200 AD, Iraq), p 282 V 2, Publisher; DAR AL-KUTUB AL-ILMIYYAH, Beirut, Lebanon, first edition 1992.

[47]AL-TABAQAT AL-KABIR, by Muhammad b. Sa'd Al-Baghdadi (d. 845 AD, Iraq), p 34 V 10, Publisher; MAKTABAH AL-KHANJI, Cairo, Egypt, year 2001.

[48] SUNAN IBN MAJAH, by Abu Abdullah Muhammad b. Yazid Al-Qazwini (d 887 AD, Iran), chapter; KITAB AL-JANAIZ, N; 1512 Narrator; Husain b. Ali, p 484 V 1, publisher; DAR IHYAA AL-KUTUB AL- ARABIYYAH, Cairo, Egypt, year 1952.

[49]AL-MU'JAM AL-KABIR, by Abu Al-Qasim Sulaiman b. Ayub Al-Tabarani (d. 918 AD, Iran), Narrator; Zubair b. Bikar b. Da'amah, p 436 V 22, Publisher; MAKTABAH IBN TAIMIYYAH, Cairo, Egypt, 1983.

AL-TABAQAT AL-KABIR, by Muhammad b. Sa'd Al-Baghdadi (d. 845 AD, Iraq), p 37 V 10, Publisher; MAKTABAH AL-KHANJI, Cairo, Egypt, year 2001.

[50]AL-JAME' AL-SAHIH, by Abu Abdullah Muhammad b. Ismael Al-Bukhari (d. 870 AD, Uzbekistan), Narrator; Anas RA, p 311, Publisher DAR IBN KATHIR, Damascus, Syria, first edition 2002.

AL-TABAQAT AL-KABIR, by Muhammad b. Sa'd Al-Baghdadi (d. 845 AD, Iraq), p 38 V 10, Publisher; MAKTABAH AL-KHANJI, Cairo, Egypt, year 2001.

[51]AL-MUNTADHAM FI TARIKH AL-MULUK WA AL-UMAM, by Abu Al-Faraj Abdul-Rahman b. Ali Ibn Al-Jawzi (d. 1200 AD, Iraq), p 95 V 4, Publisher; DAR AL-KUTUB AL-ILMIYYAH, Beirut, Lebanon, first edition 1992.
[52]AL-MU'JAM AL-KABIR, by Abu Al-Qasim Sulaiman b. Ayub Al-Tabarani (d. 918 AD, Iran), Narrator; Qatadah b. Da'amah, p 434 V 22, Publisher; MAKTABAH IBN TAIMIYYAH, Cairo, Egypt, 1983.

AL-TABAQAT AL-KABIR, by Muhammad b. Sa'd Al-Baghdadi (d. 845 AD, Iraq), p 36 V 10, Publisher; MAKTABAH AL-KHANJI, Cairo, Egypt, year 2001.

[53]AL-MU'JAM AL-KABIR, by Abu Al-Qasim Sulaiman b. Ayub Al-Tabarani (d. 918 AD, Iran), Narrator; Zubair b. Bikar, p 434 V 22, Publisher; MAKTABAH IBN TAIMIYYAH, Cairo, Egypt, 1983.

AL-TABAQAT AL-KABIR, by Muhammad b. Sa'd Al-Baghdadi (d. 845 AD, Iraq), p 36 V 10, Publisher; MAKTABAH AL-KHANJI, Cairo, Egypt, year 2001.

[54] ibid
[55]AL-SIRAH AL-NABAWIYYAH, by Abu Muhammad Abdulmalik b. Hisham Al-Himyari (d. 833 AD, Egypt), p 215 -216 V 1, Publisher DAR AL-KITAB AL-ARABI, Beirut, Lebanon, third edition 1990.
[56]AL-SIRAH AL-NABAWIYYAH, by Abu Muhammad Abdulmalik b. Hisham Al-Himyari (d. 833 AD, Egypt), p 215 – 216 V 1, Publisher DAR AL-KITAB AL-ARABI, Beirut, Lebanon, third edition 1990.
JAMHARAT ANSAB AL-ARAB, by Abu Muhammad Ali b. Ahmad Ibn Hazm Al-Andalusi (d. 1064 AD, Spain), p 16, Chapter; NASAB ABDULLAH BIN ABDUL-MUTTALIB, Publisher; DAR AL-MA'ARIF, Cairo, Egypt, 1982.

JAWAME' AL-SIRAH AL-NABAWIYYAH, by Abu Muhammad Ali b. Ahmad Ibn Hazm Al-Andalusi (d. 1064 AD, Spain), p 128, Narrator; Urwah b. Zubair, Narrator; DAR KUTUB AL-ILMIYYAH, Beirut, Lebanon, first edition 2003.

[57] ibid
[58]AL-SIRAH AL-NABAWIYYAH, by Abu Muhammad Abdulmalik b. Hisham Al-Himyari (d. 833 AD, Egypt), Narrator; Ibn Ishaq, p 216 V 1, Publisher DAR AL-KITAB AL-ARABI, Beirut, Lebanon, third edition 1990.

TARIKH MADINAT DIMISHQ, by Abu Al-Qasim Ali b. Hasan Ibn Asakir Al-Dimishqi (d. 1176 AD, Syria), Narrator; Al-Baraa RA, p 137 V 3, Publisher; DAR AL-FIKAR, Beirut, Lebanon, first edition 1998.

[59]AL-SIRAH AL-NABAWIYYAH, by Abu Muhammad Abdulmalik b. Hisham Al-Himyari (d. 833 AD, Egypt), Narrator; Ibn Ishaq, p 216 V 1, Publisher DAR AL-KITAB AL-ARABI, Beirut, Lebanon, third edition 1990.

[60]AL-JAME' AL-SAHIH, by Abu Abdullah Muhammad b. Ismael Al-Bukhari (d. 870 AD, Uzbekistan), Narrator; Aisha RA, p 1569, Publisher DAR IBN KATHIR, Damascus, Syria, first edition 2002.

AL-SUNAN AL-KUBRA, by Abu Abdul-Rahman Ahmad b. Shuaib Al-Nasai (d. 915 AD Mecca/Turkmenistan), Narrator; Aisha RA, p 393 V 7, Publisher; MUASSASAT AL-RISALAH, Beirut, Lebanon, first edition 2001.

MUSNAD AHMAD, by Abu Abdullah Ahmad b. Muhammad b. Hanbal Al-Marwazi (d.855, Iraq), Narrator; Aisha RA, p 216 V 18, Publisher; DAR AL-HADITH, Cairo, Egypt, first edition 1995.

[61] SAHIH TIRMIDHI, by Abu Isa Muhammad b. Isa Al-Tirmidhi (d. 892 AD, Uzbekistan), chapter; AL-MANAQIB, N; 3872, Narrator; Aisha RA, p 175 V 6, published by DAR AL-GHARB AL-ISLAMI, Beirut, Lebanon, first edition 1996.

AL-SUNAN AL-KUBRA, by Abu Abdul-Rahman Ahmad b. Shuaib Al-Nasai (d. 915 AD Mecca/Turkmenistan), Narrator; Aisha RA, p 393 V 7, Publisher; MUASSASAT AL-RISALAH, Beirut, Lebanon, first edition 2001.

SUNAN ABU DAWUD, by Abu Dawud Sulaiman b. Al-Ash'ath Al-Sijistani (d. 889 AD, Iraq), p 505 V 7, Publisher; DAR AL-RISALAH AL-ALAMIYYAH, Damascus, Syria, first edition 2009.

[62]AL-TABAQAT AL-KABIR, by Muhammad b. Sa'd Al-Baghdadi (d. 845 AD, Iraq), p 26 V 10, Publisher; MAKTABAH AL-KHANJI, Cairo, Egypt, year 2001.

AL-ISABAH FI TAMYEEZ AL-SAHABAH, by Shihabuddin Ahmad b. Nuriddin Ibn Hajar Al-Asqallani (d. 1449 AD, Egypt), p 268 V 8, Publisher; DAR AL-KUTUB AL-ILMIYYAH, Beirut, Lebanon, first edition 1995.

[63]AL-TABAQAT AL-KABIR, by Muhammad b. Sa'd Al-Baghdadi (d. 845 AD, Iraq), p 26 V 10, Publisher; MAKTABAH AL-KHANJI, Cairo, Egypt, year 2001.

[64]SUNAN ABU DAWUD, by Abu Dawud Sulaiman b. Al-Ash'ath Al-Sijistani (d. 889 AD, Iraq), Narrator; Thawban, p 273 V 6, Publisher; DAR AL-RISALAH AL-ALAMIYYAH, Damascus, Syria, first edition 2009.

AL-SUNAN AL-KUBRA, by Abu Bakr Ahmad b. Husain Al-Baihaqi (d. 1066 AD, Iran), Narrator; Thawban, p 41 V 1, Publisher; DAR AL-KUTUB AL-ILMIYYAH, Beirut, Lebanon, 2003.

[65]AL-JAME' AL-SAHIH, by Abu Abdullah Muhammad b. Ismael Al-Bukhari (d. 870 AD, Uzbekistan), Narrator; Anas RA, p 1092, Publisher DAR IBN KATHIR, Damascus, Syria, first edition 2002.

SUNAN IBN MAJAH, by Abu Abdullah Muhammad b. Yazid Al-Qazwini (d 887 AD, Iran), chapter; KITAB AL-JANAIZ, N; 1629-1630 Narrator; Anas, p 521 V 1, publisher; DAR IHYAA AL-KUTUB AL-ARABIYYAH, Cairo, Egypt, year 1952

AL-SUNAN AL-KUBRA, by Abu Abdul-Rahman Ahmad b. Shuaib Al-Nasai (d. 915 AD Mecca/Turkmenistan), Narrator; Anas RA, p 387 V 2, Publisher; MUASSASAT AL-RISALAH, Beirut, Lebanon, first edition 2001.

AL-TABAQAT AL-KABIR, by Muhammad b. Sa'd Al-Baghdadi (d. 845 AD, Iraq), p 270 V 2, Publisher; MAKTABAH AL-KHANJI, Cairo, Egypt, year 2001.

[66]AL-TABAQAT AL-KABIR, by Muhammad b. Sa'd Al-Baghdadi (d. 845 AD, Iraq), p 271 V 2, Publisher; MAKTABAH AL-KHANJI, Cairo, Egypt, year 2001.

[67]AL-TABAQAT AL-KABIR, by Muhammad b. Sa'd Al-Baghdadi (d. 845 AD, Iraq), p 37 V 10, Publisher; MAKTABAH AL-KHANJI, Cairo, Egypt, year 2001.

AL-MU'JAM AL-KABIR, by Abu Al-Qasim Sulaiman b. Ayub Al-Tabarani (d. 918 AD, Iran), Narrator; Abdullah b. Abbas, p 217 V 12, Publisher; MAKTABAH IBN TAIMIYYAH, Cairo, Egypt.

[68]AL-TABAQAT AL-KABIR, by Muhammad b. Sa'd Al-Baghdadi (d. 845 AD, Iraq), p 34 V 10, Publisher; MAKTABAH AL-KHANJI, Cairo, Egypt, year 2001.

[69]AL-JAME' AL-SAHIH, by Abu Abdullah Muhammad b. Ismael Al-Bukhari (d. 870 AD, Uzbekistan), Narrator; Anas RA, p 315, Publisher DAR IBN KATHIR, Damascus, Syria, first edition 2002.

SHUAB AL-IMAN, by Abu Bakr Ahmad b. Husain Al-Baihaqi (d. 1066 AD, Iran), N; 9684, chapter; FASL FI MIHNAT AL-JARAD WA AL-SABR ALAIHA, p 430, V 12, publisher; MAKTABAH AL-RUSHD LI AL-NASHR WA AL-TAWZEA, Riyadh, KSA, first edition 2003.

AL-BAHR AL-ZAKHKHAR Abu Bakr Ahmad b. Amr Al-Bazzar (d. 905 AD, Iraq), Narrator; Jabir, N; 1001, p 214 V 3, publisher; MAKTABAH AL-ULUM WA AL-HIKAM, Madinah, KSA, first edition 1988.

SAHIH TIRMIDHI, by Abu Isa Muhammad b. Isa Al-Tirmidhi (d. 892 AD, Uzbekistan), chapter; AL-JANAIZ, N; 1001, Narrator; Abdul-Rahman b. Auf RA, p 214 V 3, published by DAR AL-GHARB AL-ISLAMI, Beirut, Lebanon, first edition 1996.

[70]SAHIH MUSLIM, by Abu Al-Husain Muslim b. Hajjaj Al-Nisapuri (d. 875 AD, Iran), Narrator; Ali RA, p 2316, Publisher; DAR TAYBAH, Riyadh, KSA, first edition 2006.

TARIKH MADINAT DIMISHQ, by Abu Al-Qasim Ali b. Hasan Ibn Asakir Al-Dimishqi (d. 1176 AD, Syria), Narrator; Anas RA, p 136 V 3, Publisher; DAR AL-FIKAR, Beirut, Lebanon, first edition 1998.

[71]JAMHARAT ANSAB AL-ARAB, by Abu Muhammad Ali b. Ahmad Ibn Hazm Al-Andalusi (d. 1064 AD, Spain), p 16, Chapter; NASAB ABDULLAH BIN ABDUL-MUTTALIB, Publisher; DAR AL-MA'ARIF, Cairo, Egypt, 1982.

IMTA' AL-ASMA' BIMA LI AL-NABIYYI MIN AL-AHWAL WA AL-AMWAL WA AL-HAFADAT WA AL-MATA', by Ahmad b. Ali Al-Maqrizi (d. 1442 AD, Cairo), p 355 V 5, Publisher, DAR AL-KUTUB AL-ILMIYYAH, Beirut, Lebanon, first edition 1999.

[72]JAMHARAT ANSAB AL-ARAB, by Abu Muhammad Ali b. Ahmad Ibn Hazm Al-Andalusi (d. 1064 AD, Spain), p 16, Chapter; NASAB ABDULLAH BIN ABDUL-MUTTALIB, Publisher; DAR AL-MA'ARIF, Cairo, Egypt, 1982.

[73]JAMHARAT ANSAB AL-ARAB, by Abu Muhammad Ali b. Ahmad Ibn Hazm Al-Andalusi (d. 1064 AD, Spain), p 16, Chapter; NASAB ABDULLAH BIN ABDUL-MUTTALIB, Publisher; DAR AL-MA'ARIF, Cairo, Egypt, 1982.

[74]ibid

[75]IMTA' AL-ASMA' BIMA LI AL-NABIYYI MIN AL-AHWAL WA AL-AMWAL WA AL-HAFADAT WA AL-MATA', by Ahmad b. Ali Al-Maqrizi (d. 1442 AD, Cairo), p 369 V 5, Publisher, DAR AL-KUTUB AL-ILMIYYAH, Beirut, Lebanon, first edition 1999

[76]IMTA' AL-ASMA' BIMA LI AL-NABIYYI MIN AL-AHWAL WA AL-AMWAL WA AL-HAFADAT WA AL-MATA', by Ahmad b. Ali Al-Maqrizi (d. 1442 AD, Cairo), p 369 V 5, Publisher, DAR AL-KUTUB AL-ILMIYYAH, Beirut, Lebanon, first edition 1999.

[77]IMTA' AL-ASMA' BIMA LI AL-NABIYYI MIN AL-AHWAL WA AL-AMWAL WA AL-HAFADAT WA AL-MATA', by Ahmad b. Ali Al-Maqrizi (d. 1442 AD, Cairo), p 371 V 5, Publisher, DAR AL-KUTUB AL-ILMIYYAH, Beirut, Lebanon, first edition 1999.

[78]IMTA' AL-ASMA' BIMA LI AL-NABIYYI MIN AL-AHWAL WA AL-AMWAL WA AL-HAFADAT WA AL-MATA', by Ahmad b. Ali Al-Maqrizi (d. 1442 AD, Cairo), p 355 V 5, Publisher, DAR AL-KUTUB AL-ILMIYYAH, Beirut, Lebanon, first edition 1999.

[79] AL-BAHR AL-ZAKHKHAR Abu Bakr Ahmad b. Amr Al-Bazzar (d. 905 AD, Iraq), Narrator; Jabir, N; 742, p 314 V 2, publisher; MAKTABAH AL-ULUM WA AL-HIKAM, Madinah, KSA, first edition 1988.

TARIKH MADINAT DIMISHQ, by Abu Al-Qasim Ali b. Hasan Ibn Asakir Al-Dimishqi (d. 1176 AD, Syria), Narrator; Ali RA, p 118 V 14, Publisher; DAR AL-FIKAR, Beirut, Lebanon, first edition 1998.

AL-TABAQAT AL-KABIR, by Muhammad b. Sa'd Al-Baghdadi (d. 845 AD, Iraq), p 356 V 6, Publisher; MAKTABAH AL-KHANJI, Cairo, Egypt, year 2001.

[80]SUNAN AL-NASAI, by Abu Abdul-Rahman Ahmad b. Shuaib Al-Nasai (d. 915 AD Mecca/Turkmenistan), Narrator; Shaddad b. Al-Haad RA, p 158, Publisher; Ministry of religious affairs, KSA, 1999.

MUSNAD IBN ABU SHAYBAH, by Abu Bakr Muhammad b. Abdullah Ibn Abu Shaybah (d. 849 AD, Iraq), Narrator; Shaddad b. Al-Haad RA, p 210 V 2, Publisher; DAR AL-WATAN, Riyadh, KSA, first edition 1997.

[81]AL-SUNAN AL-KUBRA, by Abu Abdul-Rahman Ahmad b. Shuaib Al-Nasai (d. 915 AD Mecca/Turkmenistan), Narrator; Abu Qatadah RA, p 39 V 2, Publisher; MUASSASAT AL-RISALAH, Beirut, Lebanon, first edition 2001.

[82] MUSTARDAK ALA AL-SAHIHAIN, by Abu Abdullah Muhammad b. Abdullah Al-Nisapuri (d 1012 AD, Iran), chapter; KITAB MA'RIFAT AL-SAHABAH, N; 4810, Narrator; Abu Bakrah, p 192 V 3, publisher; DAR AL-KUTUB AL-ILMIYYAH, second edition 2002.

AL-JAME' AL-SAHIH, by Abu Abdullah Muhammad b. Ismael Al-Bukhari (d. 870 AD, Uzbekistan), Narrator; Hasan Al-Basri RA, p 1758, Publisher DAR IBN KATHIR, Damascus, Syria, first edition 2002.

[83]MUSANNAF IBN ABU SHAYBAH, by Abu Bakr Muhammad b. Abdullah Ibn Abu Shaybah (d. 849 AD, Iraq), Narrator; Buraidah RA, p 168 V 18, Publisher; DAR AL-QIBLAH LI AL-THAQAFAH AL-ISLAMIYYAH, Jeddah, KSA, first edition 2006.

SUNAN IBN MAJAH, by Abu Abdullah Muhammad b. Yazid Al-Qazwini (d 887 AD, Iran), chapter; KITAB AL-LIBAS, N; 3600 Narrator; Buraidah, p 1190 V 2, publisher; DAR IHYAA AL-KUTUB AL-ARABIYYAH, Cairo, Egypt, year 1952.

[84]AL-IHSAN FI TAQRIB SAHIH IBN HIBBAN, by Abu Hatim Muhammad b. Faisal Al-Busti (d. 965 AD, Afghanistan), Narrator; Umair b. Ishaq, N; 5628, Chapter; KITAB AL-HADHAR WA AL-IBAHAH, BAAB DHIKR AL-IBAHAH LI AL-MAR'I AN YUQABBILA WALADAHU, p 345 V 6, Publisher; DAR AL-TA'SIL MARKAZ AL-BUHUTH WA TIQANIYYAH AL-MA'LUMAT, Cairo, Egypt, first edition 2014.

[85]AL-MU'JAM AL-KABIR, by Abu Al-Qasim Sulaiman b. Ayub Al-Tabarani (d. 918 AD, Iran), Narrator; Aisha RA, p 162 V 7, Publisher; MAKTABAH IBN TAIMIYYAH, Cairo, Egypt, 1983.

AL-IHSAN FI TAQRIB SAHIH IBN HIBBAN, by Abu Hatim Muhammad b. Faisal Al-Busti (d. 965 AD, Afghanistan), Narrator; Abu Hurairah RA, N; 5629, Chapter; KITAB AL-HADHAR WA AL-IBAHAH, BAAB DHIKR AL-IBAHAH LI AL-MAR'I AN YUQABBILA WALADAHU, p 345 V 6, Publisher; DAR AL-TA'SIL MARKAZ AL-BUHUTH WA TIQANIYYAH AL-MA'LUMAT, Cairo, Egypt, first edition 2014.

SAHIH MUSLIM, by Abu Al-Husain Muslim b. Hajjaj Al-Nisapuri (d. 875 AD, Iran), Narrator; Aisha RA, p 2318, Publisher; DAR TAYBAH, Riyadh, KSA, first edition 2006.

[86]AL-IHSAN FI TAQRIB SAHIH IBN HIBBAN, by Abu Hatim Muhammad b. Faisal Al-Busti (d. 965 AD, Afghanistan), Narrator; Abu Huraira RA, N; 6936, p 60 V 8, Publisher; DAR AL-KUTUB AL-ISLAMIYYAH, Beirut, Lebanon,1987.
[87]SAHIH MUSLIM, by Abu Al-Husain Muslim b. Hajjaj Al-Nisapuri (d. 875 AD, Iran), Narrator; Aisha RA, p 2317, Publisher; DAR TAYBAH, Riyadh, KSA, first edition 2006.

AL-IHSAN FI TAQRIB SAHIH IBN HIBBAN, by Abu Hatim Muhammad b. Faisal Al-Busti (d. 965 AD, Afghanistan), Narrator; Aisha RA, N; 5630, Chapter; KITAB AL-HADHAR WA AL-IBAHAH, BAAB DHIKR AL-IBAHAH LI AL-MAR'I AN YUQABBILA WALADAHU, p 345 V 6, Publisher; DAR AL-TA'SIL MARKAZ AL-BUHUTH WA TIQANIYYAH AL-MA'LUMAT, Cairo, Egypt, first edition 2014.

[88]MUSANNAF IBN ABU SHAYBAH, by Abu Bakr Muhammad b. Abdullah Ibn Abu Shaybah (d. 849 AD, Iraq), Narrator; Abu Hurairah RA, p 509 V 10, Publisher; AL-FARUQ AL-HADITHAH, Cairo, Egypt, first edition 2008.

[89]AL-ADAB AL-MUFRAD by Muhammad b. Ismael Al-Bukhari Al-Ju'fi (d. 870 AD, Uzbekistan), Narrator; Abu Huraira, p 432, Publisher; DAR AL-SADIQ, Jabal, KSA, second edition 2000.
[90]AL-MU'JAM AL-KABIR, by Abu Al-Qasim Sulaiman b. Ayub Al-Tabarani (d. 918 AD, Iran), Narrator; Abu Hurairah, p 42 V 3, Publisher; MAKTABAH IBN TAIMIYYAH, Cairo, Egypt, 1983.
[91]MUSANNAF IBN ABU SHAYBAH, by Abu Bakr Muhammad b. Abdullah Ibn Abu Shaybah (d. 849 AD, Iraq), Narrator; Abu Ja'far RA, p 509 V 10, Publisher; AL-FARUQ AL-HADITHAH, Cairo, Egypt, first edition 2008.
[92] SIAR A'LAAM AL-NUBALA, by Shamsuddin Al-Dhahabi (d. 1348 AD, Syria), Narrator; Anas b. Malik, p 178 V 2, Publisher; DAR AL-KUTUB AL-ISLAMI, Beirut, Lebanon, 2010.

[93]AL-MU'JAM AL-KABIR, by Abu Al-Qasim Sulaiman b. Ayub Al-Tabarani (d. 918 AD, Iran), Narrator; Zubair b. Bikar, p 424 V 22, Publisher; MAKTABAH IBN TAIMIYYAH, Cairo, Egypt, 1983.
[94]MUSNAD AHMAD, by Abu Abdullah Ahmad b. Muhammad b. Hanbal Al-Marwazi (d.855, Iraq), Narrator; Aisha RA, p 232 V 41, Publisher; MUASSASAH AL-RISALAH, Beirut, Lebanon, first edition 2001.

AL-TABAQAT AL-KABIR, by Muhammad b. Sa'd Al-Baghdadi (d. 845 AD, Iraq), p 40 V 10, Publisher; MAKTABAH AL-KHANJI, Cairo, Egypt, year 2001.

AL-MU'JAM AL-KABIR, by Abu Al-Qasim Sulaiman b. Ayub Al-Tabarani (d. 918 AD, Iran), Narrator; Aisha RA, p 442 V 22, Publisher; MAKTABAH IBN TAIMIYYAH, Cairo, Egypt, 1983.

[95]AL-TABAQAT AL-KABIR, by Muhammad b. Sa'd Al-Baghdadi (d. 845 AD, Iraq), p 40 V 10, Publisher; MAKTABAH AL-KHANJI, Cairo, Egypt, year 2001.
[96]AL-SIRAH AL-NABAWIYYAH, by Abu Muhammad Abdulmalik b. Hisham Al-Himyari (d. 833 AD, Egypt), Narrator; Ibn Ishaq, p 216 V 1, Publisher DAR AL-KITAB AL-ARABI, Beirut, Lebanon, third edition 1990.

[97]AL-JAME' AL-SAHIH, by Abu Abdullah Muhammad b. Ismael Al-Bukhari (d. 870 AD, Uzbekistan), Narrator; Usamah b. Zaid RA, p 310, Publisher DAR IBN KATHIR, Damascus, Syria, first edition 2002.

SAHIH MUSLIM, by Abu Al-Husain Muslim b. Hajjaj Al-Nisapuri (d. 875 AD, Iran), Narrator; Usamah b. Zaid RA, p 410, Publisher; DAR TAYBAH, Riyadh, KSA, first edition 2006.

[98]AL-SIRAH AL-NABAWIYYAH, by Abu Bakr Muhammad b. Ishaq Al-Madani (d. 768 AD, Madinah/Iraq), p 282 V 1, Publisher; DAR AL-KUTUB AL-ILMIYYAH, Beirut, Lebanon, first edition 2004.

[99]AL-AHADITH AL-MUKHTARAH, by Diauddin Muhammad b. Abdul-Wahid Al-Maqdisi (d. 1245 AD, Syria), Narrator; Anas RA, p 109 V 5, Publisher; DAR AL-KHIDR, Beirut, Lebanon, third edition 2000.

[100]AL-JAME' AL-SAHIH, by Abu Abdullah Muhammad b. Ismael Al-Bukhari (d. 870 AD, Uzbekistan), Narrator; Umar b. Abu Salamah RA, p 1370, Publisher DAR IBN KATHIR, Damascus, Syria, first edition 2002.

SAHIH MUSLIM, by Abu Al-Husain Muslim b. Hajjaj Al-Nisapuri (d. 875 AD, Iran), Narrator; Umar b. Abu Salamah RA, p 972, Publisher; DAR TAYBAH, Riyadh, KSA, first edition 2006.

[101]USUD AL-GHABAH FI MA'RIFAT AL-SAHABAH, by Abu Al-Hasan Ali b. Muhammad Al-Jazari (d. 1233 AD, Iraq), p 67 V 2, Publisher; DAR AL-KUTUB AL-ILMIYYAH, Beirut, Lebanon, first edition 1996.

USUD AL-GHABAH FI MA'RIFAT AL-SAHABAH, by Abu Al-Hasan Ali b. Muhammad Al-Jazari (d. 1233 AD, Iraq), p 67 V 2, Publisher; DAR AL-KUTUB AL-ILMIYYAH, Beirut, Lebanon, first edition 1996.

[102]USUD AL-GHABAH FI MA'RIFAT AL-SAHABAH, by Abu Al-Hasan Ali b. Muhammad Al-Jazari (d. 1233 AD, Iraq), p 67 V 2, Publisher; DAR AL-KUTUB AL-ILMIYYAH, Beirut, Lebanon, first edition 1996.

[103]AL-SIRAH AL-NABAWIYYAH, by Abu Muhammad Abdulmalik b. Hisham Al-Himyari (d. 833 AD, Egypt), Narrator; Ibn Ishaq, p 186 V 1, Publisher DAR AL-KITAB AL-ARABI, Beirut, Lebanon, third edition 1990.

[104]TARIKH AL-MULUK WA AL-RUSUL, by Muhammad b. Jarir Al-Tabari (d. 923 AD, Iraq), Narrator; Yazid b. Ubaid Al-Sa'di, p 81 V 3, Publisher; DAR AL-MA'ARIF, Cairo, Egypt, second edition 1967.

[105] SUNAN IBN MAJAH, by Abu Abdullah Muhammad b. Yazid Al-Qazwini (d 887 AD, Iran), chapter; KITAB AL-ATIMAH, N; 3251 Narrator; Abdullah b. Sallam p 1083 V 2, publisher; DAR IHYAA AL-KUTUB AL- ARABIYYAH, Cairo, Egypt, year 1952

[106]AL-JAME' AL-SAHIH, by Abu Abdullah Muhammad b. Ismael Al-Bukhari (d. 870 AD, Uzbekistan), Narrator; Anas RA, p 498, Publisher DAR IBN KATHIR, Damascus, Syria, first edition 2002.

[107]AL-JAME' AL-SAHIH, by Abu Abdullah Muhammad b. Ismael Al-Bukhari (d. 870 AD, Uzbekistan), Narrator; Abu Hurairah RA, p 1504, Publisher DAR IBN KATHIR, Damascus, Syria, first edition 2002.

AL-SUNAN AL-KUBRA, by Abu Bakr Ahmad b. Husain Al-Baihaqi (d. 1066 AD, Iran), Narrator; Aisha RA, p 40 V 7, Publisher; DAR AL-KUTUB AL-ILMIYYAH, Beirut, Lebanon, 2003

[108] SUNAN IBN MAJAH, by Abu Abdullah Muhammad b. Yazid Al-Qazwini (d 887 AD, Iran), chapter; KITAB AL-JANAIZ, N; 1591 Narrator; Abdullah b. Umar, p 507 V 1, publisher; DAR IHYAA AL-KUTUB AL- ARABIYYAH, Cairo, Egypt, year 1952.

MUSTARDAK ALA AL-SAHIHAIN, by Abu Abdullah Muhammad b. Abdullah Al-Nisapuri (d 1012 AD, Iran), chapter; KITAB MA'RIFAT AL-SAHABAH, N; 4883, Narrator; Abdullah b. Umar, p 119 V 1, publisher; DAR AL-KUTUB AL-ILMIYYAH, second edition 2002.

[109] SAHIH TIRMIDHI, by Abu Isa Muhammad b. Isa Al-Tirmidhi (d. 892 AD, Uzbekistan), chapter; AL-MANAQIB, N; 3759, Narrator; Abdullah b. Abbas RA, p 109 V 6, published by DAR AL-GHARB AL-ISLAMI, Beirut, Lebanon, first edition 1996.

[110] SUNAN IBN MAJAH, by Abu Abdullah Muhammad b. Yazid Al-Qazwini (d 887 AD, Iran), chapter; KITAB AL-JANAIZ, N; 1591 Narrator; Abdullah b. Umar, p 507 V 1, publisher; DAR IHYAA AL-KUTUB AL- ARABIYYAH, Cairo, Egypt, year 1952.

MUSTARDAK ALA AL-SAHIHAIN, by Abu Abdullah Muhammad b. Abdullah Al-Nisapuri (d 1012 AD, Iran), chapter; KITAB MA'RIFAT AL-SAHABAH, N; 4883, Narrator; Abdullah b. Umar, p 119 V 1, publisher; DAR AL-KUTUB AL-ILMIYYAH, second edition 2002.

[110]AL-JAME' AL-SAHIH, by Abu Abdullah Muhammad b. Ismael Al-Bukhari (d. 870 AD, Uzbekistan), Narrator; Abu Hurairah RA, p 358, Publisher DAR IBN KATHIR, Damascus, Syria, first edition 2002.

SAHIH MUSLIM, by Abu Al-Husain Muslim b. Hajjaj Al-Nisapuri (d. 875 AD, Iran), Narrator; Abu Hurairah RA, p 436, Publisher; DAR TAYBAH, Riyadh, KSA, first edition 2006.

MUSNAD ABU YA'LA, by Abu Ya'la Ahmad b. Ali Al-Mausilli (d. 919 AD Iraq), Narrator; Ali, N; 545, p 414 V 1, Publisher; DAR AL-MA'MUN, Damascus, Syria, second edition 1989.

SAHIH TIRMIDHI, by Abu Isa Muhammad b. Isa Al-Tirmidhi (d. 892 AD, Uzbekistan), chapter; AL-MANAQIB, N; 3761, Narrator; Abdullah b. Abbas RA, p 109 V 6, published by DAR AL-GHARB AL-ISLAMI, Beirut, Lebanon, first edition 1996.

[111] SAHIH TIRMIDHI, by Abu Isa Muhammad b. Isa Al-Tirmidhi (d. 892 AD, Uzbekistan), chapter; AL-MANAQIB, N; 3762, Narrator; Abdullah b. Abbas RA, p 109 V 6, published by DAR AL-GHARB AL-ISLAMI, Beirut, Lebanon, first edition 1996.

[112] SAHIH TIRMIDHI, by Abu Isa Muhammad b. Isa Al-Tirmidhi (d. 892 AD, Uzbekistan), chapter; AL-MANAQIB, N; 3758, Narrator; Abdullah b. Abbas RA, p 109 V 6, published by DAR AL-GHARB AL-ISLAMI, Beirut, Lebanon, first edition 1996.

[113] SAHIH TIRMIDHI, by Abu Isa Muhammad b. Isa Al-Tirmidhi (d. 892 AD, Uzbekistan), chapter; KITAB AL-MANAQIB, N; 3752, Narrator; Jabir RA, p 104 V 6, published by DAR AL-GHARB AL-ISLAMI, Beirut, Lebanon, first edition 1996.
TARIKH MADINAT DIMISHQ, by Abu Al-Qasim Ali b. Hasan Ibn Asakir Al-Dimishqi (d. 1176 AD, Syria), Narrator; Jabir RA, p 332 V 20, Publisher; DAR AL-FIKAR, Beirut, Lebanon, 1995.
[114]AL-MU'JAM AL-KABIR, by Abu Al-Qasim Sulaiman b. Ayub Al-Tabarani (d. 918 AD, Iran), Narrator; Sha'bi RA, p 108 V 2, Publisher; MAKTABAH IBN TAIMIYYAH, Cairo, Egypt, 1983.

AL-SIRAH AL-NABAWIYYAH, by Abu Muhammad Abdulmalik b. Hisham Al-Himyari (d. 833 AD, Egypt), Narrator; Aamir b. Sharahbil Al-Sha'bi, p 307 V 2, Publisher DAR AL-KITAB AL-ARABI, Beirut, Lebanon, third edition 1990.

[115]MUSNAD AHMAD, by Abu Abdullah Ahmad b. Muhammad b. Hanbal Al-Marwazi (d.855, Iraq), Narrator; Asmaa bt. Umais RA, p 422 V 18, Publisher; Publisher; DAR AL-HADITH, Cairo, Egypt, first edition 1995.

AL-MU'JAM AL-KABIR, by Abu Al-Qasim Sulaiman b. Ayub Al-Tabarani (d. 918 AD, Iran), Narrator; Asmaa bt. Umais RA, p 380 V 24, Publisher; MAKTABAH IBN TAIMIYYAH, Cairo, Egypt, 1983.

DALAIL AL-NUBUWWAH, by Abu Nuaim Abdullah b. Ahmad Al-Asbahani (d. 1038 AD, Iran), Narrator; Asmaa bt. Umais p 530, V 2, publisher; DAR AL-NAFAIS, Beirut, Lebanon, first edition 1986.

[116]MUSNAD ABU YA'LA, by Abu Ya'la Ahmad b. Ali Al-Mausilli (d. 919 AD Iraq), Narrator; Anas, N; 1432, p 199 V 7, Publisher; DAR AL-MA'MUN, Damascus, Syria, second edition 1989.

AL-IHSAN FI TAQRIB SAHIH IBN HIBBAN, by Abu Hatim Muhammad b. Faisal Al-Busti (d. 965 AD, Afghanistan), Narrator; Fudhalah RA, N; 4862, Chapter; KITAB AL-JIHAD, BAAB AL-HIJRAH, p 203 V 11, Publisher; MUASSASAH AL-RISALAH, Beirut, Lebanon, first edition 1991.

AL-JAME' AL-SAHIH, by Abu Abdullah Muhammad b. Ismael Al-Bukhari (d. 870 AD, Uzbekistan), Narrator; Abdullah b. Amr RA, p 13, Publisher DAR IBN KATHIR, Damascus, Syria, first edition 2002.

AL-MUNTAKHAB MIN MUSNAD by Abd b. Humaid Al-Keshi (d. 863 AD, Shahrisabz, Uzbekistan), Narrator; Abdullah b. Amr, p 257 V 1, Publisher; DAR BALNASIYYAH. Riyadh, KSA, second edition 2002.

SUNAN IBN MAJAH, by Abu Abdullah Muhammad b. Yazid Al-Qazwini (d 887 AD, Iran), chapter; KITAB AL-FITAN, N; 3934 Narrator; Fudhalah b. Ubaid b. Ali, p 1298 V 2, publisher; DAR IHYAA AL-KUTUB AL- ARABIYYAH, Cairo, Egypt, year 1952

AL-SUNAN AL-KUBRA, by Abu Abdul-Rahman Ahmad b. Shuaib Al-Nasai (d. 915 AD Mecca/Turkmenistan), Narrator; Fudalah b. Ubaid RA, p 386 V 10, Publisher; MUASSASAT AL-RISALAH, Beirut, Lebanon, first edition 2001.

SAHIH TIRMIDHI, by Abu Isa Muhammad b. Isa Al-Tirmidhi (d. 892 AD, Uzbekistan), chapter; FADHAIL AL-JIHAD, N; 1621, Narrator; Fudhala RA, p 265 V 3, published by DAR AL-GHARB AL-ISLAMI, Beirut, Lebanon, first edition 1996.

[117] Surah 4 Al – Nisa; 36

[118]AL-JAME' AL-SAHIH, by Abu Abdullah Muhammad b. Ismael Al-Bukhari (d. 870 AD, Uzbekistan), Narrator; Anas RA, p 327, Publisher DAR IBN KATHIR, Damascus, Syria, first edition 2002.

AMAL AL-YAWM WA AL-LAYLAH, by Ibn Al-Sunniy Abu Bakr Ahmad b. Muhammad Al-Ja'fari Al-Hashimi (d. 974 AD, Iran), Narrator; Buraidah RA, p 334, Publisher; DAR AL-ARQAM, Beirut, Lebanon, first edition 1998.

MUSNAD ABU HANIFAH, by Sadruddin Musa b. Zakariya Al-Haskafi (d. 1252 AD, Turkey), with its commentary AL-MAWAHIB AL-LATIFAH SHARH MUSNAD ABI HANIFAH, by Muhammad Abid b. Ahmad Al-Ansari (d. 1841 AD, India/Madinah), p 113 V1, Publisher; DAR AL-NAWADIR, Damascus, Syria, first edition 2013.

[119] SUNAN IBN MAJAH, by Abu Abdullah Muhammad b. Yazid Al-Qazwini (d 887 AD, Iran), chapter; KITAB AL-NIKAH, N; 1899 Narrator; Anas, p 612 V 1, publisher; DAR IHYAA AL-KUTUB AL- ARABIYYAH, Cairo, Egypt, year 1952.

[120] SAHIH TIRMIDHI, by Abu Isa Muhammad b. Isa Al-Tirmidhi (d. 892 AD, Uzbekistan), chapter; AL-MANAQIB, N; 3895, Narrator; Aisha RA, p 188 V 6, published by DAR AL-GHARB AL-ISLAMI, Beirut, Lebanon, first edition 1996.

AL-MUSNAD AL-JAMEA, by Abdullah b. Abdul-Rahaman Al-Darimi (d 869 AD, Uzbekistan), chapter; HUSN MU'ASHARAH AL-NISA, N; 2439, Narrator; Aisha RA p 539, published by DAR AL-BASHAIR AL-ISLAMIYYAH, Beirut, Lebanon, first edition 2013.

[121] SAHIH TIRMIDHI, by Abu Isa Muhammad b. Isa Al-Tirmidhi (d. 892 AD, Uzbekistan), chapter; AL-IMAN, N; 2612, Narrator; Aisha RA, p 359 V 4, published by DAR AL-GHARB AL-ISLAMI, Beirut, Lebanon, first edition 1996.

MUSTARDAK ALA AL-SAHIHAIN, by Abu Abdullah Muhammad b. Abdullah Al-Nisapuri (d 1012 AD, Iran), chapter; KITAB AL-IMAN, N; 173, Narrator; Aisha, p 119 V 1, publisher; DAR AL-KUTUB AL-ILMIYYAH, second edition 2002.

SHARH USUL I'TIQAD AHL AL-SUNNAH WA AL-JAMA'AH, by Abu Al-Qasim Hibatullah b. Hasan Al-Razi Al-Lalikai (d. 1027 AD, Iran), Narrator; Aisha RA, p 901 V 3, Publisher; Umm Al-Qura University, Mecca, KSA.

SAHIH TIRMIDHI, by Abu Isa Muhammad b. Isa Al-Tirmidhi (d. 892 AD, Uzbekistan), chapter; AL-RIDHA', N; 1162, Narrator; Abu Hurairah RA, p 454 V 2, published by DAR AL-GHARB AL-ISLAMI, Beirut, Lebanon, first edition 1996.

[122]TARIKH MADINAT DIMISHQ, by Abu Al-Qasim Ali b. Hasan Ibn Asakir Al-Dimishqi (d. 1176 AD, Syria), Narrator; Ali RA, p 131 V 13, Publisher; DAR AL-FIKAR, Beirut, Lebanon, 1995.

[123]SAHIH MUSLIM, by Abu Al-Husain Muslim b. Hajjaj Al-Nisapuri (d. 875 AD, Iran), Narrator; Jabir RA, p 556, Publisher; DAR TAYBAH, Riyadh, KSA, first edition 2006.

AL-SUNAN AL-KUBRA, by Abu Bakr Ahmad b. Husain Al-Baihaqi (d. 1066 AD, Iran), Narrator; Jabir RA, p 481 V 7, Publisher; DAR AL-KUTUB AL-ILMIYYAH, Beirut, Lebanon, third edition 2003.

[124]AL-JAME' AL-SAHIH, by Abu Abdullah Muhammad b. Ismael Al-Bukhari (d. 870 AD, Uzbekistan), Narrator; Abu Hurairah RA, p 1321, Publisher DAR IBN KATHIR, Damascus, Syria, first edition 2002.

[125]AL-MUSNAD, by Aby Yaqub Ishaq b. Ibrahim Ibn Rahwayh Al-Handhali (d. 853 AD, Iran), Narrator; Amrah bt. Abdul-Rahman, p 434 V 2, Publisher; MAKTABAH AL-IMAN, Madinah, KSA, first edition 1990.

TARIKH MADINAT DIMISHQ, by Abu Al-Qasim Ali b. Hasan Ibn Asakir Al-Dimishqi (d. 1176 AD, Syria), Narrator; Amrah bt. Abdul-Rahman RA, p 46 V 4, Publisher; DAR AL-FIKAR, Beirut, Lebanon, first edition 1995.

[126]AL-JAME' AL-SAHIH, by Abu Abdullah Muhammad b. Ismael Al-Bukhari (d. 870 AD, Uzbekistan), Narrator; Al-Aswad b. Yazid Al-Nakh'i RA, p 168, Publisher DAR IBN KATHIR, Damascus, Syria, first edition 2002.

[127]MUSNAD AHMAD, by Abu Abdullah Ahmad b. Muhammad b. Hanbal Al-Marwazi (d.855, Iraq), Narrator; Urwah RA, p 289 V 43, Publisher; MUASSASAH AL-RISALAH, Beirut, Lebanon, first edition 2001.

AL-ADAB AL-MUFRAD, by Abu Abdullah Muhammad b. Ismael Al-Bukhari (d. 870 AD, Uzbekistan), Narrator; Urwah, p 142, Publisher AL-MATBA'AH AL-SALAFIYYAH, Cairo, Egypt,1956.

AL-ANWAR FI SHAMAIL AL-MUKHTAR, by Abu Muhammad Husain b. Masud Al-Farra Al-Baghawi (d. 1122 AD, Iran), Narrator; Urwah, p 300 V 1, Publisher; DAR AL-MAKTABI, Damascus, Syria, first edition 1995.

TARIKH MADINAT DIMISHQ, by Abu Al-Qasim Ali b. Hasan Ibn Asakir Al-Dimishqi (d. 1176 AD, Syria), Narrator; Urwah RA, p 58 V 4, Publisher; DAR AL-FIKAR, Beirut, Lebanon, 1995.

AL-ANWAR FI SHAMAIL AL-MUKHTAR, by Abu Muhammad Husain b. Masud Al-Farra Al-Baghawi (d. 1122 AD, Iran), Narrator; Amrah, p 301 V 1, Publisher; DAR AL-MAKTABI, Damascus, Syria, first edition 1995.

[128]MUSNAD AHMAD, by Abu Abdullah Ahmad b. Muhammad b. Hanbal Al-Marwazi (d.855, Iraq), Narrator; Aisha RA, p 144 V 40, Publisher; MUASSASAH AL-RISALAH, Beirut, Lebanon, first edition 2001.

AL-MU'JAM AL-KABIR, by Abu Al-Qasim Sulaiman b. Ayub Al-Tabarani (d. 918 AD, Iran), Narrator; Aisha RA, p 124 V 23, Publisher; MAKTABAH IBN TAIMIYYAH, Cairo, Egypt, 1983.

SUNAN IBN MAJAH, by Abu Abdullah Muhammad b. Yazid Al-Qazwini (d 887 AD, Iran), chapter; KITAB AL-NIKAH, N; 1979 Narrator; Aisha, p 636 V 1, publisher; DAR IHYAA AL-KUTUB AL-ARABIYYAH, Cairo, Egypt, year 1952.

[129]AL-JAME' AL-SAHIH, by Abu Abdullah Muhammad b. Ismael Al-Bukhari (d. 870 AD, Uzbekistan), Narrator; Aisha RA, p 1507, Publisher DAR IBN KATHIR, Damascus, Syria, first edition 2002.

[130] MUSTARDAK ALA AL-SAHIHAIN, by Abu Abdullah Muhammad b. Abdullah Al-Nisapuri (d 1012 AD, Iran), chapter; KITAB AL-IMAN, N; 40, Narrator; Aisha, p 62 V 1, publisher; DAR AL-KUTUB AL-ILMIYYAH, second edition 2002.

SAHIH TIRMIDHI, by Abu Isa Muhammad b. Isa Al-Tirmidhi (d. 892 AD, Uzbekistan), chapter; ABWAB AL-BIRR WA AL-SILAH, N; 2017, Narrator; Aisha RA, p 544 V 3, published by DAR AL-GHARB AL-ISLAMI, Beirut, Lebanon, first edition 1996.

[131] AL-BAHR AL-ZAKHKHAR Abu Bakr Ahmad b. Amr Al-Bazzar (d. 905 AD, Iraq), Narrator; Anas, N; 6868, p 290 V 13, publisher; MAKTABAH AL-ULUM WA AL-HIKAM, Madinah, KSA, first edition 2005.

AL-ADAB AL-MUFRAD, by Abu Abdullah Muhammad b. Ismael Al-Bukhari (d. 870 AD, Uzbekistan), Narrator; Anas, p 68, Publisher AL-MATBA'AH AL-SALAFIYYAH, Cairo, Egypt,1956.

[132]TARIKH MADINAT DIMISHQ, by Abu Al-Qasim Ali b. Hasan Ibn Asakir Al-Dimishqi (d. 1176 AD, Syria), Narrator; Safiyyah bt. Huyay RA, p 385 V 3, Publisher; DAR AL-FIKAR, Beirut, Lebanon, 1995.

AL-MU'JAM AL-AWSAT, by Abu Al-Qasim Sulaiman b. Ayub Al-Tabarani (d. 918 AD, Iran), Narrator; Safiyyah bt. Huyay, p 344 V 6, Publisher; DAR AL-HARAMAIN, Cairo, Egypt, 1995.

[133]SAHIH MUSLIM, by Abu Al-Husain Muslim b. Hajjaj Al-Nisapuri (d. 875 AD, Iran), Narrator; Abdullah b. Umar RA, p 785, Publisher; DAR TAYBAH, Riyadh, KSA, first edition 2006.

MUSNAD ABU AWANAH, by Abu Awanah Yaqub b. Ibrahim Al-Isfaraini (d. 928 AD, Iran), Narrator; Abdullah b. Umar RA, p 68 V 4, Publisher; DAR AL-MA'RIFAH, Beirut, Lebanon, first edition 1998.

AL-SUNAN AL-KUBRA, by Abu Bakr Ahmad b. Husain Al-Baihaqi (d. 1066 AD, Iran), Narrator; Abdullah b. Umar RA, p 17 V 8, Publisher; DAR AL-KUTUB AL-ILMIYYAH, Beirut, Lebanon, third edition 2003.

[134]SAHIH MUSLIM, by Abu Al-Husain Muslim b. Hajjaj Al-Nisapuri (d. 875 AD, Iran), Narrator; Abu Masud RA, p 785, Publisher; DAR TAYBAH, Riyadh, KSA, first edition 2006.

MUSNAD ABU AWANAH, by Abu Awanah Yaqub b. Ibrahim Al-Isfaraini (d. 928 AD, Iran), Narrator; Abu Masud Al-Ansari RA, p 70 V 4, Publisher; DAR AL-MA'RIFAH, Beirut, Lebanon, first edition 1998.

SAHIH TIRMIDHI, by Abu Isa Muhammad b. Isa Al-Tirmidhi (d. 892 AD, Uzbekistan), chapter; ABWAB AL-BIRR WA AL-SILAH, N; 1948, Narrator; Abu Masud Al-Ansari RA, p 500 V 3, published by DAR AL-GHARB AL-ISLAMI, Beirut, Lebanon, first edition 1996.

[135]AL-JAME' AL-SAHIH, by Abu Abdullah Muhammad b. Ismael Al-Bukhari (d. 870 AD, Uzbekistan), Narrator; Al-Ma'rur b. Suwaid RA, p 616, Publisher DAR IBN KATHIR, Damascus, Syria, first edition 2002.

SAHIH MUSLIM, by Abu Al-Husain Muslim b. Hajjaj Al-Nisapuri (d. 875 AD, Iran), Narrator; Al-Ma'rur RA, p 787, Publisher; DAR TAYBAH, Riyadh, KSA, first edition 2006.

[136] SAHIH TIRMIDHI, by Abu Isa Muhammad b. Isa Al-Tirmidhi (d. 892 AD, Uzbekistan), chapter; ABWAB AL-BIRR WA AL-SILAH, N; 1949, Narrator; Abdullah b. Umar RA, p 500 V 3, published by DAR AL-GHARB AL-ISLAMI, Beirut, Lebanon, first edition 1996.

AL-SUNAN AL-KUBRA, by Abu Bakr Ahmad b. Husain Al-Baihaqi (d. 1066 AD, Iran), Narrator; Abdullah b. Umar RA, p 18 V 8, Publisher; DAR AL-KUTUB AL-ILMIYYAH, Beirut, Lebanon, third edition 2003.

[137]AL-ISABAH FI TAMYEEZ AL-SAHABAH, by Shihabuddin Ahmad b. Nuriddin Ibn Hajar Al-Asqallani (d. 1449 AD, Egypt), p 495 V 2, Publisher; DAR AL-KUTUB AL-ILMIYYAH, Beirut, Lebanon, first edition 1995.

AL-SIRAH AL-NABAWIYYAH, by Abu Muhammad Abdulmalik b. Hisham Al-Himyari (d. 833 AD, Egypt), p 495 V 2, Publisher DAR AL-KITAB AL-ARABI, Beirut, Lebanon, third edition 1990.

TARIKH MADINAT DIMISHQ, by Abu Al-Qasim Ali b. Hasan Ibn Asakir Al-Dimishqi (d. 1176 AD, Syria), Narrator; Ibn Hisham RA, p 352 V 19, Publisher; DAR AL-FIKAR, Beirut, Lebanon, 1995.

AL-MU'JAM AL-KABIR, by Abu Al-Qasim Sulaiman b. Ayub Al-Tabarani (d. 918 AD, Iran), Narrator; Ibn Hisham RA, p 83 V 5, Publisher; MAKTABAH IBN TAIMIYYAH, Cairo, Egypt, 1983.

[138] ibid

[139] MAJMA' AL-AMTHAL, by Abu Al-Fadl Ahmad b. Muhammad Al-Midani (d. 1124 AD, Iran), p 374, V 1, Publisher; MATBA'AH AL-SUNNAH AL-MUHAMMADIYYAH, Cairo, Egypt, 1955.

AYYAM AL-ARABIYYAH, by Muhammad Ahmad Jaad, Ali Muhammad Al-Bijawi and Muhammad Abu Al-Fadl Ibrahim, P142, Publisher; ISA AL-BABI AL-HALABI, Cairo, Egypt 1942.

[140]USUD AL-GHABAH FI MA'RIFAT AL-SAHABAH, by Abu Al-Hasan Ali b. Muhammad Al-Jazari (d. 1233 AD, Iraq), p 195 V 1, Publisher; DAR AL-KUTUB AL-ILMIYYAH, Beirut, Lebanon, first edition 1996.

[141]TARIKH MADINAT DIMISHQ, by Abu Al-Qasim Ali b. Hasan Ibn Asakir Al-Dimishqi (d. 1176 AD, Syria), Narrator; Thawban b. Juhdur RA, p 172 V 1, Publisher; DAR AL-FIKAR, Beirut, Lebanon, 1995.

USUD AL-GHABAH FI MA'RIFAT AL-SAHABAH, by Abu Al-Hasan Ali b. Muhammad Al-Jazari (d. 1233 AD, Iraq), p 480 V 1, Publisher; DAR AL-KUTUB AL-ILMIYYAH, Beirut, Lebanon, first edition 1996.

[142]TARIKH MADINAT DIMISHQ, by Abu Al-Qasim Ali b. Hasan Ibn Asakir Al-Dimishqi (d. 1176 AD, Syria), Narrator; Thawban b. Juhdur RA, p 174 V 11, Publisher; DAR AL-FIKAR, Beirut, Lebanon, 1995.

ASBAB AL-NUZUL, by Abu Al-Hasan Ali b. Ahmad Al-Nisapuri Al-Wahidi (d. 1076 AD, Iran), p 169, Publisher; DAR AL-KUTUB AL-ILMIYYAH, Beirut, Lebanon, first edition 1991.

MA'ALIM AL-TANZIL, by Abu Muhammad Husain b. Masud Al-Baghawi (d. 1122 AD, Iran), p 247 V 82 Publisher; DAR TAYBAH, Riyadh, KSA, 1992.

JAME' AL-BAYAN 'AN TA'WIL AYI AL-QURAN, by Muhammad b. Jarir Al-Tabari (d. 923 AD, Iraq), Narrator; Sa'ed b. Jubair, p 213 V 7, Publisher; DAR HAJR, Cairo, Egypt, first edition 2001.

ASBAB AL-NUZUL, by Abu Al-Hasan Ali b. Ahmad Al-Nisapuri Al-Wahidi (d. 1076 AD, Iran), Narrator; Aisha RA, p 170, Publisher; DAR AL-KUTUB AL-ILMIYYAH, Beirut, Lebanon, first edition 1991.

[143]USUD AL-GHABAH FI MA'RIFAT AL-SAHABAH, by Abu Al-Hasan Ali b. Muhammad Al-Jazari (d. 1233 AD, Iraq), p 510 V 2, Publisher; DAR AL-KUTUB AL-ILMIYYAH, Beirut, Lebanon, first edition 1996.

[144]USUD AL-GHABAH FI MA'RIFAT AL-SAHABAH, by Abu Al-Hasan Ali b. Muhammad Al-Jazari (d. 1233 AD, Iraq), p 510 V 2, Publisher; DAR AL-KUTUB AL-ILMIYYAH, Beirut, Lebanon, first edition 1996.

[145] MUSTARDAK ALA AL-SAHIHAIN, by Abu Abdullah Muhammad b. Abdullah Al-Nisapuri (d 1012 AD, Iran), N; 6539, Narrator; Musab b. Abdullah and N; 6541 Narrator; Amr b. Auf, publisher; DAR AL-KUTUB AL-ILMIYYAH, second edition 2002.

AL-MU'JAM AL-KABIR, by Abu Al-Qasim Sulaiman b. Ayub Al-Tabarani (d. 918 AD, Iran), Narrator; Musab b. Abdullah RA, p 212 V 6, Publisher; MAKTABAH IBN TAIMIYYAH, Cairo, Egypt, 1983.

[146]AL-JAME' AL-SAHIH, by Abu Abdullah Muhammad b. Ismael Al-Bukhari (d. 870 AD, Uzbekistan), Narrator; Anas RA, p 685, Publisher DAR IBN KATHIR, Damascus, Syria, first edition 2002.

SAHIH MUSLIM, by Abu Al-Husain Muslim b. Hajjaj Al-Nisapuri (d. 875 AD, Iran), Narrator; Anas RA, p 1092, Publisher; DAR TAYBAH, Riyadh, KSA, first edition 2006.

[147] ibid

[148]MUSNAD AHMAD, by Abu Abdullah Ahmad b. Muhammad b. Hanbal Al-Marwazi (d.855, Iraq), Narrator; Anas RA, p 175 V 11, Publisher; DAR AL-HADITH, Cairo, Egypt, first edition 1995.

[149]SAHIH MUSLIM, by Abu Al-Husain Muslim b. Hajjaj Al-Nisapuri (d. 875 AD, Iran), Narrator; Anas RA, p 1093, Publisher; DAR TAYBAH, Riyadh, KSA, first edition 2006.

[150]AL-JAME' AL-SAHIH, by Abu Abdullah Muhammad b. Ismael Al-Bukhari (d. 870 AD, Uzbekistan), Narrator; Sa'd b. Abu Waqqas RA, p 313, Publisher DAR IBN KATHIR, Damascus, Syria, first edition 2002.

AL-MUWATTA, by Abu Abdullah Malik b. Anas Al-Asbahi Al-Himyari (d. 795, Madinah), Narrator; Sa'd b. Abu Waqqas, p 763, Publisher; MUSTAFA AL-BABI AL-HALABI, (DAR IHYA AL-TURATH), Cairo, Egypt, 1985.

[151]KITAB AL-AMALI, by Yahya b. Al-Husain Al-Shajari Al-Jurjani (d.1105 AD, Iran) Narrator; Anas RA, p 154 V 2, Publisher; DAR AL-KUTUB AL-ILMIYYAH, Beirut, Lebanon, first edition 2001.

[152] SAHIH TIRMIDHI, by Abu Isa Muhammad b. Isa Al-Tirmidhi (d. 892 AD, Uzbekistan), chapter; AL-JANAIZ, N; 989, Narrator; Aisha RA, p 304 V 2, published by DAR AL-GHARB AL-ISLAMI, Beirut, Lebanon, first edition 1996.

SUNAN ABU DAWUD, by Abu Dawud Sulaiman b. Al-Ash'ath Al-Sijistani (d. 889 AD, Iraq), Narrator; Aisha RA, p 75 V 5, Publisher; DAR AL-RISALAH AL-ALAMIYYAH, Damascus, Syria, first edition 2009.

SUNAN IBN MAJAH, by Abu Abdullah Muhammad b. Yazid Al-Qazwini (d 887 AD, Iran), chapter; KITAB AL-JANAIZ, N; 1456 Narrator; Aisha, p 468 V 1, publisher; DAR IHYAA AL-KUTUB AL-ARABIYYAH, Cairo, Egypt, year 1952.

[153]SUNAN ABU DAWUD, by Abu Dawud Sulaiman b. Al-Ash'ath Al-Sijistani (d. 889 AD, Iraq), Narrator; Al-Muttalib, p 115 V 5, Publisher; DAR AL-RISALAH AL-ALAMIYYAH, Damascus, Syria, first edition 2009.

SUNAN IBN MAJAH, by Abu Abdullah Muhammad b. Yazid Al-Qazwini (d 887 AD, Iran), chapter; KITAB AL-JANAIZ, N; 1561 Narrator; Anas, p 498 V 1, publisher; DAR IHYAA AL-KUTUB AL-ARABIYYAH, Cairo, Egypt, year 1952.

[154]SAHIH MUSLIM, by Abu Al-Husain Muslim b. Hajjaj Al-Nisapuri (d. 875 AD, Iran), Narrator; Aisha RA, p 431, Publisher; DAR TAYBAH, Riyadh, KSA, first edition 2006.

[155]AL-JAME' AL-SAHIH, by Abu Abdullah Muhammad b. Ismael Al-Bukhari (d. 870 AD, Uzbekistan), Narrator; Anas RA, p 1598, Publisher DAR IBN KATHIR, Damascus, Syria, first edition 2002.

SAHIH MUSLIM, by Abu Al-Husain Muslim b. Hajjaj Al-Nisapuri (d. 875 AD, Iran), Narrator; Anas RA, p 871, Publisher; DAR TAYBAH, Riyadh, KSA, first edition 2006.

[156]AL-MU'JAM AL-KABIR, by Abu Al-Qasim Sulaiman b. Ayub Al-Tabarani (d. 918 AD, Iran), Narrator; Abdullah b. Masud RA, p 77 V 9, Publisher; MAKTABAH IBN TAIMIYYAH, Cairo, Egypt, 1983.

AL-MU'JAM AL-KABIR, by Abu Al-Qasim Sulaiman b. Ayub Al-Tabarani (d. 918 AD, Iran), Narrator; Abdullah b. Masud RA, p 76 V 9, Publisher; MAKTABAH IBN TAIMIYYAH, Cairo, Egypt, 1983.

[157]AL-MU'JAM AL-KABIR, by Abu Al-Qasim Sulaiman b. Ayub Al-Tabarani (d. 918 AD, Iran), Narrator; Jubaish b. Khalid RA, p 254 V 25, Publisher; MAKTABAH IBN TAIMIYYAH, Cairo, Egypt, 1983.

[158]USUD AL-GHABAH FI MA'RIFAT AL-SAHABAH, by Abu Al-Hasan Ali b. Muhammad Al-Jazari (d. 1233 AD, Iraq), p 393 V 2, Publisher; DAR AL-KUTUB AL-ILMIYYAH, Beirut, Lebanon, first edition 1996.

[159]MUSNAD ABU YA'LA, by Abu Ya'la Ahmad b. Ali Al-Mausilli (d. 919 AD Iraq), Narrator; Abdullah b. Abbas, N; 899, p 69 V 5, Publisher; DAR AL-THAQAFAH AL-ARABIYYAH, Damascus, Syria, second edition 1992.

[160]AL-SIRAH AL-NABAWIYYAH, by Abu Muhammad Abdulmalik b. Hisham Al-Himyari (d. 833 AD, Egypt), Narrator; Yahya b. Saed, p 58 V 4, Publisher DAR AL-KITAB AL-ARABI, Beirut, Lebanon, third edition 1990.

[161]AL-JAME' AL-SAHIH, by Abu Abdullah Muhammad b. Ismael Al-Bukhari (d. 870 AD, Uzbekistan), Narrator; Anas RA, p 900, Publisher DAR IBN KATHIR, Damascus, Syria, first edition 2002.

[162]TARIKH MADINAT DIMISHQ, by Abu Al-Qasim Ali b. Hasan Ibn Asakir Al-Dimishqi (d. 1176 AD, Syria), Narrator; Anas RA, p 271 V 35, Publisher; DAR AL-FIKAR, Beirut, Lebanon, first edition 1998.

[163]SAHIH MUSLIM, by Abu Al-Husain Muslim b. Hajjaj Al-Nisapuri (d. 875 AD, Iran), Narrator; Anas RA, p 296, Publisher; DAR TAYBAH, Riyadh, KSA, first edition 2006.

AL-JAME' AL-SAHIH, by Abu Abdullah Muhammad b. Ismael Al-Bukhari (d. 870 AD, Uzbekistan), Narrator; Anas RA, p 106, Publisher DAR IBN KATHIR, Damascus, Syria, first edition 2002.

[164]AL-SUNAN AL-KUBRA, by Abu Bakr Ahmad b. Husain Al-Baihaqi (d. 1066 AD, Iran), Narrator; Abu Sa'ed Al-Khudri RA, p 462 V 4, Publisher; DAR AL-KUTUB AL-ILMIYYAH, Beirut, Lebanon, third edition 2003.

[165]AL-JAME' AL-SAHIH, by Abu Abdullah Muhammad b. Ismael Al-Bukhari (d. 870 AD, Uzbekistan), Narrator; Jabir RA, p 1008, Publisher DAR IBN KATHIR, Damascus, Syria, first edition 2002.

SAHIH MUSLIM, by Abu Al-Husain Muslim b. Hajjaj Al-Nisapuri (d. 875 AD, Iran), Narrator; Jabir RA, p 978, Publisher; DAR TAYBAH, Riyadh, KSA, first edition 2006.

[166] Surah 9 Al-Tawbah; 128.

[167]AL-JAME' AL-SAHIH, by Abu Abdullah Muhammad b. Ismael Al-Bukhari (d. 870 AD, Uzbekistan), Narrator; Anas RA, p 1008, Publisher DAR IBN KATHIR, Damascus, Syria, first edition 2002.

SAHIH MUSLIM, by Abu Al-Husain Muslim b. Hajjaj Al-Nisapuri (d. 875 AD, Iran), Narrator; Anas RA, p 979, Publisher; DAR TAYBAH, Riyadh, KSA, first edtion 2006.

[168]SAHIH MUSLIM, by Abu Al-Husain Muslim b. Hajjaj Al-Nisapuri (d. 875 AD, Iran), Narrator; Abu Hurairah RA, p 978, Publisher; DAR TAYBAH, Riyadh, KSA, first edition 2006.

[169]AL-JAME' AL-SAHIH, by Abu Abdullah Muhammad b. Ismael Al-Bukhari (d. 870 AD, Uzbekistan), Narrator; Sahl b. Sa'd Al-Sa'idi RA, p 1320, Publisher DAR IBN KATHIR, Damascus, Syria, first edition 2002.

SAHIH MUSLIM, by Abu Al-Husain Muslim b. Hajjaj Al-Nisapuri (d. 875 AD, Iran), Narrator; Sahl RA, p 967, Publisher; DAR TAYBAH, Riyadh, KSA, first edition 2006.

[170] Matthew; 26, John; 12.

[171]AL-JAME' AL-SAHIH, by Abu Abdullah Muhammad b. Ismael Al-Bukhari (d. 870 AD, Uzbekistan), Narrator; Abu Hurairah RA, p 1509, Publisher DAR IBN KATHIR, Damascus, Syria, first edition 2002.

SAHIH MUSLIM, by Abu Al-Husain Muslim b. Hajjaj Al-Nisapuri (d. 875 AD, Iran), Narrator; Abu Hurairah RA, p 41, Publisher; DAR TAYBAH, Riyadh, KSA, first edition 2006.

[172] DALAIL AL-NUBUWWAH, by Abu Bakr Ahmad b. Husain Al-Baihaqi (d. 1066 AD, Iran), Narrator; Abu Umamah Al-Bahili, p 307, V 2, publisher; DAR AL-KUTUB AL-ILMIYYAH, Beirut, Lebanon, and DAR AL-RAYYAN LI AL-TURATH, Cairo, Egypt, first edition 1988.

AL-MU'JAM AL-KABIR, by Abu Al-Qasim Sulaiman b. Ayub Al-Tabarani (d. 918 AD, Iran), Narrator; Abu Qatadah RA, p 224 V 25, Publisher; MAKTABAH IBN TAIMIYYAH, Cairo, Egypt, 1983.

[173]AL-SIRAH AL-NABAWIYYAH, by Abu Bakr Muhammad b. Ishaq Al-Madani (d. 768 AD, Madinah/Iraq), p 651 V 2, Publisher; DAR AL-KUTUB AL-ILMIYYAH, Beirut, Lebanon, third edition 2003.

AL-KAMIL FI AL-TARIKH, by Abu Al-Hasan Ali b. Muhammad Al-Jazari Ibn Al-Athir (d. 1233 AD, Turkey/Iraq), p 156 V 2, Publisher; DAR AL-KUTUB AL-ILMIYYAH, Beirut, Lebanon, first edition 1987.

[174] SHAMAIL MUHAMMADIYYAH, by Abu Isa Muhammad b. Isa Al-Tirmidhi (d. 892 AD, Uzbekistan), chapter; MA JAA FI TAWADHU RASULULLAH, N; 337, Narrator; Hsan b. Ali RA, p 247, published by MAKTABAH AL-ULUM WA AL-HIKAM, Cairo, Egypt, first edition 2008.

DALAIL AL-NUBUWWAH, by Abu Bakr Ahmad b. Husain Al-Baihaqi (d. 1066 AD, Iran), N; 565, Narrator; Hasan b. Ali p 627, V 2, publisher; DAR AL-NAFAIS, Beirut, Lebanon, first edition 1986.

AL-MU'JAM AL-KABIR, by Abu Al-Qasim Sulaiman b. Ayub Al-Tabarani (d. 918 AD, Iran), Narrator; Hasan b. Ali RA, p 155 V 22, Publisher; MAKTABAH IBN TAIMIYYAH, Cairo, Egypt, 1983.

[175] SAHIH TIRMIDHI, by Abu Isa Muhammad b. Isa Al-Tirmidhi (d. 892 AD, Uzbekistan), chapter; ABWAB AL-TAFSIR, N; 3340, Narrator; Abu Talha RA, p 182 V 4, published by DAR AL-GHARB AL-ISLAMI, Beirut, Lebanon, first edition 1996

[176]SAHIH MUSLIM, by Abu Al-Husain Muslim b. Hajjaj Al-Nisapuri (d. 875 AD, Iran), Narrator; Abu Hurairah RA, p 986, Publisher; DAR TAYBAH, Riyadh, KSA, first edition 2006

AL-JAME' AL-SAHIH, by Abu Abdullah Muhammad b. Ismael Al-Bukhari (d. 870 AD, Uzbekistan), Narrator; Abu Hurairah RA, p 930, Publisher DAR IBN KATHIR, Damascus, Syria, first edition 2002.

[177] SAHIH TIRMIDHI, by Abu Isa Muhammad b. Isa Al-Tirmidhi (d. 892 AD, Uzbekistan), chapter; AL-MANAQIB, N; 3640, Narrator; Aisha RA, p 29 V 6, published by DAR AL-GHARB AL-ISLAMI, Beirut, Lebanon, first edition 1996.

[178] SAHIH TIRMIDHI, by Abu Isa Muhammad b. Isa Al-Tirmidhi (d. 892 AD, Uzbekistan), chapter; KALAM AL-NABIY SA, N; 3639, Narrator; Aisha RA, p 29 V 6, published by DAR AL-GHARB AL-ISLAMI, Beirut, Lebanon, first edition 1996.

AL-JAME' AL-SAHIH, by Abu Abdullah Muhammad b. Ismael Al-Bukhari (d. 870 AD, Uzbekistan), Narrator; Aisha RA, p 878, Publisher DAR IBN KATHIR, Damascus, Syria, first edition 2002.

SAHIH MUSLIM, by Abu Al-Husain Muslim b. Hajjaj Al-Nisapuri (d. 875 AD, Iran), Narrator; Aisha RA, p 1366, Publisher; DAR TAYBAH, Riyadh, KSA, first edition 2006.

SUNAN ABU DAWUD, by Abu Dawud Sulaiman b. Al-Ash'ath Al-Sijistani (d. 889 AD, Iraq), Narrator; Aisha, p 496 V 5, Publisher; DAR AL-RISALAH AL-ALAMIYYAH, Damascus, Syria, special edition 2009.

[179]SUNAN ABU DAWUD, by Abu Dawud Sulaiman b. Al-Ash'ath Al-Sijistani (d. 889 AD, Iraq), Narrator; Aisha RA, p 208 V 7, Publisher; DAR AL-RISALAH AL-ALAMIYYAH, Damascus, Syria, special edition 2009.

MUSNAD AHMAD, by Abu Abdullah Ahmad b. Muhammad b. Hanbal Al-Marwazi (d.855, Iraq), Narrator; Aisha RA, p 520 V 41, Publisher; MUASSASAH AL-RISALAH, Beirut, Lebanon, first edition 2001.

[180] Surah 14 Ibrahim; 24-25

[181]AL-JAME' AL-SAHIH, by Abu Abdullah Muhammad b. Ismael Al-Bukhari (d. 870 AD, Uzbekistan), Narrator; Abu Hurairah RA, p 930, Publisher DAR IBN KATHIR, Damascus, Syria, first edition 2002.

SAHIH MUSLIM, by Abu Al-Husain Muslim b. Hajjaj Al-Nisapuri (d. 875 AD, Iran), Narrator; Abu Hurairah RA, p 300, Publisher; DAR TAYBAH, Riyadh, KSA, first edition 2006.

AL-MUNTAKHAB MIN MUSNAD by Abd b. Humaid Al-Keshi (d. 863 AD, Shahrisabz, Uzbekistan), Narrator; Jabir RA, p 134 V 2, Publisher; DAR BALNASIYYAH. Riyadh, KSA, second edition 2002.

[182]SAHIH MUSLIM, by Abu Al-Husain Muslim b. Hajjaj Al-Nisapuri (d. 875 AD, Iran), Narrator; Anas, Jabir, and Abu Musa RA, p 463, Publisher; DAR TAYBAH, Riyadh, KSA, first edtion 2006.

SAHIH TIRMIDHI, by Abu Isa Muhammad b. Isa Al-Tirmidhi (d. 892 AD, Uzbekistan), chapter; AL-ZUHD, N; 2337, Narrator; Anas RA, p 161 V 4 published by DAR AL-GHARB AL-ISLAMI, Beirut, Lebanon, first edition 1996.

[183]AL-JAME' AL-SAHIH, by Abu Abdullah Muhammad b. Ismael Al-Bukhari (d. 870 AD, Uzbekistan), Narrator; Abdullah b. Umar RA, pp 26-27, Publisher DAR IBN KATHIR, Damascus, Syria, first edition 2002.

SAHIH MUSLIM, by Abu Al-Husain Muslim b. Hajjaj Al-Nisapuri (d. 875 AD, Iran), Narrator; Abdullah b. Umar RA, p 1293, Publisher; DAR TAYBAH, Riyadh, KSA, first edtion 2006.

[184]AL-JAME' AL-SAHIH, by Abu Abdullah Muhammad b. Ismael Al-Bukhari (d. 870 AD, Uzbekistan), Narrator; Abu Musa RA, p 32, Publisher DAR IBN KATHIR, Damascus, Syria, first edition 2002.

SAHIH MUSLIM, by Abu Al-Husain Muslim b. Hajjaj Al-Nisapuri (d. 875 AD, Iran), Narrator; Abu Musa RA, p 1083, Publisher; DAR TAYBAH, Riyadh, KSA, first edition 2006.

[185]AL-JAME' AL-SAHIH, by Abu Abdullah Muhammad b. Ismael Al-Bukhari (d. 870 AD, Uzbekistan), Narrator; Abu Musa RA, p 1612, Publisher DAR IBN KATHIR, Damascus, Syria, first edition 2002.

SAHIH MUSLIM, by Abu Al-Husain Muslim b. Hajjaj Al-Nisapuri (d. 875 AD, Iran), Narrator; Abu Musa RA, p 1084, Publisher; DAR TAYBAH, Riyadh, KSA, first edition 2006.

[186]AL-JAME' AL-SAHIH, by Abu Abdullah Muhammad b. Ismael Al-Bukhari (d. 870 AD, Uzbekistan), Narrator; Jabir and Abu Huraira RA, p 873, Publisher DAR IBN KATHIR, Damascus, Syria, first edition 2002.
SAHIH MUSLIM, by Abu Al-Husain Muslim b. Hajjaj Al-Nisapuri (d. 875 AD, Iran), Narrator; Abu Hurairah RA, p 1085, Publisher; DAR TAYBAH, Riyadh, KSA, first edition 2006.
[187]AL-JAME' AL-SAHIH, by Abu Abdullah Muhammad b. Ismael Al-Bukhari (d. 870 AD, Uzbekistan), Narrator; Abdullah b. Masud RA, p 1574, Publisher DAR IBN KATHIR, Damascus, Syria, first edition 2002.
SAHIH MUSLIM, by Abu Al-Husain Muslim b. Hajjaj Al-Nisapuri (d. 875 AD, Iran), Narrator; Abdullah b. Masud RA, p 2744, Publisher; DAR TAYBAH, Riyadh, KSA, first edition 2006.
[188]AL-JAME' AL-SAHIH, by Abu Abdullah Muhammad b. Ismael Al-Bukhari (d. 870 AD, Uzbekistan), Narrator; Anas RA, p 27, Publisher DAR IBN KATHIR, Damascus, Syria, first edition 2002.
SUNAN IBN MAJAH, by Abu Abdullah Muhammad b. Yazid Al-Qazwini (d 887 AD, Iran), chapter; KITAB AL-IQAMAT AL-SALAT WA AL-SUNNAH FIHA, N; 1402 Narrator; Anas, p 449 V 1, publisher; DAR IHYAA AL-KUTUB AL- ARABIYYAH, Cairo, Egypt, year 1952.
AL-SUNAN AL-KUBRA, by Abu Bakr Ahmad b. Husain Al-Baihaqi (d. 1066 AD, Iran), Narrator; Anas RA, p 13 V 7, Publisher; DAR AL-KUTUB AL-ILMIYYAH, Beirut, Lebanon, third edition 2003.

[189]SAHIH MUSLIM, by Abu Al-Husain Muslim b. Hajjaj Al-Nisapuri (d. 875 AD, Iran), Narrator; Anas RA, p 144, Publisher; DAR TAYBAH, Riyadh, KSA, first edition 2006.
AL-JAME' AL-SAHIH, by Abu Abdullah Muhammad b. Ismael Al-Bukhari (d. 870 AD, Uzbekistan), Narrator; Anas RA, p 66, Publisher DAR IBN KATHIR, Damascus, Syria, first edition 2002.
[190] SAHIH TIRMIDHI, by Abu Isa Muhammad b. Isa Al-Tirmidhi (d. 892 AD, Uzbekistan), chapter; AL-ILM, N; 2678, Narrator; Anas RA, p 410 V 4, published by DAR AL-GHARB AL-ISLAMI, Beirut, Lebanon, first edition 1996.
[191]MUSNAD AHMAD, by Abu Abdullah Ahmad b. Muhammad b. Hanbal Al-Marwazi (d.855, Iraq), Narrator; Abdullah b. Abbas RA, p 244 V 3, Publisher; DAR AL-HADITH, Cairo, Egypt, first edition 1995.
SAHIH TIRMIDHI, by Abu Isa Muhammad b. Isa Al-Tirmidhi (d. 892 AD, Uzbekistan), chapter; ABWAB SIFAT AL-QIYAMAH WA AL-RAQAIQ WA AL-WARA', N; 2516, Narrator; Abdullah b. Abbas RA, p 284 V 4 published by DAR AL-GHARB AL-ISLAMI, Beirut, Lebanon, first edition 1996.
[192]AL-JAME' AL-SAHIH, by Abu Abdullah Muhammad b. Ismael Al-Bukhari (d. 870 AD, Uzbekistan), Narrator; Abdullah b. Abbas RA, p 31, Publisher DAR IBN KATHIR, Damascus, Syria, first edition 2002.
SAHIH MUSLIM, by Abu Al-Husain Muslim b. Hajjaj Al-Nisapuri (d. 875 AD, Iran), Narrator; Mu'awiyah b. Abu Sufyan, p 459, Publisher; DAR TAYBAH, Riyadh, KSA, first edition 2006.
[193]AL-JAME' AL-SAHIH, by Abu Abdullah Muhammad b. Ismael Al-Bukhari (d. 870 AD, Uzbekistan), Mu'awiyah b. Abu Sufyan, p 30, Publisher DAR IBN KATHIR, Damascus, Syria, first edition 2002.
SAHIH MUSLIM, by Abu Al-Husain Muslim b. Hajjaj Al-Nisapuri (d. 875 AD, Iran), Narrator; Abdullah b. Abbas RA, p 1158, Publisher; DAR TAYBAH, Riyadh, KSA, first edition 2006.

[194]SAHIH MUSLIM, by Abu Al-Husain Muslim b. Hajjaj Al-Nisapuri (d. 875 AD, Iran), Narrator; Muawiyah b. Al-Hakam Al-Sulami RA, p 242, Publisher; DAR TAYBAH, Riyadh, KSA, first edition 2006.
SUNAN ABU DAWUD, by Abu Dawud Sulaiman b. Al-Ash'ath Al-Sijistani (d. 889 AD, Iraq), Narrator; Muawiah b. Al-Hakam Al-Sulami, p 191 V 2, Publisher; DAR AL-RISALAH AL-ALAMIYYAH, Damascus, Syria, special edition 2009.
[195]AL-SIRAH AL-NABAWIYYAH, by Abu Muhammad Abdulmalik b. Hisham Al-Himyari (d. 833 AD, Egypt), Narrator; Yahya b. Saed, p 82 V 2, Publisher DAR AL-KITAB AL-ARABI, Beirut, Lebanon, third edition 1990.
[196]AL-JAME' AL-SAHIH, by Abu Abdullah Muhammad b. Ismael Al-Bukhari (d. 870 AD, Uzbekistan), Narrator; Anas RA, p 898, Publisher DAR IBN KATHIR, Damascus, Syria, first edition 2002.

SAHIH MUSLIM, by Abu Al-Husain Muslim b. Hajjaj Al-Nisapuri (d. 875 AD, Iran), Narrator; Anas RA, p 1119, Publisher; DAR TAYBAH, Riyadh, KSA, first edition 2006

[197] Surah 9 Al-Tawbah; 40.
[198]AL-SIRAH AL-NABAWIYYAH, by Abu Bakr Muhammad b. Ishaq Al-Madani (d. 768 AD, Madinah/Iraq), p 124 V 1, Publisher; DAR AL-KUTUB AL-ILMIYYAH, Beirut, Lebanon, first edition 2004.

DIWAN ABU TALIB, by Dr. Muhammad Al-Tunji, p 38, Publisher; DAR AL-KITAB AL-ARABI, Beirut, Lebanon, first edition 1994.

[199]AL-SIRAH AL-NABAWIYYAH, by Abu Bakr Muhammad b. Ishaq Al-Madani (d. 768 AD, Madinah/Iraq), p 127 V 2, Publisher; DAR AL-KUTUB AL-ILMIYYAH, Beirut, Lebanon, first edition 2004.
[200]AL-SIRAH AL-NABAWIYYAH, by Abu Bakr Muhammad b. Ishaq Al-Madani (d. 768 AD, Madinah/Iraq), p 143 V 2, Publisher; DAR AL-KUTUB AL-ILMIYYAH, Beirut, Lebanon, first edition 2004.
[201] AL-MUSNAD AL-JAMEA, by Abdullah b. Abdul-Rahaman Al-Darimi (d 869 AD, Uzbekistan), chapter; HUSN MU'ASHARAH AL-NISA, N; 2, Narrator; Wadin RA p 93, published by DAR AL-BASHAIR AL-ISLAMIYYAH, Beirut, Lebanon, first edition 2013.
[202]AL-MU'JAM AL-KABIR, by Abu Al-Qasim Sulaiman b. Ayub Al-Tabarani (d. 918 AD, Iran), Narrator; Umar RA, p 337 V 18, Publisher; MAKTABAH IBN TAIMIYYAH, Cairo, Egypt, 1983.

AL-TAFSIR, by Abdul-Razzaq b. Hammam Al-San'ani (d. 828 AD, Yemen), Narrator; uMAR, p 397 V 3, Publisher; DAR KUTUB AL-ILMIYYAH, Beirut, Lebanon, first edition 1999.

[203]AL-JAME' AL-SAHIH, by Abu Abdullah Muhammad b. Ismael Al-Bukhari (d. 870 AD, Uzbekistan), Narrator; Abdullah b. Abbas RA, p 1720, Publisher DAR IBN KATHIR, Damascus, Syria, first edition 2002.

JAME' AL-BAYAN 'AN TA'WIL AYI AL-QURAN, by Muhammad b. Jarir Al-Tabari (d. 923 AD, Iraq), Narrator; Abdullah b. Abbas, p 526 V 6, Publisher; DAR HAJR, Cairo, Egypt, first edition 2001.

[204] ibid

[205] Surah 4 Al-Nisa; 19.

[206]MA'ALIM AL-TANZIL, by Abu Muhammad Husain b. Masud Al-Baghawi (d. 1122 AD, Iran), p 422 V 8, Publisher; DAR TAYBAH, Riyadh, KSA, 1992.

[207] Surah 4 Al-Nisa; 7.

[208]AL-JAME' AL-SAHIH, by Abu Abdullah Muhammad b. Ismael Al-Bukhari (d. 870 AD, Uzbekistan), Narrator; Abdullah b. Masud RA, p 1097, Publisher DAR IBN KATHIR, Damascus, Syria, first edition 2002.

SAHIH MUSLIM, by Abu Al-Husain Muslim b. Hajjaj Al-Nisapuri (d. 875 AD, Iran), Narrator; Abdullah b. Masud RA, p 53, Publisher; DAR TAYBAH, Riyadh, KSA, first edition 2006.

[209] Surah 17 Al-Israa; 31.

[210]AL-SIRAH AL-NABAWIYYAH, by Abu Bakr Muhammad b. Ishaq Al-Madani (d. 768 AD, Madinah/Iraq), p 249 V 1, Publisher; DAR AL-KUTUB AL-ILMIYYAH, Beirut, Lebanon, third edition 2003.

[211] Surah 62 Al-Jum'ah; 2.

[212] SAHIH TIRMIDHI, by Abu Isa Muhammad b. Isa Al-Tirmidhi (d. 892 AD, Uzbekistan), chapter; AL-FITAN AN RASULILLAH, N; 2175, Narrator; Khabbab b. Al-Aratt RA, p 45 V 4, published by DAR AL-GHARB AL-ISLAMI, Beirut, Lebanon, first edition 1996.

SUNAN AL-NASAI, by Abu Abdul-Rahman Ahmad b. Shuaib Al-Nasai (d. 915 AD Mecca/Turkmenistan), Narrator; Khabbab b. Al-Aratt, p 236, Publisher; DAR AL-HADARAH, Riyadh, KSA, second edition 2015.

SUNAN IBN MAJAH, by Abu Abdullah Muhammad b. Yazid Al-Qazwini (d 887 AD, Iran), chapter; KITAB AL-FITAN, N; 3951 Narrator; Muadh, p 1303 V 2, publisher; DAR IHYAA AL-KUTUB AL-ARABIYYAH, Cairo, Egypt, year 1952.

MUSANNAF IBN ABU SHAYBAH, by Abu Bakr Muhammad b. Abdullah Ibn Abu Shaybah (d. 849 AD, Iraq), Narrator; Muadh RA, p 260 V 16, Publisher; DAR AL-QIBLAH LI AL-THAQAFAH AL-ISLAMIYYAH, Jeddah, KSA, first edition 2006.

[213]MUSANNAF IBN ABU SHAYBAH, by Abu Bakr Muhammad b. Abdullah Ibn Abu Shaybah (d. 849 AD, Iraq), Narrator; Suhaib RA, p 261 V 16, Publisher; DAR AL-QIBLAH LI AL-THAQAFAH AL-ISLAMIYYAH, Jeddah, KSA, first edition 2006.

SAHIH TIRMIDHI, by Abu Isa Muhammad b. Isa Al-Tirmidhi (d. 892 AD, Uzbekistan), chapter; AL-TAFSIR, N; 3340, Narrator; Suhaib RA, p 362 V 5, published by DAR AL-GHARB AL-ISLAMI, Beirut, Lebanon, first edition 1996.

[214] SAHIH TIRMIDHI, by Abu Isa Muhammad b. Isa Al-Tirmidhi (d. 892 AD, Uzbekistan), chapter; AL-TAFSIR, N; 3297, Narrator; Abdullah b. Abbas RA, p 325 V 6, published by DAR AL-GHARB AL-ISLAMI, Beirut, Lebanon, first edition 1996.

MUSTARDAK ALA AL-SAHIHAIN, by Abu Abdullah Muhammad b. Abdullah Al-Nisapuri (d 1012 AD, Iran), chapter; KITAB AL-TAFSIR, N; 3777, Narrator; Abdullah b. Abbas, p 518 V 2, publisher; DAR AL-HARAMAIN, Cairo, Egypt, first edition 1997.

[215] MUSTARDAK ALA AL-SAHIHAIN, by Abu Abdullah Muhammad b. Abdullah Al-Nisapuri (d 1012 AD, Iran), chapter; KITAB AL-IMAN, N; 226, Narrator; Abdul-Rahman b. Abu Uqail Al-Thaqafi, p 127 V 1, publisher; DAR AL-HARAMAIN, Cairo, Egypt, first edition 1997.

MUSANNAF IBN ABU SHAYBAH, by Abu Bakr Muhammad b. Abdullah Ibn Abu Shaybah (d. 849 AD, Iraq), Narrator; Abdul-Rahman b. Abu Uqail Al-Thaqafi RA, p 40 V 11, Publisher; MAKTABAT AL-RUSHD NARHIRUN, Riyadh, KSA, first edition 2004.

[216]MUSNAD AHMAD, by Abu Abdullah Ahmad b. Muhammad b. Hanbal Al-Marwazi (d.855, Iraq), Narrator; Umm Salamah RA, p 327 V 16, Publisher; DAR AL-HADITH, Cairo, Egypt, first edition 1995.

AL-SIRAH AL-NABAWIYYAH, by Abu Bakr Muhammad b. Ishaq Al-Madani (d. 768 AD, Madinah/Iraq), p 249 V 1, Publisher; DAR AL-KUTUB AL-ILMIYYAH, Beirut, Lebanon, third edition 2003.

[217]AL-JAME' AL-SAHIH, by Abu Abdullah Muhammad b. Ismael Al-Bukhari (d. 870 AD, Uzbekistan), Narrator; Aisha RA, p 7, Publisher DAR IBN KATHIR, Damascus, Syria, first edition 2002.

SAHIH MUSLIM, by Abu Al-Husain Muslim b. Hajjaj Al-Nisapuri (d. 875 AD, Iran), Narrator; Aisha RA, p 83, Publisher; DAR TAYBAH, Riyadh, KSA, first edition 2006.

[218]AL-JAME' AL-SAHIH, by Abu Abdullah Muhammad b. Ismael Al-Bukhari (d. 870 AD, Uzbekistan), Narrator; Abdullah b. Masud RA, p 861, Publisher DAR IBN KATHIR, Damascus, Syria, first edition 2002.

[219]AL-JAME' AL-SAHIH, by Abu Abdullah Muhammad b. Ismael Al-Bukhari (d. 870 AD, Uzbekistan), Narrator; Urwah b. Al-Zubair RA, p 943, Publisher DAR IBN KATHIR, Damascus, Syria, first edition 2002.

[220] MUSTARDAK ALA AL-SAHIHAIN, by Abu Abdullah Muhammad b. Abdullah Al-Nisapuri (d 1012 AD, Iran), chapter; KITAB MA'RIFAT AL-SAHABAH, N; 4424, Narrator; Abu Bakr b. Abu Quhafah, p 70 V 3, publisher; DAR AL-HARAMAIN, Cairo, Egypt, first edition 1997.

[221]TARIKH AL-MULUK WA AL-RUSUL, by Muhammad b. Jarir Al-Tabari (d. 923 AD, Iraq), Narrator; Muhammad b. Ka'b Al-Quradhi, p 344 V 2, Publisher; DAR AL-MA'ARIF, Cairo, Egypt, second edition 1967.

[222]AL-JAME' AL-SAHIH, by Abu Abdullah Muhammad b. Ismael Al-Bukhari (d. 870 AD, Uzbekistan), Narrator; Aisha RA, p 798, Publisher DAR IBN KATHIR, Damascus, Syria, first edition 2002.

SAHIH MUSLIM, by Abu Al-Husain Muslim b. Hajjaj Al-Nisapuri (d. 875 AD, Iran), Narrator; Aisha RA, p 864, Publisher; DAR TAYBAH, Riyadh, KSA, first edition 2006.

[223]AL-TABAQAT AL-KABIR, by Muhammad b. Sa'd Al-Baghdadi (d. 845 AD, Iraq), Narrators; Ali, Aisha and Abdullah b. Masud RA, p 193 V 1, Publisher; DAR AL-KUTUB AL-ILMIYYAH, Beirut, Lebanon, first edition 1990.

[224] Surah 42 Al-Shura; 39.

[225] Surah 41 Fussilat; 34.

[226]AL-JAME' AL-SAHIH, by Abu Abdullah Muhammad b. Ismael Al-Bukhari (d. 870 AD, Uzbekistan), Narrator; Jabir RA, p 1013, Publisher DAR IBN KATHIR, Damascus, Syria, first edition 2002.

SAHIH MUSLIM, by Abu Al-Husain Muslim b. Hajjaj Al-Nisapuri (d. 875 AD, Iran), Narrator; Jabir RA, p 1083, Publisher; DAR TAYBAH, Riyadh, KSA, first edition 2006.

[227]AL-JAME' AL-SAHIH, by Abu Abdullah Muhammad b. Ismael Al-Bukhari (d. 870 AD, Uzbekistan), Narrator; Abu Hurairah RA, p 1070, Publisher DAR IBN KATHIR, Damascus, Syria, first edition 2002.

SAHIH MUSLIM, by Abu Al-Husain Muslim b. Hajjaj Al-Nisapuri (d. 875 AD, Iran), Narrator; Abu Hurairah RA, p 844, Publisher; DAR TAYBAH, Riyadh, KSA, first edition 2006.

[228]AL-SIRAH AL-NABAWIYYAH, by Abu Muhammad Abdulmalik b. Hisham Al-Himyari (d. 833 AD, Egypt), Narrator; Ibn Ishaq, p 54 V 4, Publisher DAR AL-KITAB AL-ARABI, Beirut, Lebanon, third edition 1990.

TARIKH AL-MULUK WA AL-RUSUL, by, Muhammad b. Jarir Al-Tabari (d. 923 AD, Iraq), Narrator; Qatadah Al-Sadusi, p 60 V 2, Publisher; DAR AL-MA'ARIF, Cairo, Egypt, second edition 1967.

[229]AL-SIRAH AL-NABAWIYYAH, by Abu Bakr Muhammad b. Ishaq Al-Madani (d. 768 AD, Madinah/Iraq), p 442 V 2, Publisher; DAR AL-KUTUB AL-ILMIYYAH, Beirut, Lebanon, first edition 2004.

AL-SIRAH AL-NABAWIYYAH, by Abu Muhammad Abdulmalik b. Hisham Al-Himyari (d. 833 AD, Egypt), Narrator; Aisha RA, p 240 V 2, Publisher DAR AL-KITAB AL-ARABI, Beirut, Lebanon, third edition 1990.

AL-SUNAN AL-KUBRA, by Abu Bakr Ahmad b. Husain Al-Baihaqi (d. 1066 AD, Iran), Narrator; Aisha RA, p 127 V 9, Publisher; DAR AL-KUTUB AL-ILMIYYAH, Beirut, Lebanon, third edition 2003.

AL-MAGHAZI AL-NABAWIYYAH, by Abu Abdullah Muhammad b. Umar Al-Waqidi (d. 823 AD, Iraq), Narrator; Aisha, p 411 V 1, Publisher; Oxford University Press, London, UK, 1965, (Re-prented; third edition 1984).

MUSTARDAK ALA AL-SAHIHAIN, by Abu Abdullah Muhammad b. Abdullah Al-Nisapuri (d 1012 AD, Iran), chapter; KITAB MA'RIFAT AL-SAHABAH, N; 6860, Narrator; Aisha, p 110 V 4, publisher; DAR AL-KUTUB AL-ILMIYYAH, second edition 2002.

[230] Surah 2 Al-Baqarah; 177.
[231]MUSNAD ABU YA'LA, by Abu Ya'la Ahmad b. Ali Al-Mausilli (d. 919 AD Iraq), Narrator; Ali, N; 3478, p 194 V 6, Publisher; DAR AL-MA'MUN, Damascus, Syria, second edition 1989.
[232]SAHIH MUSLIM, by Abu Al-Husain Muslim b. Hajjaj Al-Nisapuri (d. 875 AD, Iran), Narrator; Abu Hurairah RA, p 1242, Publisher; DAR TAYBAH, Riyadh, KSA, first edition 2006.
[233]SAHIH MUSLIM, by Abu Al-Husain Muslim b. Hajjaj Al-Nisapuri (d. 875 AD, Iran), Narrator; Abu Hurairah RA, p 1360, Publisher; DAR TAYBAH, Riyadh, KSA, first edition 2006.
AL-JAME' AL-SAHIH, by Abu Abdullah Muhammad b. Ismael Al-Bukhari (d. 870 AD, Uzbekistan), Narrator; Abu Hurairah RA, p 5353, Publisher DAR IBN KATHIR, Damascus, Syria, first edition 2002.
[234]SAHIH MUSLIM, by Abu Al-Husain Muslim b. Hajjaj Al-Nisapuri (d. 875 AD, Iran), Narrator; Abu Sa'ed Al-Khudri RA, p 827, Publisher; DAR TAYBAH, Riyadh, KSA, first edition 2006.
[235]ibid
[236]AL-JAME' AL-SAHIH, by Abu Abdullah Muhammad b. Ismael Al-Bukhari (d. 870 AD, Uzbekistan), Narrator; Hudhaifah b. Al-Yaman RA, p 500, Publisher DAR IBN KATHIR, Damascus, Syria, first edition 2002.
SAHIH MUSLIM, by Abu Al-Husain Muslim b. Hajjaj Al-Nisapuri (d. 875 AD, Iran), Narrator; Abu Qatadah RA, p 736, Publisher; DAR TAYBAH, Riyadh, KSA, first edition 2006.
[237] SHUAB AL-IMAN, by Abu Bakr Ahmad b. Husain Al-Baihaqi (d. 1066 AD, Iran), Narrator; Ali RA, N; 3089, p 57, V 5, publisher; MAKTABAH AL-RUSHD LI AL-NASHR WA AL-TAWZEA, Riyadh, KSA, first edition 2003.
[238]AL-JAME' AL-SAHIH, by Abu Abdullah Muhammad b. Ismael Al-Bukhari (d. 870 AD, Uzbekistan), Narrator; Abdullah b. Qais RA, p 351, Publisher DAR IBN KATHIR, Damascus, Syria, first edition 2002.

SAHIH MUSLIM, by Abu Al-Husain Muslim b. Hajjaj Al-Nisapuri (d. 875 AD, Iran), Narrator; Abdullah b. Qais RA, p 448, Publisher; DAR TAYBAH, Riyadh, KSA, first edition 2006.

[239]AL-SIRAH AL-NABAWIYYAH, by Abu Muhammad Abdulmalik b. Hisham Al-Himyari (d. 833 AD, Egypt), p 153 V 1, Publisher DAR AL-KITAB AL-ARABI, Beirut, Lebanon, third edition 1990.

MUSNAD AHMAD, by Abu Abdullah Ahmad b. Muhammad b. Hanbal Al-Marwazi (d.855, Iraq), Narrator; Abdul-Rahman b. Auf RA, p 193 V 3, Publisher; MUASSASAH AL-RISALAH, Beirut, Lebanon, first edition 2001.

AL-KAMIL FI AL-TARIKH, by Abu Al-Hasan Ali b. Muhammad Al-Jazari Ibn Al-Athir (d. 1233 AD, Turkey/Iraq), p 570 V 1, Publisher; DAR AL-KUTUB AL-ILMIYYAH, Beirut, Lebanon, first edition 1987.

[240]MUSNAD ABU AWANAH, by Abu Awanah Yaqub b. Ibrahim Al-Isfaraini (d. 928 AD, Iran), Narrator; Qatadah RA, p 348 V 4, Publisher; DAR AL-MA'RIFAH, Beirut, Lebanon, first edition 1998.

[241]AL-JAME' AL-SAHIH, by Abu Abdullah Muhammad b. Ismael Al-Bukhari (d. 870 AD, Uzbekistan), Narrator; Anas RA, p 637, Publisher DAR IBN KATHIR, Damascus, Syria, first edition 2002.

SAHIH MUSLIM, by Abu Al-Husain Muslim b. Hajjaj Al-Nisapuri (d. 875 AD, Iran), Narrator; Anas RA, p 1091, Publisher; DAR TAYBAH, Riyadh, KSA, first edition 2006

[242] Surah 2 Al-Baqarah; 165.

[243] Surah 3 Aal Imran; 31.

[244] Surah 5 Al-Maidah; 54.

[245]SAHIH MUSLIM, by Abu Al-Husain Muslim b. Hajjaj Al-Nisapuri (d. 875 AD, Iran), Narrator; Abu Hurairah RA, p 44, Publisher; DAR TAYBAH, Riyadh, KSA, first edition 2006.

[246] Surah 3 Aal-Imran; 31

[247]AL-ADAB AL-MUFRAD, by Abu Abdullah Muhammad b. Ismael Al-Bukhari (d. 870 AD, Uzbekistan), Narrator; Anas RA, p 187, Publisher DAR AL-SIDDIQ, Al-Jubail, KSA, second edition 2000.

[248]SAHIH MUSLIM, by Abu Al-Husain Muslim b. Hajjaj Al-Nisapuri (d. 875 AD, Iran), Narrator; Abu Hurairah RA, p 1194, Publisher; DAR TAYBAH, Riyadh, KSA, first edition 2006.

[249]AL-JAME' AL-SAHIH, by Abu Abdullah Muhammad b. Ismael Al-Bukhari (d. 870 AD, Uzbekistan), Narrator; Anas RA, p 14, Publisher DAR IBN KATHIR, Damascus, Syria, first edition 2002.

[250]AL-JAME' AL-SAHIH, by Abu Abdullah Muhammad b. Ismael Al-Bukhari (d. 870 AD, Uzbekistan), Narrator; Anas RA, p 14, Publisher DAR IBN KATHIR, Damascus, Syria, first edition 2002.

[251]AL-MU'JAM AL-KABIR, by Abu Al-Qasim Sulaiman b. Ayub Al-Tabarani (d. 918 AD, Iran), Narrator; Abu Malik Al-Ash'ari RA, p 329 V 3, Publisher; MAKTABAH IBN TAIMIYYAH, Cairo, Egypt, 1983.

TARIKH MADINAT DIMISHQ, by Abu Al-Qasim Ali b. Hasan Ibn Asakir Al-Dimishqi (d. 1176 AD, Syria), Narrator; Abu Malik Al-Ash'ari RA, p 195 V 67, Publisher; DAR AL-FIKAR, Beirut, Lebanon, first edition 1998.

[252]SAHIH MUSLIM, by Abu Al-Husain Muslim b. Hajjaj Al-Nisapuri (d. 875 AD, Iran), Narrator; Abu Hurairah RA, p 131, Publisher; DAR TAYBAH, Riyadh, KSA, first edition 2006.

[253] AL-MAQASID AL-HASANA FI BAYAN KATHIR MIN AL-AHADITH AL-MUSHTAHIRA ALA AL-ALSINA, by Muhammad Abdul-Rahman Al-Skhawi (d. 1497 AD, Egypt), Narrator; Ali RA, p 73,

Publisher; DAR AL-KITAB AL-ARABI, first edition 1985. (Sakhawi has concluded that the hadith does not have an authentic chain however its meaning is authentic.)

[254] SAHIH TIRMIDHI, by Abu Isa Muhammad b. Isa Al-Tirmidhi (d. 892 AD, Uzbekistan), chapter; N; 3638, Narrator; Ali RA, p 27 V 6, published by DAR AL-GHARB AL-ISLAMI, Beirut, Lebanon, first edition 1996

[255]AL-SHIFA BI TA'RIF HUQUQ AL-MUSTAFA, by Ayad b. Musa (d. 1149 AD, Morocco), Narrator; Ali, p 497, Publisher; JAIZAT DUBAI AL-DAWLIYYAH LI AL-QURAN AL-KARIM, Dubai, UAE, first edition 2013.

[256]MA'RIFAT AL-SAHABA, by Abu Nuaim Abdullah b. Ahmad Al-Asbahani (d. 1038 AD, Iran), Narrator; Aisha RA, p 3490, Publisher; DAR AL-WATAN, Riyadh, KSA, first edition 1998.

TARIKH MADINAT DIMISHQ, by Abu Al-Qasim Ali b. Hasan Ibn Asakir Al-Dimishqi (d. 1176 AD, Syria), Narrator; Aisha RA, p 120 V 17, Publisher; DAR AL-KUTUB AL-ILMIYYAH, Beirut, Lebanon, first edition 2012.

[257]AL-SIRAH AL-NABAWIYYAH, by Abu Muhammad Abdulmalik b. Hisham Al-Himyari (d. 833 AD, Egypt), Narrator; Sa'd b. Abu Qaqqas, p 63 V 3, Publisher DAR AL-KITAB AL-ARABI, Beirut, Lebanon, third edition 1990.

TARIKH AL-MULUK WA AL-RUSUL, by Muhammad b. Jarir Al-Tabari (d. 923 AD, Iraq), Narrator; Sa'd b. Abu Waqqas, p 532 V 2, Publisher; DAR AL-MA'ARIF, Cairo, Egypt, second edition 1967.

[258]AL-TABAQAT AL-KABIR, by Muhammad b. Sa'd Al-Baghdadi (d. 845 AD, Iraq), p 43 V 2, Publisher; DAR AL-KUTUB AL-ILMIYYAH, Cairo, Egypt, third edition 2017.

AL-SIRAH AL-NABAWIYYAH, by Abu Muhammad Abdulmalik b. Hisham Al-Himyari (d. 833 AD, Egypt), Narrator; Ibn Ishaq, p 126 V 3, Publisher DAR AL-KITAB AL-ARABI, Beirut, Lebanon, third edition 1990.

[259]KITAB AL-ZUHD WA AL-RAQAIQ, by Abdullah b. Mubarak Al-Marwazi (d. 797 AD, Turkemnistan/Iraq), Narrator; Zaid b. Aslam, p 908, Publisher; DAR AL-ME'RAJ AL-DAWLIYYAH, Riyad, KSA, first edition 1995.

[260]AL-TABAQAT AL-KABIR, by Muhammad b. Sa'd Al-Baghdadi (d. 845 AD, Iraq), p 142 V 3, Publisher; MAKTABAH AL-KHANJI, Cairo, Egypt, year 2001.

[261]AL-JAME' AL-SAHIH, by Abu Abdullah Muhammad b. Ismael Al-Bukhari (d. 870 AD, Uzbekistan), Narrator; Anas RA, p 930, Publisher DAR IBN KATHIR, Damascus, Syria, first edition 2002.

[262]AL-JAME' AL-SAHIH, by Abu Abdullah Muhammad b. Ismael Al-Bukhari (d. 870 AD, Uzbekistan), Narrator; Abu Sa'ed Al-Khudri RA, p 899, Publisher DAR IBN KATHIR, Damascus, Syria, first edition 2002.

[263]MAFATIH AL-GHAIB, by Fakhruddin Abu Abdullah Muhammad b. Umar Al-Razi (d. 1210 AD, Iran/Afghanistan), p 175 V 10, Publisher; DAR AL-FIKAR, Beirut, Lebanon, 1981.

AL-BAHR AL-MUHIT, by Abu Hayyan Muhammad b. Yusuf Al-Gharnati (d. 1344 AD, Spain/Egypt), p 299 V 3, Publisher; DAR AL-KUTUB AL-ILMIYYAH, Beirut, Lebanon, first edition 1993.

AL-JAME' LI AHKAM AL-QURAN, by Abu Abdullah Muhammad b. Ahmad Al-Ansari Al-Qurtubi (d. 1273 AD, Spain/Egypt), p 448 V 6, Publisher; MUASSASAT AL-RISALAH, Beirut, Lebanon, first edition 2006.

[264]SAHIH MUSLIM, by Abu Al-Husain Muslim b. Hajjaj Al-Nisapuri (d. 875 AD, Iran), Narrator; Anas RA, p 1097, Publisher; DAR TAYBAH, Riyadh, KSA, first edition 2006.

[265]AL-ISABAH FI TAMYEEZ AL-SAHABAH, by Shihabuddin Ahmad b. Nuriddin Ibn Hajar Al-Asqallani (d. 1449 AD, Egypt), p 276 V 1, Publisher; DAR AL-KUTUB AL-ILMIYYAH, Beirut, Egy[pt, 1995.

[266]AL-MUWATTA, by Abu Abdullah Malik b. Anas Al-Asbahi Al-Himyari (d. 795, Madinah), Narrator; Yahya b. Sa'ed, p 465, Publisher; MUSTAFA AL-BABI AL-HALABI, (DAR IHYA AL-TURATH), Cairo, Egypt, 1985.

AL-SIRAH AL-NABAWIYYAH, by Abu Muhammad Abdulmalik b. Hisham Al-Himyari (d. 833 AD, Egypt), Narrator; Muhammad b. Abdullah Al-Mazini, p 57 V 3, Publisher DAR AL-KITAB AL-ARABI, Beirut, Lebanon, third edition 1990.

MUSTARDAK ALA AL-SAHIHAIN, by Abu Abdullah Muhammad b. Abdullah Al-Nisapuri (d 1012 AD, Iran), chapter; KITAB MA'RIFAT AL-SAHABAH, N; 4906, Narrator; Abu Bakr b. Abu Quhafah, p 221 V 3, publisher; DAR AL-HARAMAIN, Cairo, Egypt, first edition 1997.

[267]SAHIH MUSLIM, by Abu Al-Husain Muslim b. Hajjaj Al-Nisapuri (d. 875 AD, Iran), Narrator; Abu Hurairah RA, p 1300, Publisher; DAR TAYBAH, Riyadh, KSA, first edition 2006.

[268]HILYAT AL-AWLIA WA TABAQAT AL-ASFIA, by Abu Nuaim Ahmad b. Abdullah Al-Asbahani (d. 1038 AD, Iran), Narrator Khalid b. Ma'dan RA, p 210 V 6, Publisher; DAR AL-KUTUB AL-ILMIYYAH, Beirut, Lebanon, 1988.

[269] MUSTARDAK ALA AL-SAHIHAIN, by Abu Abdullah Muhammad b. Abdullah Al-Nisapuri (d 1012 AD, Iran), chapter; KITAB AL-IMAN, N; 226, Narrator; Abu Hurairah, p 212 V 1, publisher; DAR AL-HARAMAIN, Cairo, Egypt, first edition 1997.

[270] SAHIH TIRMIDHI, by Abu Isa Muhammad b. Isa Al-Tirmidhi (d. 892 AD, Uzbekistan), chapter; AL-ILM, N; 2678, Narrator; Abu Dharr RA, p 506 V 3, published by DAR AL-GHARB AL-ISLAMI, Beirut, Lebanon, first edition 1996.

[271]SAHIH MUSLIM, by Abu Al-Husain Muslim b. Hajjaj Al-Nisapuri (d. 875 AD, Iran), Narrator; Abu Dharr RA, p 1214, Publisher; DAR TAYBAH, Riyadh, KSA, first edition 2006.

[272]AL-JAME' AL-SAHIH, by Abu Abdullah Muhammad b. Ismael Al-Bukhari (d. 870 AD, Uzbekistan), Narrator; Jarir b. Abdullah RA, p 936, Publisher DAR IBN KATHIR, Damascus, Syria, first edition 2002.

SAHIH MUSLIM, by Abu Al-Husain Muslim b. Hajjaj Al-Nisapuri (d. 875 AD, Iran), Narrator; Jarir RA, p 1157, Publisher; DAR TAYBAH, Riyadh, KSA, first edition 2006.

[273]MUSNAD AHMAD, by Abu Abdullah Ahmad b. Muhammad b. Hanbal Al-Marwazi (d.855, Iraq), Narrator; Umm Dardaa RA, p 77 V 16, Publisher; DAR AL-HADITH, Cairo, Egypt, first edition 1995.

[274] Referenced earlier.

[275]AL-JAME' AL-SAHIH, by Abu Abdullah Muhammad b. Ismael Al-Bukhari (d. 870 AD, Uzbekistan), Narrator; Aisha RA, p 1676, Publisher DAR IBN KATHIR, Damascus, Syria, first edition 2002.

SAHIH MUSLIM, by Abu Al-Husain Muslim b. Hajjaj Al-Nisapuri (d. 875 AD, Iran), Narrator; Aisha RA, p 1459, Publisher; DAR TAYBAH, Riyadh, KSA, first edition 2006.

[276] AL-ANWAR FI SHAMAIL AL-MUKHTAR SALLALLAHU ALAIHI WA SALLAM, by Husain b. Masud Al-Baghawi (d. 1122 AD, Iran), Narrator; Jabir b. Samurah RA, 267 V1, Publisher; DAR AL-MAKTABI, Damascus, Syria, first edition 1995.

[277]AL-JAME' AL-SAHIH, by Abu Abdullah Muhammad b. Ismael Al-Bukhari (d. 870 AD, Uzbekistan), Narrator; Aisha RA, p 1524, Publisher DAR IBN KATHIR, Damascus, Syria, first edition 2002.

SUNAN ABU DAWUD, by Abu Dawud Sulaiman b. Al-Ash'ath Al-Sijistani (d. 889 AD, Iraq), Narrator; Aisha, p 427 V 7, Publisher; DAR AL-RISALAH AL-ALAMIYYAH, Damascus, Syria, first edition 2009.

[278] SAHIH TIRMIDHI, by Abu Isa Muhammad b. Isa Al-Tirmidhi (d. 892 AD, Uzbekistan), chapter; AL-MANAQIB, N; 3641, Narrator; Abdullah b. Al-Harith RA, p 30 V 6, published by DAR AL-GHARB AL-ISLAMI, Beirut, Lebanon, first edition 1996.

[279] SAHIH TIRMIDHI, by Abu Isa Muhammad b. Isa Al-Tirmidhi (d. 892 AD, Uzbekistan), chapter; AL-MANAQIB, N; 3642, Narrator; Abdullah b. Al-Harith RA, p 30 V 6, published by DAR AL-GHARB AL-ISLAMI, Beirut, Lebanon, first edition 1996.

[280]AL-JAME' AL-SAHIH, by Abu Abdullah Muhammad b. Ismael Al-Bukhari (d. 870 AD, Uzbekistan), Narrator; Aisha RA, p 1524, Publisher DAR IBN KATHIR, Damascus, Syria, first edition 2002.

SUNAN ABU DAWUD, by Abu Dawud Sulaiman b. Al-Ash'ath Al-Sijistani (d. 889 AD, Iraq), Narrator; Aisha, p 427 V 7, Publisher; DAR AL-RISALAH AL-ALAMIYYAH, Damascus, Syria, first edition 2009.

[281] MUSTARDAK ALA AL-SAHIHAIN, by Abu Abdullah Muhammad b. Abdullah Al-Nisapuri (d 1012 AD, Iran), chapter; KITAB AL-ISTISQA, N; 1226, Narrator; Aisha, p 468 V 1, publisher; DAR AL-HARAMAIN, Cairo, Egypt, first edition 1997.

KITAB AL-DU'A, by Abu Al-Qasim Sulaiman b. Ayub Al-Tabarani (d. 918 AD, Iran), Narrator; Anas RA, p 1773, Publisher; DAR AL-BASHAIR AL-ISLAMIYYAH, Beirut, Lebanon, first edition 1987.

[282]MUSNAD AHMAD, by Abu Abdullah Ahmad b. Muhammad b. Hanbal Al-Marwazi (d.855, Iraq), Narrator; Sa'ed b. Abu Rashid RA, p 244 V 27, Publisher; MUASSASAH AL-RISALAH, Beirut, Lebanon, first edition 2001.

[283] Surah 58 Al-Mujadalah; 2.

[284] SUNAN IBN MAJAH, by Abu Abdullah Muhammad b. Yazid Al-Qazwini (d 887 AD, Iran), chapter; KITAB AL-TALAQ, N; 2065 Narrator; Abdullah b. Abbas, p 666 V 1, publisher; DAR IHYAA AL-KUTUB AL- ARABIYYAH, Cairo, Egypt, year 1952.

[285]SAHIH MUSLIM, by Abu Al-Husain Muslim b. Hajjaj Al-Nisapuri (d. 875 AD, Iran), Narrator; Abu Dharr RA, p 105, Publisher; DAR TAYBAH, Riyadh, KSA, first edition 2006.

[286]AL-JAME' AL-SAHIH, by Abu Abdullah Muhammad b. Ismael Al-Bukhari (d. 870 AD, Uzbekistan), Narrator; Anas RA, p 1524, Publisher DAR IBN KATHIR, Damascus, Syria, first edition 2002.

SAHIH MUSLIM, by Abu Al-Husain Muslim b. Hajjaj Al-Nisapuri (d. 875 AD, Iran), Narrator; Anas RA, p 466, Publisher; DAR TAYBAH, Riyadh, KSA, first edition 2006.

[287] SUNAN IBN MAJAH, by Abu Abdullah Muhammad b. Yazid Al-Qazwini (d 887 AD, Iran), chapter; KITAB AL-ADAB, N; 3719 Narrator; Abdullah b. Abbas, p 1225 V 2, publisher; DAR IHYAA AL-KUTUB AL- ARABIYYAH, Cairo, Egypt, year 1952.

[288]AL-ISABAH FI TAMYEEZ AL-SAHABAH, by Shihabuddin Ahmad b. Nuriddin Ibn Hajar Al-Asqallani (d. 1449 AD, Egypt), p 366 V 6, Publisher; DAR AL-KUTUB AL-ILMIYYAH, Beirut, Lebanon, 2010.

[289] SHAMAIL MUHAMMADIYAH, by Abu Isa Muhammad b. Isa Al-Tirmidhi (d. 892 AD, Uzbekistan), chapter; AL-MANAQIB, N; 3759, Narrator; Anas RA, p 112, published by DAR AL-HADITH, Beirut, Lebanon, third edition 1998.

[290]AL-JAME' AL-SAHIH, by Abu Abdullah Muhammad b. Ismael Al-Bukhari (d. 870 AD, Uzbekistan), Narrator; Abu Hurairah RA, p 1529, Publisher DAR IBN KATHIR, Damascus, Syria, first edition 2002.

[291]FAWAID IBN SHAHIN, by Abu Hafs Umar b. Ahmad Al-Baghdadi (d. 995 AD, Iraq), Narrator; Abu Huraira RA, p 73, (published in the collection of MAJMU' MUSANNAFAT IBN SHAHIN), Publisher; DAR IBN ATHIR, Kuwait, first edition 1994.

[292]MUSNAD AHMAD, by Abu Abdullah Ahmad b. Muhammad b. Hanbal Al-Marwazi (d.855, Iraq), Narrator; Abdullah b. Abbas RA, p 39 V 4, Publisher; MUASSASAH AL-RISALAH, Beirut, Lebanon, first edition 2001.

[293] SHAMAIL MUHAMMADIYYAH, by Abu Isa Muhammad b. Isa Al-Tirmidhi (d. 892 AD, Uzbekistan), chapter; MA JAA FI TAWADHU RASULULLAH, N; 337, Narrator; Hsan b. Ali RA, p 247, published by MAKTABAH AL-ULUM WA AL-HIKAM, Cairo, Egypt, first edition 2008.

DALAIL AL-NUBUWWAH, by Abu Bakr Ahmad b. Husain Al-Baihaqi (d. 1066 AD, Iran), N; 565, Narrator; Hasan b. Ali p 627, V 2, publisher; DAR AL-NAFAIS, Beirut, Lebanon, first edition 1986.

AL-MU'JAM AL-KABIR, by Abu Al-Qasim Sulaiman b. Ayub Al-Tabarani (d. 918 AD, Iran), Narrator; Hasan b. Ali RA, p 155 V 22, Publisher; MAKTABAH IBN TAIMIYYAH, Cairo, Egypt, 1983.

[294] Referenced in the previous chapter.
[295]SAHIH MUSLIM, by Abu Al-Husain Muslim b. Hajjaj Al-Nisapuri (d. 875 AD, Iran), Narrator; Abu Masud Al-Ansari RA, p 215, Publisher; DAR TAYBAH, Riyadh, KSA, first edition 2006

AL-JAME' AL-SAHIH, by Abu Abdullah Muhammad b. Ismael Al-Bukhari (d. 870 AD, Uzbekistan), Narrator; Abu Masud Al-Ansari RA, p 35, Publisher DAR IBN KATHIR, Damascus, Syria, first edition 2002.

[296]SUNAN ABU DAWUD, by Abu Dawud Sulaiman b. Al-Ash'ath Al-Sijistani (d. 889 AD, Iraq), Narrator; Abdullah b. Amr, p 489 V 5, Publisher; DAR AL-RISALAH AL-ALAMIYYAH, Damascus, Syria, first edition 2009.
[297]AL-JAME' AL-SAHIH, by Abu Abdullah Muhammad b. Ismael Al-Bukhari (d. 870 AD, Uzbekistan), Narrator; Usamah b. Zaid RA, p 1045, Publisher DAR IBN KATHIR, Damascus, Syria, first edition 2002.

SAHIH MUSLIM, by Abu Al-Husain Muslim b. Hajjaj Al-Nisapuri (d. 875 AD, Iran), Narrator; Usamah b. Zaid RA, p 57, Publisher; DAR TAYBAH, Riyadh, KSA, first edition 2006.

[298]AL-SIRAH AL-NABAWIYYAH, by Abu Muhammad Abdulmalik b. Hisham Al-Himyari (d. 833 AD, Egypt), Narrator; Muhammad b. Ja'far b. Al-Zubair, p 58 V 3, Publisher DAR AL-KITAB AL-ARABI, Beirut, Lebanon, third edition 1990.
[299]AL-SIRAH AL-NABAWIYYAH, by Abu Bakr Muhammad b. Ishaq Al-Madani (d. 768 AD, Madinah/Iraq), p 378 V 1, Publisher; DAR AL-KUTUB AL-ILMIYYAH, Beirut, Lebanon, third edition 2003.

AL-SIRAH AL-NABAWIYYAH, by Abu Muhammad Abdulmalik b. Hisham Al-Himyari (d. 833 AD, Egypt), Narrator; Ibn Ishaq, p 137 V 3, Publisher DAR AL-KITAB AL-ARABI, Beirut, Lebanon, third edition 1990.

[300]AL-JAME' AL-SAHIH, by Abu Abdullah Muhammad b. Ismael Al-Bukhari (d. 870 AD, Uzbekistan), Narrator; Abdullah b. Umar RA, p 315, Publisher DAR IBN KATHIR, Damascus, Syria, first edition 2002.

SAHIH MUSLIM, by Abu Al-Husain Muslim b. Hajjaj Al-Nisapuri (d. 875 AD, Iran), Narrator; Abdullah b. Umar RA, p 410, Publisher; DAR TAYBAH, Riyadh, KSA, first edition 2006.

[301]AL-TABAQAT AL-KABIR, by Muhammad b. Sa'd Al-Baghdadi (d. 845 AD, Iraq), p 37 V 10, Publisher; MAKTABAH AL-KHANJI, Cairo, Egypt, year 2001.

AL-MU'JAM AL-KABIR, by Abu Al-Qasim Sulaiman b. Ayub Al-Tabarani (d. 918 AD, Iran), Narrator; Abdullah b. Abbas, p 217 V 12, Publisher; MAKTABAH IBN TAIMIYYAH, Cairo, Egypt.

SAHIH TIRMIDHI, by Abu Isa Muhammad b. Isa Al-Tirmidhi (d. 892 AD, Uzbekistan), chapter; AL-JANAIZ, N; 989, Narrator; Aisha RA, p 304 V 2, published by DAR AL-GHARB AL-ISLAMI, Beirut, Lebanon, first edition 1996.

SUNAN ABU DAWUD, by Abu Dawud Sulaiman b. Al-Ash'ath Al-Sijistani (d. 889 AD, Iraq), Narrator; Aisha RA, p 75 V 5, Publisher; DAR AL-RISALAH AL-ALAMIYYAH, Damascus, Syria, first edition 2009.

SUNAN IBN MAJAH, by Abu Abdullah Muhammad b. Yazid Al-Qazwini (d 887 AD, Iran), chapter; KITAB AL-JANAIZ, N; 1456 Narrator; Aisha, p 468 V 1, publisher; DAR IHYAA AL-KUTUB AL-ARABIYYAH, Cairo, Egypt, year 1952

[302]AL-MUSANNAF, by Abdul-Razzaq b. Hammam Al-San'ani (d. 828 AD, Yemen), Narrator; Abdullah b. Masud, p 420 V 3, Publisher; DAR AL-TASIL, Cairo, Egypt, first edition 2015.

[303] MUSTARDAK ALA AL-SAHIHAIN, by Abu Abdullah Muhammad b. Abdullah Al-Nisapuri (d 1012 AD, Iran), chapter; KITAB MA'RIFAT AL-SAHABAH, N; 4818, Narrator; Abu Bakr b. Abu Quhafah, p 194 V 3, publisher; DAR AL-KUTUB AL-ILMIYYAH, Beirut, Lebanon, second edition 2002.

TARIKH MADINAT DIMISHQ, by Abu Al-Qasim Ali b. Hasan Ibn Asakir Al-Dimishqi (d. 1176 AD, Syria), Narrator; Ali RA, p 189 V 14, Publisher; DAR AL-FIKAR, Beirut, Lebanon, first edition 1998.

MUSTARDAK ALA AL-SAHIHAIN, by Abu Abdullah Muhammad b. Abdullah Al-Nisapuri (d 1012 AD, Iran), chapter; KITAB MA'RIFAT AL-SAHABAH, N; 4818, Narrator; Umm Al-Fadl bt. Al-Harith, p 194 V 3, publisher; DAR AL-KUTUB AL-ILMIYYAH, second edition 2002.

SUNAN IBN MAJAH, by Abu Abdullah Muhammad b. Yazid Al-Qazwini (d 887 AD, Iran), chapter; KITAB AL-TA'BIR AL-RU'YAA, N; 3923 Narrator; Umm Al-Fadl, p 1293 V 2, publisher; DAR IHYAA AL-KUTUB AL- ARABIYYAH, Cairo, Egypt, year 1952.

[304] SUNAN IBN MAJAH, by Abu Abdullah Muhammad b. Yazid Al-Qazwini (d 887 AD, Iran), chapter; KITAB AL-IQAMAT AL-SALAT WA AL-SUNNAH FIHA, N; 4195 Narrator; Al-Barraa b. Azib, p 1403 V 2, publisher; DAR IHYAA AL-KUTUB AL- ARABIYYAH, Cairo, Egypt, year 1952.

[305]SAHIH MUSLIM, by Abu Al-Husain Muslim b. Hajjaj Al-Nisapuri (d. 875 AD, Iran), Narrator; Abdullah b. Amr RA, p 114, Publisher; DAR TAYBAH, Riyadh, KSA, first edition 2006.

[306]AL-JAME' AL-SAHIH, by Abu Abdullah Muhammad b. Ismael Al-Bukhari (d. 870 AD, Uzbekistan), Narrator; Abdullah b. Masud RA, p 1288, Publisher DAR IBN KATHIR, Damascus, Syria, first edition 2002.

[307]SAHIH IBN KHUZAIMA, by Abu Bakr Muhammad bin Ishaq Ibn Khuzaimah (d. 923 AD, Iran), Narrator; Ali b. Abu Talib RA, p 450 V1, Publisher; AL-MAKTAB AL-ISLAMI, Beirut, Lebanon, 2003.

MUSNAD ABU YA'LA, by Abu Ya'la Ahmad b. Ali Al-Mausilli (d. 919 AD Iraq), Narrator; Ali, N; 899, p 450 V 1, Publisher; DAR AL-MA'MUN, Damascus, Syria, second edition 1989.

[308]SUNAN ABU DAWUD, by Abu Dawud Sulaiman b. Al-Ash'ath Al-Sijistani (d. 889 AD, Iraq), Narrator; Abdullah b. Al-Shukhair, p 173 V 2, Publisher; DAR AL-RISALAH AL-ALAMIYYAH, Damascus, Syria, special edition 2009.

AL-SUNAN AL-KUBRA, by Abu Bakr Ahmad b. Husain Al-Baihaqi (d. 1066 AD, Iran), Narrator; Abdullah b. Al-Shukhair RA, p 357 V 2, Publisher; DAR AL-KUTUB AL-ILMIYYAH, Beirut, Lebanon, third edition 2003.

[309]AL-IHSAN FI TAQRIB SAHIH IBN HIBBAN, by Abu Hatim Muhammad b. Faisal Al-Busti (d. 965 AD, Afghanistan), Narrator; Ata, N; 620, Chapter; KITAB AL-RIQAQ, BAAB AL-TAWBAH, p 386 V 2, Publisher; MUASSASAH AL-RISALAH, Beirut, Lebanon, first edition edition 1988.

[310]SAHIH IBN KHUZAIMAH, by Abu Bakr Muhammad b. Ishaq b. Khuzaimah Al-Sulami Al-Nisapuri (d. 923 AD, Iran), Narrator; Jabir, p 1285 V 2, Publisher; AL-MAKTAB AL-ISLAMI, Beirut, Lebanon, 2003.

[311]AL-SIRAH AL-NABAWIYYAH, by Abu Muhammad Abdulmalik b. Hisham Al-Himyari (d. 833 AD, Egypt), p 298 V 1, Publisher DAR AL-KITAB AL-ARABI, Beirut, Lebanon, third edition 1990.

[312]AL-MU'JAM AL-KABIR, by Abu Al-Qasim Sulaiman b. Ayub Al-Tabarani (d. 918 AD, Iran), Narrator; Abdullah b. Abbas RA, p 141 V 12, Publisher; MAKTABAH IBN TAIMIYYAH, Cairo, Egypt, 1983.

[313]AL-JAME' AL-SAHIH, by Abu Abdullah Muhammad b. Ismael Al-Bukhari (d. 870 AD, Uzbekistan), Narrator; Aisha RA, p 1569, Publisher DAR IBN KATHIR, Damascus, Syria, first edition 2002.

[314] SUNAN IBN MAJAH, by Abu Abdullah Muhammad b. Yazid Al-Qazwini (d 887 AD, Iran), chapter; KITAB AL-JANAIZ, N; 3023 Narrator; Jabir, p 1006 V 2, publisher; DAR IHYAA AL-KUTUB AL- ARABIYYAH, Cairo, Egypt, year 1952

SAHIH TIRMIDHI, by Abu Isa Muhammad b. Isa Al-Tirmidhi (d. 892 AD, Uzbekistan), chapter; AL-HAJJ, N; 886, Narrator; Jabir RA, p 223 V 2, published by DAR AL-GHARB AL-ISLAMI, Beirut, Lebanon, first edition 1996.

[315]AL-MU'JAM AL-KABIR, by Abu Al-Qasim Sulaiman b. Ayub Al-Tabarani (d. 918 AD, Iran), Narrator; Muadh RA, p 120-121 V 20, Publisher; MAKTABAH IBN TAIMIYYAH, Cairo, Egypt, 1983.

[316]AL-JAME' AL-SAHIH, by Abu Abdullah Muhammad b. Ismael Al-Bukhari (d. 870 AD, Uzbekistan), Narrator; Abdullah b. Abbas RA, p 1269, Publisher DAR IBN KATHIR, Damascus, Syria, first edition 2002.

[317]AL-JAME' AL-SAHIH, by Abu Abdullah Muhammad b. Ismael Al-Bukhari (d. 870 AD, Uzbekistan), Narrator; Uqbah b. Aamir RA, p 1601, Publisher DAR IBN KATHIR, Damascus, Syria, first edition 2002.

SAHIH MUSLIM, by Abu Al-Husain Muslim b. Hajjaj Al-Nisapuri (d. 875 AD, Iran), Narrator; Uqbah b. Aamir RA, p 1088, Publisher; DAR TAYBAH, Riyadh, KSA, first edition 2006.

[318]AL-MU'JAM AL-KABIR, by Abu Al-Qasim Sulaiman b. Ayub Al-Tabarani (d. 918 AD, Iran), Narrator; Al-Fadl b. Al-Abbas RA, p 279 V 25, Publisher; MAKTABAH IBN TAIMIYYAH, Cairo, Egypt, 1983.
MUSNAD ABU YA'LA, by Abu Ya'la Ahmad b. Ali Al-Mausilli (d. 919 AD Iraq), Narrator; Al-Fadl b. Al-Abbas RA, N; 6824, p 201 V 12, Publisher; DAR AL-MA'MUN, Damascus, Syria, first edition 1988.
[319] Surah 57 Al-Hadid; 25.

[320]AL-JAME' AL-SAHIH, by Abu Abdullah Muhammad b. Ismael Al-Bukhari (d. 870 AD, Uzbekistan), Narrator; Aisha RA, p 166, Publisher DAR IBN KATHIR, Damascus, Syria, first edition 2002.

SAHIH MUSLIM, by Abu Al-Husain Muslim b. Hajjaj Al-Nisapuri (d. 875 AD, Iran), Narrator; Aisha RA, p 198, Publisher; DAR TAYBAH, Riyadh, KSA, first edition 2006.

[321]MUSANNAF IBN ABU SHAYBAH, by Abu Bakr Muhammad b. Abdullah Ibn Abu Shaybah (d. 849 AD, Iraq), Narrator; Umm Salamah RA, p 95 V 17, Publisher; DAR AL-QIBLAH LI AL-THAQAFAH AL-ISLAMIYYAH, Jeddah, KSA, first edition 2006.

AL-SUNAN AL-KUBRA, by Abu Abdul-Rahman Ahmad b. Shuaib Al-Nasai (d. 915 AD Mecca/Turkmenistan), Narrator; Umm Salamah RA, p 465 V 7, Publisher; MUASSASAT AL-RISALAH, Beirut, Lebanon, first edition 2001.

TARIKH MADINAT DIMISHQ, by Abu Al-Qasim Ali b. Hasan Ibn Asakir Al-Dimishqi (d. 1176 AD, Syria), Narrator; Urwah RA, p 490 V 23, Publisher; DAR AL-KUTUB AL-ILMIYYAH, Beirut, Lebanon, first edition 2012.

[322]AL-JAME' AL-SAHIH, by Abu Abdullah Muhammad b. Ismael Al-Bukhari (d. 870 AD, Uzbekistan), Narrator; Aisha RA, p 1601, Publisher DAR IBN KATHIR, Damascus, Syria, first edition 2002.